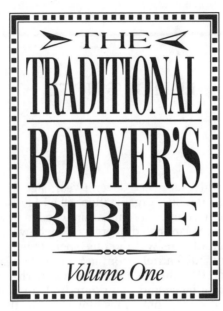

# THE TRADITIONAL BOWYER'S BIBLE

## Volume One

Steve Allely
Tim Baker
Paul Comstock
Jim Hamm
Ron Hardcastle
Jay Massey
John Strunk

# THE LYONS PRESS

GUILFORD, CONNECTICUT

AN IMPRINT OF THE GLOBE PEQUOT PRESS

# EDITOR'S NOTE

This book was, in reality, launched several years ago at an archery tournament in Michigan, when the host organization asked Jay Massey, John Strunk, Ron Hardcastle, and me to conduct a seminar on wooden bows. The subject was well enough received by the laminated fiberglass longbow and recurve shooters, but the real highlight for all of us was the time spent together, often far into the night, discussing bows made entirely from natural materials. One of us would trot out a pet theory, and the others would chip in with their opinions, opinions based upon years of experience and many hundreds of bows. Sometimes the original theory was confirmed, sometimes blown out of the water, and sometimes transformed into a new, revolutionary theory – though we all recognized we were mostly tilling ground which had been plowed for the last ten thousand years by men who depended upon their weapons for the necessities of life.

In any case, sharing the experience and intuition of the others was the most enlightening three days I have ever spent, and Ron coined the perfect term for our interaction, "Cross-pollination."

Afterwards, we kept in touch, sharing information, ideas, and raw materials. The informal circle soon came to include others who were inexorably drawn to the primordial lure of these weapons, men who devote vast amounts of time and energy toward keeping the ancient art of wooden bowmaking alive.

Through our common bond and cross-pollination, the seed for a series of books slowly took root and grew, finally resulting in these *Traditional Bowyer's Bible* volumes. It is the authors' sincerest wish that by sharing our accumulated knowledge our ideas will cross-pollinate with your own, further expanding the delight and satisfaction these lovely weapons have to offer.

Jim Hamm
Spring, 1992

# TABLE OF CONTENTS

Originally published in 1992 by Bois d'Arc Press

First Lyons Press Edition ©2000

The Lyons Press is an imprint of The Globe Pequot Press.

Printed in Canada

First Lyons Edition/Fourth Printing

Library of Congress Cataloging-in-Publication Data

ISBN 1-58574-085-3

# ABOUT THE AUTHORS

**Steve Allely** is an artist who enjoys painting the landscapes, wildlife, and historical subjects of the West. In addition to being a full time painter, he is also an accomplished flintknapper and replicates Native American knives, bows, and arrows, particularly those used in the Far West. Steve has made items for a number of museum exhibits around the country, private collections, and has worked on exhibits for the U.S. Forest Service and the National Park Service. Steve and his wife Susie make their home in central Oregon. To contact Steve about artwork or replications write: PO Box 1648, Sisters, OR, 97759.

**Tim Baker,** like many others, first became interested in archery after reading about Ishi and the remarkable weapons he made with only stone tools. Upon reading the available archery texts, it became clear to Tim that there was a great deal of contradiction and confusion about wooden bows and their design. He decided the only way to get reliable information was to make every conceivable type of bow of every conceivable material while keeping complete statistics on each one. By comparing stats, the qualities which produce superior bows slowly became apparent. Based upon his research, he has written articles on wooden bows and their construction, as well as teaching at archery meets and primitive skills workshops. Tim is presently assembling the first edition of *Woodbow - A Conference-in-Print* for wood and natural material bowmakers. To subscribe, write: *Woodbow,* 6609 Whitney, Oakland, CA, 94609. He also operates the Primitive Archery Switchboard at 510/654-2417, offering advice on bow design, construction, and information on sources of raw materials.

**Paul Comstock** never used a hunting weapon he really liked until he started carrying a wooden bow. He earlier tagged whitetails and black bears using a center-fire rifle, muzzleloader, shotgun, compound bow, and glass-laminated recurve bow. Since switching to wooden bows, he has abandoned modern hunting weapons entirely. Where legal, he also uses stone-tipped arrows exclusively. His largest game so far with a wooden bow is a 300-pound black bear.

He began making wooden bows in 1984. From the onset he began experimenting with woods other than yew and Osage orange, curious because old bowmaking books ignored these woods almost completely. In 1988 he published the first edition of *The Bent Stick,* the first bowmaking manual to describe in comprehensive detail how to get the best results from some of North America's most common trees. Subsequent findings have been incorporated into updated editions of *The Bent Stick.* Some of these findings stem from investigative projects conducted with Tim Baker. Paul sells the *The Bent Stick* for $11 a copy, postpaid. He can be reached at PO Box 1102, Delaware, OH 43015.

**Jim Hamm** was born in Texas in 1952, and practically grew up with a bow in his hands, graduating from small game to deer hunting when only twelve. His interest in archery never faded, and about the time he married discovered bows made entirely from wood, a discovery which was to consume his adult life. Though spending his early years operating heavy equipment, working freight docks, and "becoming a promising young executive," Jim finally went into archery full-time. He has been, as he puts it, "self-unemployed" for the past twelve years: making bows, researching, writing about bows, and recently, teaching others the age-old skill of wooden bowmaking through intensive, hands-on seminars conducted at his home. He also owns and operates Bois d'Arc Press, publishing archery books both old and new. Jim's first book, *Bows and Arrows of the Native Americans,* is available for $16.95 postpaid. To order books or inquire about bowmaking seminars write; Bois d'Arc Press 4, PO Box 233, Azle, TX, 76020.

**Ron Hardcastle** of Austin, Texas, began seriously making wooden bows in the mid-70's. He is a high school science teacher with a strong background in botany and ethnobotany. He made the bows and arrows for the CBS miniseries *Lonesome Dove*, as well as for other feature films. Ron specializes in Osage orange self bows, bias-ring self bows, and Indian reproduction bows and arrows. He is a professional bowyer and an instructor with Jim Hamm in the Bois d'Arc Bowyer School. To inquire about Ron's bows, contact him at PO Box 91692, Oak Hill, TX, 78709-1692.

A native of Oklahoma, **Jay Massey** has lived in Alaska for the past 23 years and is a registered guide/outfitter and a former member of the Alaska Board of Game. He operates an outfitting business, Moose John Outfitters, which caters to archery hunters, wilderness enthusiasts and salmon fishermen. He has written four archery books and is currently at work on a fifth which will combine fiction with fact to dramatize significant archery-related events of medieval England, the Steppes of Asia and pre-contact Indian America.

Jay's other books can be ordered through Bear Paw Publications, PO Box 429, Girdwood, AK 99587: *Bowhunting Alaska's Wild Rivers* ($15.95); *A Thousand Campfires* ($14.95); *The Bowyer's Craft* ($16.95); and *The Book of Primitive Archery* ($18.95). Add $2 for postage and handling.

**John Strunk's** interest in bowmaking started when he was a youngster trying to build his own archery equipment. Even though it was a child's attempt to satisfy his own fantasies, the flame of archery was kindled. This love of the bow and archery naturally led to bowhunting and eventually to creation of his Spirit Longbow Company 11 years ago. Today, he builds more selfbows than laminated bows. He has found a great challenge in fashioning nature's materials into archery tackle.

In the future, John plans to combine his teaching and bowmaking skills to help others find the love of archery through the development of their own talents. This will be "the greatest conclusion to my bowmaking experience." Contact him about bows or classes at: The Spirit Longbow Company, 5513 Third Street, Tillamook, OR, 97141.

*The authors would like to dedicate this book to Cliff Coe, Bill Crawford, Harry Drake, Frank Garske, Bert Grayson, Gilman Keasey, Wally Miles, Carney Saupitty, Glenn St. Charles, and all of the other men who kept "real" archery alive through the lean years, and passed it on to the present generation.*

# WHY TRADITIONAL?

*Jay Massey*

The drooping boughs of the giant conifers were cloaked in a thin shroud of fog as I drove toward my hunting area in western Oregon on that morning in 1966. It was the opening day of archery hunting season. Soon the pastel light of dawn was filtering through the gloom of the forest and I began sneaking along an old logging road that led toward an abandoned farm. In my left hand was a rawhide-backed yew longbow; on my back was a quiver of well-oiled leather, filled with a dozen hand-fletched wood arrows. Ahead was an open meadow, partially obscured in the morning mist. Beyond the meadow was the grown-over apple orchard where I had seen deer sign.

This would be my first day of hunting with the bow and arrow, my interest in archery having been sparked the previous winter by an accidental discovery I had made while browsing through the Oregon State University library. Tucked away in one wing of the library was a large collection of old archery books and literature. The dusty volumes of *Ye Sylvan Archer*, containing writings by such early archers as Chet Stevenson, B.G. Thompson, Earl Stanley Gardner and Earl Ullrich, had fired my imagination. Within days I found myself venturing forth into the snowy mountains of the nearby coastal range, drawn by some instinctive urge that I didn't yet fully comprehend. I was armed with a copy of Adrian Eliot Hodgkin's classic book, *The Archer's Craft*, and a small hand axe.

After a great deal of searching, I found a rather short, semi-straight yew tree and cut it down. I carted the small log home – it was barely five feet long – and whittled out a bow in short order. Of course, the bow took a horrible string-follow the first time I shot it. It broke within a week. But by then I was hooked on archery like a fish on a line.

A few days later I had the good fortune to meet old-time archer/bowyer Gilman Keasey. Keasey had twice been national archery champion back in the 1930's, but by 1966 considered himself sort of an "archery dropout." As he explained to me, the new laminated fiberglass bows, with their weighted handle risers and superior speed, had not only taken the fun out of tournament shooting, but also made it nearly impossible for him to compete. Keasey was a superb craftsman of English-style longbows, and he was also a die-hard traditionalist; he refused to compromise, preferring to shoot his yew longbows with their horn nocks while everybody else was switching to more sophisticated equipment. By 1966 everybody was excited about the new laminated recurved bows and fiberglass and aluminum arrows; the demand for wood bows and arrows was practically zero. As a result, Keasey had a barn filled with fine-grained red Oregon yew billets and staves. For a few dollars I became the owner of three well-seasoned staves, two of yew and one of Osage orange.

So now, on the opening day of archery season, I skirted the meadow in anticipation, carrying the yew longbow which I had made from one of Keasey's fine staves. I eased toward the brushy knoll that overlooked the orchard and peeked cautiously over the rise. Suddenly a grayish form appeared in front of me, like an apparition. On top of the deer's head were antlers. Big ones.

The buck stamped the ground once, twice. I froze in my tracks. The buck didn't bound away, perhaps because it was the first day of hunting season and he wasn't yet on the alert. Instead, he stepped cautiously forward, head held high and tail twitching as he tried to identify me.

My fingers tightened on the bowstring. My heart was beating like a triphammer. I had hunted with guns since I was barely seven years old, and I had experienced "buck fever" many times before, but this sensation was ridiculous. My nerves were stretched as taut as my bowstring. My hands shook like an aspen in an October windstorm.

A mere 25 yards away, the buck suddenly decided this was not a safe place to be. He turned broadside to leave. My heart racing wildly, I drew the bowstring quickly to my cheek. All of my brain cells were screaming: *Shoot before he runs away!*

I released the arrow and it streaked harmlessly over the buck. The deer snorted loudly, leaped high into the air and bounded away toward the safety of an alder thicket.

That botched first shot is burned forever into my memory. Though I had missed the deer, there was something intensely satisfying about the sight of the arrow sailing over his back. Right then I knew I wouldn't trade the missed shot for the biggest rifle-killed deer in the world.

I eventually managed to kill a little buck that season – using a homemade yew flatbow backed with rawhide – but only after two months of hard hunting. Those weeks were my initiation into this ancient sport of archery hunting. Those first days I spent roaming the woods with a simple wooden bow and back quiver are among my most treasured memories of 25 years of hunting with the bow and arrow. I wouldn't trade those days for a den filled with big game trophies gained through lesser means.

Few archers today know the joys of hunting with traditional equipment and stalking from the ground – the way Pope and Young did it. Almost none knows the keen sense of satisfaction which comes from taking game with their own homemade weapons. If modern archery gear seems cold and inanimate, it could be because it is manufactured and mass-produced by some faceless machinist who might as well be cranking out worm gears or ball bearings.

During the past two decades there has been a disturbing trend in American sports, a trend in which our "toys" have evolved from the simple to the intricate. No matter whether it's boating, bicycling, skiing or backpacking, the goal seems to be the same: to improve the performance and efficiency of the equipment.

Outdoor equipment today becomes "obsolete" after only a season or two, made so by the constant introduction of newer, more sophisticated models. Manufacturers of recreational equipment – who have the most to gain from the complication of leisure – spend millions to promote "new, improved" products.

And at what cost to our sense of fun and play? We seem so bent on results – on being "successful" – that we often forget why we took up a particular sport in the first place.

In other words, play is beginning to look more and more like work. And, at the same time, the price tag on our toys has gone sky-high.

One of the primary benefits of using traditional archery gear – aside from saving lots of money, especially when you make your own gear – is that it promotes a sense of fun and encourages a carefree spirit. Archers who go traditional always seem to agree that once they make the switch, archery is once again exciting. Stump-shooting and roving – roaming the woods and shooting at various targets – becomes an adventure in its own right. See that clump of leaves beneath the giant spreading oak? – it looks almost like a ruffed grouse. That rotten log on the ground looks like a deer lying down. A blackened tree stump against the hillside becomes a bear standing on his hind legs. Soon we are drawn into this ancient game and a simple stroll through the woods becomes an adventure in Sherwood Forest. For a moment, we are taken away from the complexities of a modern world and into a realm of mystery and romance. For a moment we have recaptured the spirit of traditional archery.

From my years of shooting the bow and observing hundreds of other archers, one truth emerges again and again: the tradition-oriented archer loves his tackle and will shoot with it continually. As Maurice Thompson wrote in *The Witchery of Archery*, "What a glorious weapon the longbow is!" Forty years later, in *Hunting With The Bow and Arrow*, Saxton Pope wrote, "Every good bow is a work of love." These attitudes live on in the hearts of archery traditionalists today. That's because traditional bows and arrows are things of warmth and beauty, not cold, inanimate machines.

After more than 12 years of outfitting and guiding archery hunters in Alaska, I never met a traditional archer who didn't practice with his equipment constantly while in the field. On the other hand, I've never seen a high-tech archer who seemed to enjoy roving or stump-shooting while on a hunt. The traditional archer carries his bow lightly and casually, almost as if it's an extension of his body. The high-tech archers – those who shoot the heavy, mechanized devices – almost invariably carry their bows like some sort of burden – the way a novice rifle hunter carries a firearm.

Small wonder! Is there any romance in a steel cable or a magnesium pulley? Does an aluminum arrow generate any feeling of warmth for the archer? Studying the cables and pulleys and electronics and machined parts of the modern bow tempts one to ask whether such equipment truly has any redeeming value, aside from increased efficiency and aside from making it easier for a novice archer to kill game. Does the modern gear contribute anything to the perpetuation of the sport of archery and archery hunting? Does it have cultural value?

What, you might ask, do cultural values have to do with archery and archery hunting? The answer is – plenty!

Today, archery hunting is coming increasingly under fire by people who are opposed to hunting and killing animals. Much of this opposition, I feel, is the result of our own doing. The old-time archers – Saxton Pope, Art Young, Will and Maurice Thompson and others – were seen as representing such early American values as woodcraft, hardiness and self-reliance. The gear they used was no different from that used by the English longbowman or the American Indian; their fair-chase hunting methods both reflected and nurtured our American sense of sportsmanship and fair play. Although these early archers took plenty of game – probably too much, by today's standards – their endeavors had cultural value. As the great American conservationist Aldo Leopold said, there is cultural value in any activity which serves to remind us of our own unique origins, history and heritage.

Now look at archery hunting today. Does it serve to remind us of our early American traditions and values?

Archery hunting – "bowhunting" as it is now called – seems characterized by a "get-em-any-way-you-can" attitude. The archery hunter has now become a "bowhunter" – a word which slowly, over the years, has come to have bad connotations. To the average non-hunting American, the word probably conjures up images of a hunter who seeks an unfair advantage over his prey by using space-age equipment and unfair methods. The modern bowhunter does not wear wool or buckskins, as did Meriwether Lewis or William Clark or Jim Bridger; he wears the latest high-dollar fashions in camo clothing. Few follow the advice of Saxton Pope, who wrote in his book *Hunting With the Bow and Arrow*, "We scorned to shoot from a tree." The modern bowhunter does not use bows and arrows crafted by his own hands; he purchases them fresh from the factory, precision-made. Indeed, the typical archer today buys his gear wrapped in plastic – which ironically is the same way an urban dweller purchases his meat. Neither the "bowhunter" nor the urban meat-buyer has any concept of what is involved in the manufacture of his product.

However, not all archery hunters have sunk to such depressing levels. We have not yet completely become a nation of sheep. Many archers today are fed up with the "new archery" and are looking for ways of restoring early American values to their sport. They want greater rewards and personal fulfillment and are willing to learn such out-of-date skills as woodcraft, self-reliance and hardiness. They are discovering that the more they put into archery, the more they get out of it. In short, these archers refuse to settle for things wrapped in plastic. And their ranks are growing!

I believe I speak for all the other contributors of this book – and they represent the finest craftsmen in the field of traditional archery – when I say this work has been a labor of love for us all. I'm sure they feel, as I do, that traditional archery will enrich your life and extend the pleasures you derive from this ancient sport. I'm sure they would agree that the values to be rediscovered in traditional archery can provide a means of maintaining our equilibrium in these often distressing times.

Certainly, traditional archery will offer new – sometimes difficult – challenges to the archer. But at the same time, it offers new rewards and an opportunity for greater personal growth and fulfillment. It also provides an avenue for learning – for discovering things about our origins and history, our forebears and ourselves.

There's a certain lure of traditional archery that is sometimes difficult to express either verbally or in writing. It must be experienced. But when a handmade arrow from your first homemade bow slams into a rotten stump with a satisfying Thunk!, you'll know it. When you kneel down and reverently place your homemade bow beside the form of that hard-earned deer, you'll feel it. At such moments there'll be no question why you chose the traditional archery path.

# CUTTING AND SEASONING WOOD

*Ron Hardcastle*

In 1983, a box of 175 English longbows of yew was found in the wreckage of the HMS Mary Rose in Plymouth Harbor, England, (the ship sank in 1545). To everyone's astonishment, the bows appeared in near pristine condition and were shootable after they dried out. Some even had backsets! I've often wondered how the makers of those bows would have reacted had they been told their bows would be shooting 450 years hence. It speaks well of their skill and the character of yew (and possibly of the preserving silts of Plymouth Harbor).

My first intense experience with the lure of wooden bows occurred when I was ten, while being pursued by your average neighborhood psychopathic bully. He chased me into a house under construction, where I found a pile of thin pine slats and some twine. I quickly fashioned a crude "bow and arrow" from the debris. I let fly in the general direction of my adversary, hoping merely to hold him at bay, when to my astonishment the featherless arrow darted and whipped to a fateful rendezvous with his lower lip, piercing it completely. He bolted with my unorthodox missile dangling from his lip, as terrified as I was. I now estimate that the "bow" pulled less than ten pounds, but as an engine of destruction it was truly and regrettably effective.

My pine slat weapon was destined for just that one shot, but it was linked across 450 years to those old English masterpieces by a kindred spirit which transcends time. That spirit is now being felt by people from every walk of life. Some live in cities, some in the country, and some in still primitive places like the jungles of New Guinea. The wooden bow is still alive and well as the year 2000 approaches.

Many old bows are still performing after decades of shooting. I own many myself, as do many of my archer-bowyer friends. Most of these long-lived bows are made from Osage orange, with yew and lemonwood coming in second and third respectively, since these were the primary woods used in the first half of this century. We have learned in recent years that there are other woods which can be made into excellent bows, like hickory, ash, elm, mulberry, and juniper, to name some of the front-runners. These days, energetic bowyers are using many diverse woods, enlightened designs, and inventive new techniques to optimize the efficiency of wood as a bow material.

As you read this chapter, you will notice that I favor Osage orange for bow wood (that's not a new conclusion, Art Young and the Comanches felt the same), so keep my admitted sentiments in mind. But also be aware that nothing in bowyery is true 100% of the time, that no two bowyers agree on everything, and a great deal of what happens in wood bow-making is not totally predictable, as it usually is with fiberglass and graphite.

I once made a bow from a stave which was cut in 1939, and since the bow had slept as a stave for fifty years, I named it "Sleeping Beauty." The friend to whom I gave the bow successfully used it on a hunt in Michigan in four degree weather, and was so moved by the bow's performance he wrote a poem about it and inscribed it on the lower limb. Such stuff could easily be called schmaltzy if it weren't so much fun.

To make a bow you will feel compelled to write verse about, to become a truly competent maker of wood bows, you must understand the structure of wood and its properties. Since wood comes from trees, someone has to decide which trunks or limbs to cut, how to store, cure, and protect them, and how and when to convert them into bowstaves. If you are not prepared to make these decisions you are not in full control of the bow making process.

If you purchase wood and depend upon someone else to make decisions for you, then you eventually (probably sooner rather than later) will get burned by spending hard currency on unusable wood. When a non-bowyer has sent me wood, even after my careful and extensive instructions on the requisite wood qualities, I have usually been grievously disappointed. Generally, non-bowyers don't intend to dupe us when they sell, or give, unsatisfactory wood, they just do not comprehend what we need. Too often I have seen neophyte bowyers spend hard-earned money and time on trash wood, making what I term faux bows, destined with a mathematical certainty to break.

Consider certain legitimate wood experts, like the craftsmen who make fine furniture and cabinets. They must be knowledgeable about wood selection, design, glues, use of power tools, finishes, and many other details. But they make things designed to function in some permutation of "sitting there." Now consider wood bows, which are forced to perform tortuous physical work, to undergo enormous forces of compression, tension, and shearing, shot after shot, year after year. These factors make wooden bows quite unique among everything made from wood, a fact which non-bowyers have a difficult time grasping.

I once paid "only" the freight on 800 pounds of "perfect" Osage, sent to me as a gift by a friend, a talented maker of fine furniture. You can guess what happened. Not one self bow in the pile: it was all walking sticks, firewood, and grubworm chow. "He meant well," I said through clenched teeth as I wrote the check for well over two hundred dollars in freight costs.

Of all the Osage biomass now in existence, considerably less than five percent of it is suited for making good, serious, dependable self bows. Yew experts make a similar pronouncement about their wood. With ash, hickory, elm, and other straight growing wood the percentage is considerably higher. But there are still many choices to be made during the interval between choosing a tree and actually beginning a bow. Armed with the expertise to select, cut, store, and cure his wood, the complete bowyer can procure his own wood as well as make the right choices on the offerings of other wood cutters.

What will serve you well is an understanding of how a tree grows, on the interior, tissue level. Many are surprised to learn that most of the mass of a tree is non-living, or to put it another way, dead. The outer bark and virtually ALL of the wood are dead tissues. That's a shocker, is it not, after all we have heard about the wood in a bow or an arrow coming from a living tree? It's true that wood performs an essential role in the tree's life, but wood cells and tissues themselves are dead. Leaves, flowers, fruits or nuts, and seeds are alive, but they come and go in a cycle. The main part of a tree that stays alive is a tissue-thin layer, a conoid cylinder of cells, called the **vascular cambium,** lying between the

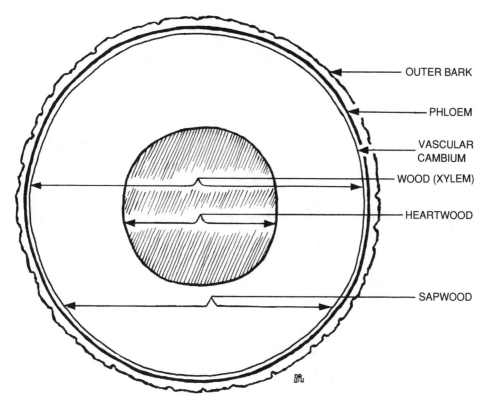

OUTER BARK

PHLOEM

VASCULAR CAMBIUM

WOOD (XYLEM)

HEARTWOOD

SAPWOOD

*Cross section of a tree.*

bark and the wood of a tree. As the tree grows outward in girth and upward in height, the vascular cambium lays down cells of wood, or **xylem,** to its interior. Soon after new wood cells are laid down they die, but their rigid walls of cellulose and other polymers continue to serve the living parts of the tree. Wood, or xylem, has three primary functions: wood recently formed, or sapwood, conducts water up through the plant, older wood, or heartwood, stores water, wastes, and other materials, and all of the wood provides structural support for the tree.

Potential bow wood trees fall into three classifications: the **ring-porous hardwoods** (Osage, ash, elm, hickory, oak, black locust, walnut, mulberry, and others), the **diffuse-porous hardwoods** (maple, poplar, and others), and the coniferous, cone-bearing woods, or **softwoods** (yew, cedar, juniper, pine, fir).

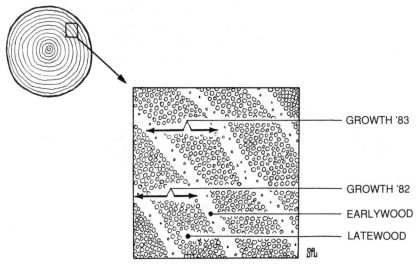

*Magnified representation of the annual growth rings of ring porous hardwoods, such as Osage orange, ash, hickory, elm, oak, and mulberry (for clarity, sapwood and heartwood are not shown as differentiated, and pore size is exaggerated).*

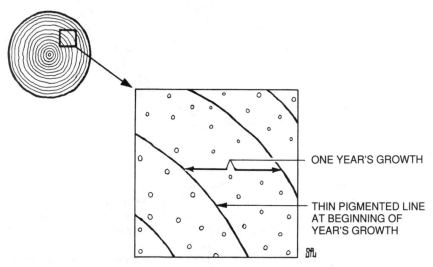

*Magnified representation of the annual growth rings of diffuse porous hardwoods, such as maple and poplar (for clarity, sapwood and heartwood are not shown as differentiated, and pore size is exaggerated).*

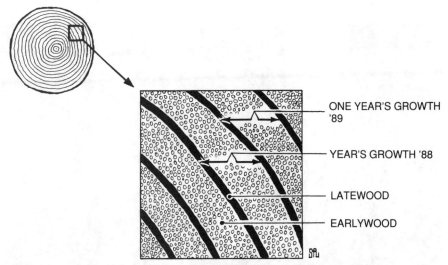

ONE YEAR'S GROWTH '89

YEAR'S GROWTH '88

LATEWOOD

EARLYWOOD

*Magnified representation of the annual growth rings of conifers, or softwoods, such as yew, cedar, juniper, and spruce (for clarity, sapwood and heartwood are not shown as differentiated, and pore size is exaggerated).*

In ring-porous hardwoods and conifers, when wood is first laid down by the vascular cambium, it is comparatively lighter in color (white to light tan), and is called **sapwood.** When you cut a tree and examine it in cross-section, you will see a band of white sapwood around the outer margin of log (the width of this band varies from species to species). As the years pass and the vascular cambium continues to move outward, the innermost rings of sapwood are overtaken by the tideline of another phenomenon that moves steadily outward as well: the conversion of sapwood into dark-colored **heartwood.**

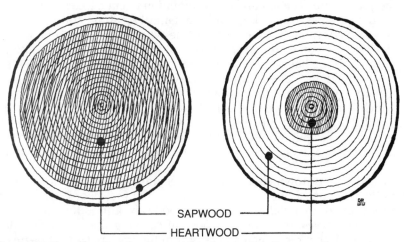

SAPWOOD

HEARTWOOD

*Left) Representation of heartwood and sapwood in trees such as Osage, mulberry, and yew, among others, i.e. mostly heartwood. Right) Heartwood and sapwood in trees such as hickory, elm, and ash, among others, i.e. mostly sapwood.*

*Bow staves, left to right; black locust, yew, Osage orange, cedar, ash, and hickory.*

It should be mentioned that sap, a very complex substance analogous to blood, is not found in wood (water, resins, and other substances are present but sap is not). Sap is carried only in a very thin layer of tissue called the **phloem,** which is also deposited by the vascular cambium, but which lies just outside it. Sap is scarce in phloem during cold weather, but the wood contains a lot of water the year round. The old archery admonition to cut a tree in winter "while the sap is down" does not hold up under botanical scrutiny, nor in the opinions of many knowledgeable bowyers. Cut a tree when you want to or when you can, just make sure you treat it properly once it is down. More on this later.

In the ring-porous hardwoods, as in conifers, a cross-section of a log shows obvious annual "rings." Closer inspection reveals that they are really alternating rings of porous wood, called **springwood** or **earlywood,** and relatively denser wood which is much less porous, called **latewood** or **summerwood.** Whatever the color of the latewood, the earlywood will usually be a somewhat lighter shade (a notable exception to this is ash, wherein the earlywood is darker). One full year's growth of wood will include one ring of both earlywood and late-wood.

Earlywood is laid down first each year, beginning with the spring growth surge as the tree comes out of hibernation. It is the first poor attempt to make wood after being dormant all winter. Earlywood is produced for a few days to a few weeks and serves its porous purpose of carrying the year's first flow of water up through the tree. When all systems in the tree are "go," it begins making latewood and continues this until the cessation of growth in the fall, at which time it becomes dormant again during the winter. The following spring

*Osage orange, showing earlywood to latewood ratios in various pieces. From left to right the wood gets better, as the proportional amount of earlywood drops.*

the cycle begins again, with another layer of earlywood, and so on. Don't lose sight of the fact that with each year's growth, the diameter of the tree increases.

Understand the significance of the above; in ring-porous hardwoods, latewood is the virtuous, dense material of which toxophilic dreams are made. It contains those special fiber cells which give the wood its springiness. In a word, latewood is "good" stuff. Earlywood, on the other hand, is, for a bow-maker, almost without virtue. It is weak, treacherous, has no springiness, and if exposed improperly on the back of a self bow can spell doom for the weapon. Of course, here is the bowyer's rub; you have to take them together. It is like dating a knockout, a "10", but having to take her goofy brother along, every time.

*The thickness of the yearly growth rings is not nearly as important as the earlywood/latewood ratio. The piece on the right is above average for Osage, though the wood on the left could certainly make an acceptable bow if made a bit wider or longer than normal.*

25

*Opposite ends of the earlywood/latewood spectrum. The Osage on the left is mostly earlywood, and is therefore nearly worthless, while the piece on the right is exceptional and made an excellent bow.*

The better logs and staves will have thinner earlywood and wider, denser latewood. In other words, the less total additive earlywood, and the more total additive latewood in your stave, the better the wood and the better the bow will be. The thickness of the yearly rings is not nearly as important as the ratio of early to late wood. In this regard, notice the piece of wood to the far left in the photo. There is virtually no latewood in the outer 60% of this wood, only early-wood deposition year in, year out. I would expect a bow made from this wood to take a hideous, permanent horseshoe shaped set, if it didn't break outright. Even sinewing would not save it. An aspiring young bowyer I know actually paid United States dollars for this piece of wood.

In the outer part of older trees with very wide yearly growth rings, 3/8" or larger, sometimes "mini" rings are evident within the layers of latewood. I call these tiny rings monthly, or **lunar rings,** (they can be seen with a magnifying glass) and they seem to be composed of thin layers of earlywood within the late-wood. The end result is that a piece of wood which, upon first glance, appears wonderful, with thick yearly rings and a low early to latewood ratio, sometimes contains more earlywood than it appears and will be correspondingly weaker.

As a rule, one would expect that for a given species of tree (like Osage) warmer climes, with longer growing seasons, would produce faster growing trees with wider annual rings than would colder climates. However, this is by no means universally true. I have found beautiful wide growth rings in Osage from Indiana and Michigan, states far north of my beloved, and HOT, Texas.

Conversely, I have cut Texas Osage with growth rings too narrow to discern. Even more to the point, Jim Hamm has chronicled extreme variations in Osage wood along a quarter-mile stretch of creek near his home. He notes that out of a total of two dozen trees cut, some had 3/8" annual growth rings, or 3 to the inch, while some had annual rings twenty to the inch. Some had very little early-wood in relation to latewood while others were a 50-50 ratio. This stark variation in wood properties and quality in an area where the available sun, soil, and water are virtually the same suggests strongly that there is more at work here than simply climate; thus the *genetics* of a given tree may play an even more important role in determining the quality of the wood. I once germinated Osage seeds and treated them identically for several years. After that time they ranged in height from four inches to four feet! That's an extreme variation in genetic make-up.

One factor that, to my knowledge, has never been investigated relative to Osage wood quality is that of sex. This is a **dioeceous** tree, meaning each plant is either a male OR a female. Perhaps the best bows come from one sex or the other. No one knows. There are certainly botanical precedents for this speculation. In the 1920's and 30's, female Tonkin cane was highly prized for surf rods, while the male cane was vastly inferior. Someone should investigate "Sex and the Single Osage," to determine if the sex of the tree matters where bow wood quality is concerned.

Now that we have a view of the bigger picture, let's dot some needed I's and cross some specific T's.

Coniferous woods such as yew grow in the same earlywood-latewood pattern as the ring-porous trees, such as Osage and hickory, but there is a significant difference with regard to the earlywood. In yew and many other conifers the earlywood has some strength and integrity, unlike the worthless earlywood of ring-porous hardwoods. Also, the earlywood of conifers is a larger percentage of the year's total growth, though with yew this is not as evident as with cedar, for example.

In most species of trees, the white, or tan, sapwood is very strong and virtuous, and in many trees, like the "white" woods of elm, ash, and hickory, most of the good bow wood IS sapwood, which makes up the bulk of one of these logs. Ax handles made of hickory are mostly sapwood, with only the occasional presence of darker heartwood. The sapwood of hickory possesses incredible tensile strength, perhaps the strongest of any wood. Yew is another tree with outstanding sapwood, which appears as a creamy white margin around the edge of the reddish-brown heartwood; not so thick as in hickory but with excellent tensile strength. It is therefore a natural backing to protect the springy heartwood of a yew bow.

Strange as it may seem, the sapwood of Osage orange is less than worthless. It is to the noble yellow heartwood what an egg-sucking cur is to the family's Best-of-Show Labrador Retriever. While I have successfully made small bows having a layer of sapwood on the back, I have never seen the sapwood of Osage sustain its role as an integral part of any serious, legitimate bow. It is profoundly ironic that the yellow heartwood of Osage (or to be more precise, the collective latewood of the heartwood), is on balance probably the best bow wood material in the world, while the sapwood may be the worst. The irony goes yet deeper, because the heartwood we value so highly began its role in the tree AS sapwood. How convenient it is that the cryptic and wonderful metamorphosis by which the useless sapwood becomes noble heartwood is attended by a color change from white to electric yellow!

Several years ago I came across a remarkable young Osage tree. It was only three inches in diameter, though with a beautiful straight trunk. It spoke to me, "Ron, cut me down an make me into two longbows. Please." (Delusions like this are one of the occupational hazards for wood bowyers). Once cut and split, the heartwood of this tree was obviously exceptional, with pencil-line thin early-wood rings and wide latewood rings. In addition, both split halves took an enormous backset after a few weeks, indicating that "the wood badly wanted to be a bow." One drawback, however, was that there wasn't enough wood in either half to make an all-heartwood bow. So, against my better instincts, I incorporated a thin layer of sapwood into the bow's back in order to have enough wood, and it made one of the fastest bows I've ever seen, a true rocket launcher. But after three months of shooting, I began to hear the tell-tale "tick" from each new crack as it appeared in the sapwood back. The failures were both longitudinal and transverse, failures which are unheard of in an all-heartwood back. At any rate, one warm afternoon the bow suffered a violent death while at full draw. Alas, the bow was brilliant but flawed, due to the ignobility of the sapwood.

When critically evaluating any tree, the type of bow you wish to make is a prime consideration. Obviously, a piece of wood for a short, thin, and narrow bow, as in many Indian designs, is much easier to find than for a long bow with wide limbs and a deep, rigid handle. Don't overlook pieces only thirty five to forty inches long, they can be split and joined with a fish-tail splice to make long bows. A bit of terminology may be in order here. A **stave** is a full-length piece of wood used to make a bow, while **billets** are two shorter pieces joined at the handle. **Sister billets** refers to pieces split side-by-side from the same log, giving each limb of a bow identical characteristics.

The tree you select should be a minimum of eight inches in diameter (if this is

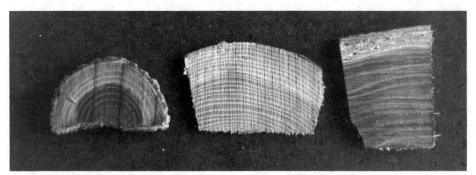

*Cross sections from different size trees. A small branch, on the left, would require de-crowning, or flattening of the back, a difficult task for a beginner. The center piece is from an eight inch diameter tree and its back will be only slightly crowned for an average width bow. The section on the right is from a fifteen inch tree, and the back of the bow will be almost flat.*

your first bow), and at least a couple of inches longer than the finished bow. Why the stated diameter? First, a stave from it will be deep enough in the belly to accommodate a thick handle section. Second, it will be fairly flat across the back, without a pronounced hump. The selected tree should be as straight as possible, though this is a relative term depending on the species. Straight ash or elm is, indeed, straight, while good quality Osage or yew sometimes exhibits some crooks, or character. A perfect eight inch log will probably yield four perfect staves, but "perfect" for the wood bowyer is like the 29th of February to everyone else.

The tree you cut, especially if you're just beginning to make bows, should be free of knots or other deformities. Very young Osage trees, though resilient and springy, are full of pins and knots, which are a daunting proposition without considerable experience. After you've made a few bows, you'll probably want to try for a young, hyper-knotty character bow. A prevalent quirk among bowyers is that the knottier and weirder it looks, the more desirable it becomes.

But bow-making will be more enjoyable, at first, if you stay with trees which are straight. This is not always easy with yew and Osage, though the white woods – ash, hickory, and elm, – are a bow-maker's delight. It is far better to spend a couple of extra hours searching for a few select trees than to spend days wrestling, and ultimately cursing, a great pile of worthless, crooked wood.

It should be noted that even carefully selected trees will not always be perfectly straight. They may curve slightly in one plane, like a parenthesis mark ( . You can get one stave from the very outside of the tree and one from the inside. The latter will have a built-in backset and the former a "taken" set, though with some seasoning it may come to be nearly straight. Both staves, however, will yield bows in which the string will be centered down its length. Again, after you've made some bows you might grow bold and go for a dog-leg in one or both limbs by trying a shallow S-shaped log. I've made some fine-shooting, interesting bows from such logs, but it requires a bit of dues-paying to pull it off.

What if there is a big limb growing from one side of the trunk, or a split, or rotten place, or some other deformity? Think like Saxton Pope; if there is one good stave in the tree, proceed to cut it down.

Before cutting a tree, look closely at the bark, because its appearance is a sure indicator of major grain characteristics of the wood. (Minor grain squiggles and snaky grain can often be hidden by the bark and can be a pleasant, or perhaps unpleasant, surprise.) **Grain** is a word often misunderstood and misused, which is not surprising, considering how many aspects there are to the three-dimensional structure of wood. It is important that you understand what the term really means, because grain is a crucial factor in laying out a bow. First, grain is completely different from growth rings. If we use a spoked bicycle wheel and tire as an analogy of a tree's cross-section, then the tire would represent an outer yearly growth ring, and the spokes would represent the grain, which radiates out from the center of the log, through all of the growth rings. If you've split firewood with an ax, you know exactly how grain runs, and how the split will follow it precisely. The grain determines how a log will split: it can be straight, spiraled, or snaky. So, examine the bark of a tree because it is an expression of

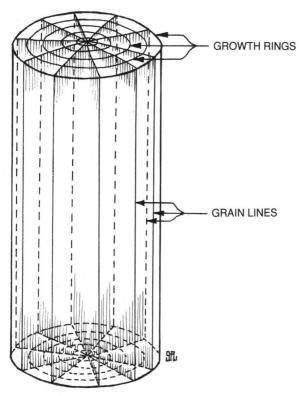

*Representation of the annual growth rings and the grain of a log. The growth rings are concentric cylinders, while the grain radiates out from the center of the log and runs lengthwise. In this "log", the grain is perfectly straight, and has been exaggerated and simplified for clarity. Growth rings are very obvious to the naked eye while the grain can be difficult to see, especially in cut lumber.*

*A tree with bark which spirals up the trunk will split like this, and be worthless for making bows*

the grain. If the bark spirals up the trunk, search on. Even if the tree is stovepipe straight, the spiral grain makes it worthless. An orthodox bow made from a spiral-grain tree will have the grain running diagonally across the limbs, making it prone to breakage. The more pronounced the spiral, the greater the risk. As a footnote, it seems that spiral-grain growth in a tree often correlates to a wind blown habitat, though it's not a 1:1 correlation.

Now, at last, we stand ready near the chosen tree (drum roll, please). No matter what the species, the trunk is the right diameter and length, and the straight bark indicates that the grain is straight.

The two things needed are a saw and some type of film-forming liquid to seal the ends of the log. Varnish, paint, and such will work, but I recommend a white, vinyl base glue, such as Elmer's™. It comes in a handy squeeze container, it is easy to spread with the fingers, clean up is easy since it is water soluble, it dries fast, and it dries clear. This last feature is important when you have many logs curing and want to visually inspect the rings of a particular piece.

Using a bow saw or chain saw, cut the tree down, placing the cut to save as much length as possible. Now, cut the section you've chosen free from the remainder of the tree and quickly cover the exposed ends of the log with glue, extending the coverage well onto the bark for two inches or so.

Why such a rush to seal the log's end? Within minutes of being cut, a log begins losing water vapor from the exposed ends, sometimes so fast that cracks appear. With Osage, you can often hear audible cracking sounds within moments of felling a tree. These cracks are called heart checks, or end checks. The way to minimize them is to seal the ends so that water can escape along the length of the log only, and NOT out of the ends. This is a fundamental concept of all wood drying which you must appreciate and observe.

In some cases, a log will require splitting before it can be transported, and there is no harm in reducing it to manageable sections at once. This is another

*Using a sledgehammer and wedges to split half of a small Osage log.*

*Two quarters of the log, now in stave form.*

reason to cut eight and ten inch logs; they can be handled by two average sized men with no problem. When I began my journey down the toxophilic highway, I lusted after huge Osage trees, reflecting upon all of the bows locked up inside. After wrestling with a few to the point of herniation, however, I realized I wasn't being smart and that two ten inch logs were better than one twenty-four incher. Even if a big log can be transported intact, it is a nightmare to split. When a student bowyer once asked Jim Hamm how he split a monster thirty inch Osage log, he replied, "I just beat on the wedges with a sledgehammer until I passed out. Then when I came to, I'd get up and beat on them some more."

There are not many reasons to wait to split a log of bow wood. As soon as it can be conveniently done, split four inch logs in half, eight inches logs into quarters, and ten to twelve inches logs into six pieces if practical. The staves should be two to two and a half inches wide. Never try to squeeze too many bows from a log: greed breeds wasted wood. Usually, in an attempt to get eight staves from a log instead of six ("if I'm real careful how I split it") three or four staves will be the resulting yield.

Split the log using a sledgehammer, wedges, and a single bladed ax (flat on the back). Begin the process by looking to see if any spontaneous grain splits have started in the ends. Smaller trees will often exhibit one straight grain split, inviting you to split it into two equal halves. Larger pieces will frequently develop two splits, at right angles, yielding four staves from the log. Consider natural cleavages as possible guidelines, but you decide where to make splits in order to obtain the most efficient use of the log.

Start by positioning the blade of the ax on the edge of the log where you want it to split. The split will usually run a bit straighter if it is begun on the larger end of the log. Strike the flat back of the ax sharply with the sledge so that it enters the wood. Continue hammering until a split begins and the ax is mostly buried in the wood. Position a wedge in the split and drive it in until only an inch or two are showing. Now the split will be well up the sides of the piece. Another wedge is driven into the split on the opposite side of the log, which should free the first wedge. The ax is used to cut any splinters connecting the two sides of the split. By alternating sides with the wedges, the log can be separated into two halves. Splitting the halves into quarters is done similarly, but the wedges are placed only from the bark side.

By splitting the logs you will A) get a good reading on the run of the grain, and B) speed up the drying process. Green logs are loaded with water: freshly cut logs of Osage, hickory, and elm can have more than 35% water in their total weight. Splitting the logs allows the water a place to quickly exit the wood, which greatly speeds up drying times.

Green wood is not stable and will occasionally have a tendency to shift or warp until the water content has fallen considerably. The most frequent movement of a split log, especially Osage, is 1) taking a backset (particularly common when a small piece is split in half), which is advantageous, 2) torquing into some degree of longitudinal twist, or 3) both of the above at once. Looking at this on the tissue level, loss of water causes wood to shrink substantially, thus becoming harder and more dense. If logs are allowed to dry whole, they will spontaneously develop cleavages or cracks along lines of the grain as the wood

*Sometimes wood from a small tree, and Osage in particular, will take a backset upon drying. This piece was flat when first split.*

shrinks.

An interesting alternative for drying logs less than 6 inches in diameter involves a hand-held circular saw. If the log is straight, with an obvious straight grain, you can make one straight cut with the saw down the entire length of the log, the kerf approaching or, indeed, going to the center of the log. As water escapes, the kerf will open up to a V, indicating shrinkage and curing of the wood. This method helps prevent any warpage in the wood while allowing the water vapor a place to escape.

A band saw, 14 inches in size, or larger, will greatly aid in reducing bigger

*Eight to fifteen inch logs split into quarters to be more easily handled when sawing.*

*A large bandsaw with a powerful motor and wide blade will allow precise reduction of quarter logs and reduce waste.*

logs once they are split into quarters which can be more easily handled. By using a bandsaw, the optimum amount of staves can be obtained from the log through precise cuts and reduction. The saw will also earn its keep later by allowing you to cut out bows and splices.

Water loss in a log is inevitable, as it should and has to be, but the rate of this drying depends on the temperature and ventilation in the drying area. Assuming adequate ventilation, wood dries quite nicely in any warm to hot environment protected from sun and rain, such as a garage.

There are two modes of proper storage if the wood is Osage: either leave the bark and sapwood on the stave, or remove them both. In other words, it is a patently bad idea to take off the bark and leave the sapwood on. The sapwood has little integrity and strength and will crack upon drying, carrying these cracks right into the heartwood and potentially ruining a stave. If the bark and sapwood are removed, drying is facilitated and the insidious drying cracks will

*A quarter log usually has several staves within it.*

*The first cut with the bandsaw is made here.*

*And the second cut made here.*

*A stack of bandsawn staves, arranged so that air can circulate between them.*

*It is a good idea to write a date on each stave, or even a date and the location where the tree was cut, so the drying and the characteristics of the wood can be closely followed.*

rarely occur in the heartwood without the sapwood to begin them.

If only green wood is at hand, and the bowyer is itching to make a bow, there is a simple technique for greatly reducing drying times. Most wood dries (to 7-12% moisture) at about the rate of an inch a year from the outside of the wood toward the center. It is easy to see that an entire log will take years to dry, and a two inch by two inch stave at least a year. But if green wood is worked to a single growth ring on the back, and the shape of the bow cut out with the thickness reduced to near finished dimensions, then the wood will dry in a matter of a month and be ready to tiller and finish. It is simply a matter of there being much less mass for the water vapor to escape from. A bowyer can work several pieces to this stage from a stock of green wood and have plenty of seasoned wood within a short time.

One of the darker demons which bedevils the Osage bow-maker is the sapwood grub worm, the larval form of a kind of wood wasp. No one knows for sure when the eggs are laid. I personally feel they are laid after the logs are cut,

*Mature wood wasp.*

*Wood wasp grub, in a cavity in an Osage stave.*

*Grub damage in a stave. Note that the holes are all in or near the sapwood.*

*Tell-tale clue of wood grub presence, small piles of sawdust on the back of a stave.*

because the worst ravaging by these grubs occurs in open air sheds where the mature wasps have access to the logs. In closed storage, such as a garage, much less damage occurs. If I had my way, and if the sapwood grub would pay attention to his work, he could eat ALL of the sapwood from Osage with my blessing. The problem is that while 85% of his munching is, indeed, done in sapwood, the 15% done down into the heartwood can damage a stave, especially one destined to become a self bow. It seems that in staves from larger logs, the grub rarely advances more than a yearly ring or two into the heartwood, but with smaller pieces, especially those small enough to split into two halves, the grubs sometimes eat entirely through the heartwood all the way to the pith in the center. The cure for these grubs, if you are working with only a few staves of wood and have time, is to remove bark AND sapwood with a drawknife down to the heartwood.

Yew wood bowyers are not so cursed with wood-eating critters as are Osage bowyers, since every part of the yew contains a toxic substance which protects the tree from insect invaders. Woodpeckers and bears, however, can maul a yew tree. Chain saws are now the biggest threat to yew, since the revelation that its bark contains an anti-cancer principle.

John Strunk prefers to cut his yew wood in the spring or fall, but will readily harvest available trees any time of the year. He mentions that summer-cut wood is more inclined to develop cracks if not properly end-sealed with some appropriate agent. After splitting it into stave size, he air dries it for a year, leaving the bark in place. The finer-ringed yew, with forty or more rings to the inch, seems to be stronger than coarser wood. The finer wood is usually found at higher elevations.

Paul Comstock has become adept at using **white woods** for bows: ash, hickory, and elm. He pioneered a beautiful procedure for treating these woods so as to make the back of the self bow a continuous, uninterrupted yearly ring, which is the ideal for a wood bow. He does this by cutting trees in August, when the sap in the phloem is at a maximum and a solid layer of latewood has been laid down for the year. After quickly treating the ends, he splits the logs into staves as usual. The wet, sappy bark is then pulled from the stave in long strips, exposing the wood underneath, which will be the perfect, intact back of the bow. The staves are then air dried until ready for use. The secret is cutting the wood during hot weather; in the winter the bark bonds tightly to the tree and its removal becomes more difficult. In such a case, Paul places the stave in a steamy shower for twenty minutes or so which allows the bark to be scraped free more easily.

In my experience, a lot of misinformation exists about the advisability of using kiln-dried wood to make bows. I have heard people of all ages condemn it categorically. I've also read some negative reviews on kiln-drying from some of the patriarchal bowyer-authors. To state, "Kiln dried wood is no good for bows" is like saying, "People with red hair have hot tempers." Both statements are unsubstantiated opinions. I have made many bows, both self and backed, from kiln-dried wood and they have performed as well as air-dried wood. The reason? A kiln is simply a chamber with an elevated temperature (usually about 140 degrees F) used to drive moisture from green wood more quickly. A car with the windows rolled up in summer can be considered a "kiln," as can an attic in summer. There IS a legitimate concern over leaving wood in a kiln of any kind for too long. It is easy to "overshoot" the runway of desired moisture and end up with wood that is too dry, and therefore brittle, because of the speed with which water can exit the wood.

The remedy is to ride herd on the moisture level with a **moisture meter.** It is an invaluable aid to the bow-maker in controlling drying.

A few years ago, before he bought a moisture meter, Jim Hamm placed some young tree staves in his attic for ninety days during the West Texas spring and summer, unknowingly lowering the moisture content well below five percent. Taking one of these staves from his attic, he began work on a long beautiful self bow as several student bowyers watched. As he finally approached full draw with the near finished bow, it exploded with a deafening CRACK! Small pieces of bow filled the air. Before the last piece hit the floor, Jim quietly said, "I have a better piece of wood right over here," whereupon he fetched it and began work.

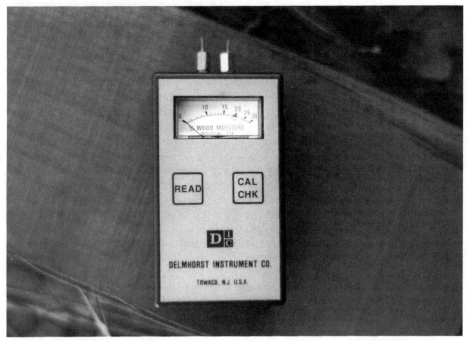

*A moisture meter, a worthwhile investment for monitoring the drying of bow wood.*

I mention this not only to illustrate the lethality of low moisture content from too much drying, but to extoll the virtues of all-conference, industrial-strength persistence in wood bow-making. You will need it. Indeed, you must have it. You will learn a lot from every bow you make, but you will learn far more from every bow you break.

Here are some guidelines for wood moisture. Five percent moisture, or below, in most bow woods is dangerously low, and over fifteen percent can be too wet to make a stable, finished bow. Seven to twelve percent is generally the window of desirability, depending on the relative humidity and time of year. In most species, green wood is very limber and of low strength, and as the moisture content is lowered, it gains strength while losing flexibility. Green wood can be very springy, especially Osage and yew, and a quickie survival bow can be made from a branch right from the tree. But these bows are usually of short draw length, low draw weight, and have a short life, although I must note that some green Osage bows over the years have been delightful and notable exceptions to this rule.

I have shagbark hickory kiln-dried in Arkansas, from its 40% down to about 20%, then shipped to me as two inch thick boards for air drying to about 10% in my hot, Austin, Texas garage. This initial kiln-drying saves paying freight on the 20% moisture difference and allows me to closely control the final "cured" water content before making bows or backing strips from the hickory. Osage, which I cut locally, is dried in the attic initially, until it reaches 15-20% moisture, then in the garage until it reaches 8%, as measured with a meter.

Tim Baker has added to his numerous Toxophilic credits a technique for determining when wood has stabilized moisture-wise. Keeping his wood in a warm environment, he simply weighs a piece of it until it stops losing moisture (and weight), waits another week, and *voilà* it's ready. He has even used a crude balance scale to accomplish this, with good results. With green pieces which have been worked close to bow shape, the drying usually takes two to four weeks.

Frequently, you can tell by visual inspection when wood has been over-dried. This is handy if you find a stash of bow quality wood in a lumber store and don't have a moisture meter. Look for numerous small cracks throughout the wood, and/or separation of the annual rings. You can also secretly get a sliver of wood and play with it; demonstrated brittleness will usually signal an elevated risk of bow breakage.

*Cutting your own wood allows more control of the bowmaking process.*

Jim Hamm, once intensely opposed to kiln-dried wood as a result of incidents like the one related previously, has softened that stance considerably since obtaining a moisture meter. In fact, he has conducted preliminary tests which indicate that even wood which has been dried to below 5%, if allowed to naturally re-hydrate through relative humidity to an equilibrium of seven to twelve percent, suffers little, if any, degradation in strength. Which is good news for the prospective bowyer. Most lumber at a commercial yard will have reached equilibrium with the local environment, which means that if a piece has the characteristics of a bow, i.e, straightness, and no tell-tale signs of drying abuse, as outlined above, then it can confidently be bought and used. I have made scores of bows from hickory and ash lumber, as has Tim Baker, among others.

No matter where you obtain your wood in the beginning, from a lumberyard or a wood dealer, at some point you will undoubtedly want to cut your own. It is profoundly satisfying to participate in the entire bow-making process, from choosing the tree all the way through to applying the finish. And if you are a hunter, there is an atavistic delight in knowing that your weapons were fashioned from materials found growing in the very sanctuary of the quarry you seek. Imagine the predatory irony of killing a deer with a bow made from a tree the deer had used for a scrape. Talk about Toxophilic dreams!

# BOW DESIGN AND PERFORMANCE

*Tim Baker*

There is magic in a wooden bow. A simple stick of wood bent to crescent shape, suddenly alive with power, straining to do far distant deeds. A wooden bow has a fascination quite apart from utility. Few can hold one and not be affected by complicated subterranean emotions.

It is not surprising that archery is so often embraced with near-religious devotion. This may be the reason archery lore is saturated with unquestioned dogma.

If you want to start a good fistfight, walk into a bowmaker's bar and say, for example, that a host of common woods can equal Osage and yew in cast, that kiln-dried and air-dried wood can make equally good bows, or that bow wood does not stack before breaking.

This would be like walking into a medieval Bishops' bar and saying the world is round, the earth orbits the sun, and man descended from lower forms.

Much of archery's doctrine, when examined in an unbiased manner, is seen as incorrect or inhibiting. Such misinformation, especially concerning "other" woods, has long been a serious bottle-neck to the rebirth and growth of natural archery.

Imagine the number of would-be bowmakers, influenced by writers of the yew-based, stacked-limb English tradition, who never made a bow because they couldn't find or afford sufficient staves of Osage or yew with which to learn the craft. If natural archery hopes to become even marginally as popular as synthetic archery there simply will not be enough Osage and yew to go around.

Paul Comstock, in his 1988 publication, *The Bent Stick,* surfaces as natural archery's Copernicus. This book adds a host of woods to Osage and yew at the center of the archery universe. His wide, flat-bellied designs let more abundant woods display their high-cast potential. These designs are not new. They are as old as archery itself. But their value was not appreciated by inheritors of the English tradition.

10,000-plus years have passed since the first bow cast the first arrow. A variety of designs have emerged through the ages, each with scores of sub-designs. An equal number of material choices exist. From this rich variety, which is the best choice for you? The answer depends on what you want a bow to do.

This chapter will explain design and performance characteristics of each of the principal designs, whether new or ancient. It should help you choose the type of bow best suited to your needs and shows how best to design it.

The best bow for you will likely contain some mix of the following ten qualities:

- Arrow speed
- Accuracy
- Comfort of draw and release
- Durability
- Suitability for its use environment

- Beauty
- Ease of construction
- Ease of Maintenance
- Cost, or availability of materials
- Unobtrusiveness

Following are the benefits and trade-offs of each of these design qualities. Arrow speed is covered first, because design factors affecting arrow speed affect most other aspects of bowmaking as well.

## ARROW SPEED

An obsessive pursuit of ever-higher arrow speed can distract from the satisfaction of natural archery. But so can a disregard of arrow speed.

Higher arrow speed has at least three benefits: 1) A flatter flight path, making aiming easier at varying distances. 2) Faster arrows have more penetrating power, and 3) Game can dodge a slow arrow.

It's easy to make an arrow fly faster – shoot it from a stronger bow. But there is a limit to the weight each of us can accurately draw, aim and release. Better than making a too-heavy bow is designing a bow which shoots an arrow faster per pound of draw weight. An efficient 50 lb straight-stave bow, for example, can cast a given arrow as fast as an inefficient 70 lb straight-stave bow. Arrow speed disparity is even greater when comparing bows of different designs.

The word "efficiency" when applied to archery bows, as with other machines, means the difference between work put in and work taken out.

But a quest for this specific type of efficiency in a bow is irrelevant to the purpose of archery.

What matters to an archer is *how fast a bow shoots per pound of draw weight.*

A 50 lb bow which stores 100 units of energy and imparts 80% of it to an arrow is energy efficient. But such a bow is not as desirable as a 50 lb bow which stores 200 units of energy and releases 60% to the arrow. This cast-per-pound definition of efficiency is more useful, and unless otherwise indicated will apply in this chapter.

*Only two factors determine the speed of a given arrow :*
1) The amount of muscle energy put into the bow while drawing the arrow.
2) Impediments to the transfer of that energy to the arrow.

If you take nothing else away with you from this chapter, take this away. This simple insight, if worked over with common sense, will lead to full fluency in bow design.

The amount of muscle energy put into the bow is determined by:

- draw weight
- draw length
- string height
- bow profile

Impediments to the transfer of stored energy to the arrow are:

- limb mass
- mass placement
- hysterisis ("internal friction" in the limb)
- string weight
- string stretch

Understanding how these energy modifiers operate and interact lets you design a more efficient bow, one which shoots faster per pound of draw weight.

First, the factors which affect the stored energy in a bow, and thus the arrow speed:

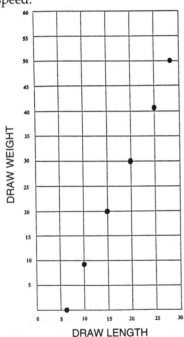
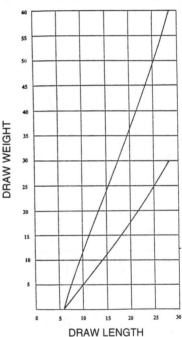

*Left: To measure a bow's stored energy draw the bow using a spring scale, noting its draw weight at various lengths of draw. A typical 50 lb. longbow will weigh: 10" = 8 lb; 15" = 20 lb; 20" = 30 lb; 25" = 41 lb; 28" = 50 lb. Label the bottom and side of the graph as shown. Make a dot where the 8 lb line and the 10" line cross. Make a dot where the 20 lb line and the 15" line cross, and so on. When finished, connect the dots. The resulting line is called the force-draw curve. Area under the line represents energy stored.*

*Right: F-d curves for a 30 pound and a 60 pound bow. Squares under a curve represent energy stored.*

## Draw Weight

Everything else being equal, higher draw weight stores more energy.

These force-draw curves show the energy stored in typical bows made from straight staves. One having a draw weight of 30 lb at 28", the other 60 lb at 28". The number of squares below a curve represents total energy stored.

This stored energy is the ONLY means available for propelling the arrow.

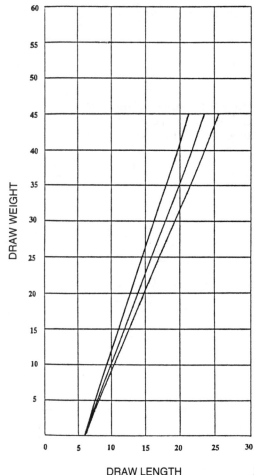

DRAW LENGTH

*Longer draw lengths store more energy.*

## Draw Length

Everything else being equal, longer draw lengths store more energy.

A 59" maple bow, made from a straight, unaltered stave, shooting a 500 grain arrow, was tillered to draw 45 pounds at 22", shooting 128 fps. This bow pulled 14 pounds at 10" of draw, and after being unstrung had taken a 1/2" set.

It was retillered to draw 45 pounds at 24", shooting 133 fps. Weight at 10" dropped to 11.5 pounds and set rose to 3/4".

Retillering continued to 45 pounds at 26", shooting 137 fps. Ten-inch draw weight fell to 10 pounds, with 1" set.

Each re-tillered version was equally hard to draw to length, but stored increasing amounts of energy. Note how early draw weight fell as set increased. As will be seen in this chapter, set would have remained even lower if limbs had been wider, longer, or made of a more elastic material. Early-draw weight would then remain high, storing more energy, raising arrow speed even more.

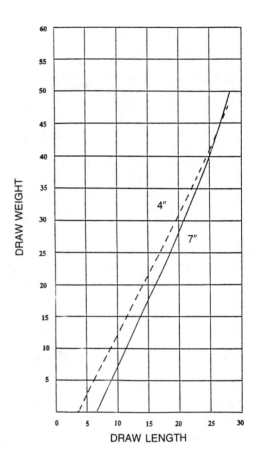

*A low-strung bow stores more energy.*

## String Height

Within a reasonable range lower string, or brace heights yields faster arrows.

Picture two identical bows strung 7" high drawing 50 lbs at 28". Lower the string on one bow to 4". At 28" of draw, this bow's weight will drop to about 47.5 lb. Its first few inches of draw will now be considerably weaker than the 7" bow's. When plucked, the string feels limp and sounds dead. The 7" bow feels taut and robust. Intuitively we know the 7" bow will throw an arrow farther and drive it deeper.

But, as will repeatedly be true in archery design, intuition has lead us astray.

The 4" bow, despite its lower weight and spongy early draw, will out-shoot the 7" bow by a couple of feet per second. It does so because a low-strung bow stores more energy.

More energy is stored principally because a 4" string travels 24", while a 7" string travels only 21". At ten inches of draw the 4" string has been drawn 6 inches and the bow weighs 13 lb.; the 7" string has been drawn only 3 inches and the bow weighs 9 lb.

A high-strung bow is more strained. Tips, in this case, are advanced three inches farther, causing considerably more bend, therefore, limb strain. For this reason low-strung bows can be left strung longer, take less set, and are in less danger of breaking.

But there are disadvantages to low string heights. If not identically spined, arrows tend to spray right and left as each struggles to "paradox" around the grip. And low strings slap the wrist.

Each archer will find a personal string height which balances performance and comfort. For hunters, string height choice is less flexible. To avoid the game-spooking noise of feathers scratching as a bow is drawn, brace height must exceed feather length.

Varying string heights on a recurved bow cause larger performance differences than on straight-stave bows. Low strings make contact lower on the curve, the bow is therefore even "shorter" during early stages of draw.

How string height affects arrow flight, and how to tune a bow, will be dealt with in Volume II of *The Traditional Bowyer's Bible*.

### Bow Profile, or Side-View Shape

This is the final factor affecting the amount of energy stored in a bow, and while the explanation is somewhat lengthy, it is by far the most important.

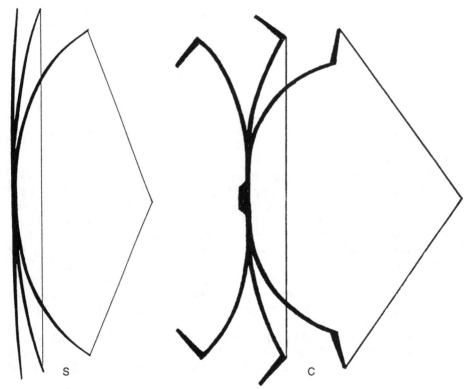

A straight-stave bow relaxed, braced, and drawn.

Composite bow relaxed, braced, and drawn.

Shown are two 50 lb bows of equal draw length. The straight-stave bow shoots a 500 grain arrow 150 fps; the Asiatic composite shoots the same arrow 175 fps. Why? Both take equal effort to hold at full draw, yet note how much more energy is stored by the composite, especially during early-draw. The secret to the difference in energy storage rests in their profiles.

A braced but undrawn bow has no ability to throw an arrow. The only energy available to a bow for the casting of arrows is energy taken from the arm as the bow is drawn. The more work your arm is made to do, the faster the arrow will fly.

Even when comparing bows of identical draw weight and length, certain bow profiles cause the arm to do more work.

The only way to put more energy into a given draw weight, draw length bow is to design it to be harder to pull in the early and mid stages of draw. In this way the total effort, or accumulated effort of drawing the bow is greater, even though its weight at full draw is the same.

No mystical capacity for arrow speed resides in any particular wood, fiberglass, sinew or horn. There is little difference in recovery speed or efficiency between various bowmaking materials. Virtually all such magic resides in a

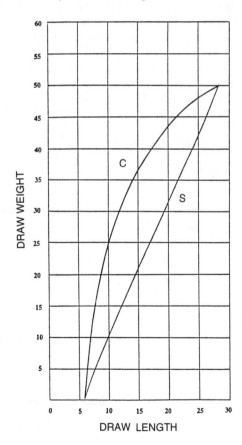

*Due to its reflexed limbs and tips, the Asiatic composite design "C", is much harder to pull during the early and mid-stages of draw, as its f-d curve indicates, thereby storing more energy.*

bow's profile. When making wood bows, proper design and craftsmanship are far more important than wood type. I have many birch, ash, hickory, elm, etc. bows which pound for pound out-shoot many of my yew and Osage bows. But only because they were better designed and crafted - the same reason some yew and Osage bows will out-shoot other yew and Osage bows.

Sinew advocate: "Give me any one of your wooden bows. I'll sinew-back it and it will shoot faster.

Profile advocate: "That's true, but only because sinewing will raise the weight of my bow, and slightly reflex it. Give me any of your sinew-backed bows and let me make an all-wood bow with the same reflex, draw weight, and draw length, and its cast will be identical to your sinewed bow."

Since different profiles cause greater and lesser amounts of energy to be stored, greater and lesser limb strains result. High energy-storing profiles therefore require wider limbs, or more energy-absorbing material, in order to retain their profiles. Some excellent original profile which no longer exists doesn't count. Its worked-in profile, its as-is profile after being pulled to full draw several times determines energy storage.

The energy storing benefits of varied profiles can be seen even within a given design. Shown are four bows made of fairly straight staves, one slightly reflexed. All would be classified as straight-stave, "D" bows. All are 50 lb at 28", and show varying worked-in profiles.

Such profiles may be due to natural stave deflex or due to set. Set may be because of limbs being too narrow for the strength of wood used, an incompletely dried stave, overstrain during tillering, being overdrawn once made, or other reasons. *The cause of set, deflex, or string follow is irrelevant to a bow's performance.* Its as-is profile, *its side-view-shape after being worked to full draw determines energy storage.*

It doesn't matter if bow "A" is made of pine, Osage, sinew/horn, fiberglass, or dried pasta. If it displays this profile after being worked in it will, CAN ONLY, store precisely the amount of energy indicated on line "A" – the same amount of energy which would be stored by any other bow of the same profile.

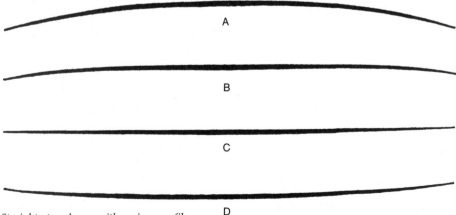

*Straight-stave bows, with various profiles.*

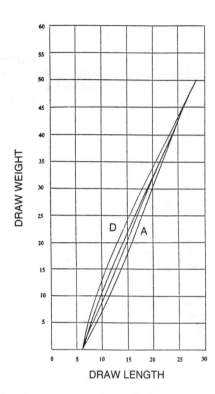

*F-d curves of the four bows,
illustrating energy storing capacities
of the different profiles.*

The task then is *to design limbs which maintain superior side-view shapes after break-in.* But how?

Different woods have different bending strengths, breaking strength, and degree of elasticity. For bows made of "inferior" wood to take the same set, and therefore shoot as fast as bows made of "superior" wood, their limbs must be made wider. Wider in proportion to differences in strength and elasticity.

Wider, thinner (therefore more flexible) weak-wood limbs can do the work of narrower, strong-wood limbs in the same way that a wider line of weaker men can lift as much weight as a narrower line of stronger men.

Wider limbs contain more wood, which would normally raise limb mass, which would normally slow the bow, but this wider wood is lighter wood, so limb mass remains about the same.

How to choose materials and limb widths to insure low-set profiles will be covered in "A Standard Bend Test" later in this chapter.

To restate: If by proper craft a bow is made to have less string follow after break-in, as with "B" and "C", it will store more energy. If an after-break-in reflex is achieved, even more energy is stored.

All four bows depicted above have the same draw length and weight. All four are equally hard to hold at full draw. Yet "D" stores considerably more energy than "A" because its profile requires more arm work in the early and mid stages of draw. "A" will feel extremely weak its first few inches of draw. "D" will feel taut and firm from the first inch of draw.

To keep set, or string follow, low requires wider limbs or stronger, more elastic material.

Straight-stave bows can be purposely, or unintentionally, tillered to a variety of different profiles. Each affects a bow's storage and release of energy.

For this to make complete sense the effects of **string angle** must be understood. *String angle affects the storage of energy as much as any other factor.*

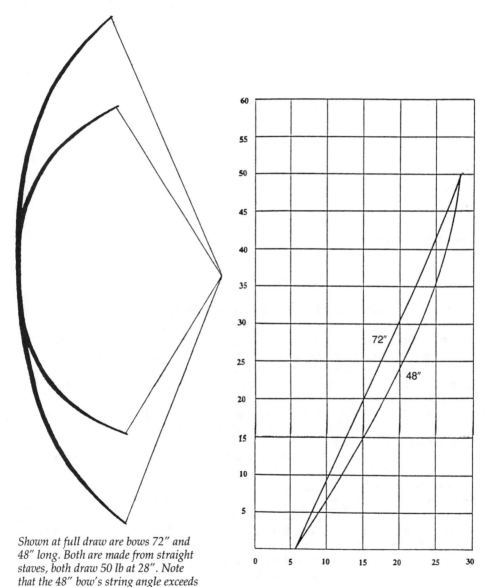

*Shown at full draw are bows 72" and 48" long. Both are made from straight staves, both draw 50 lb at 28". Note that the 48" bow's string angle exceeds 90 degrees.*

*The f-d curves of the two bows.*

Note how the 48" bow's f-d line rises almost vertically during the last few inches of draw. When a bow becomes suddenly harder to pull during these last inches, it is said to **stack**. When trying to understand the cause, our intuition outsmarts us again.

Between 15" to 20" the 48" bow draws smoothly, with weight increasing at 2 lb per inch of draw. Beyond 20" a mild sensation of stack begins, with weight increasing just under 3 lb per inch. Beyond 25" the bow starts to "hit the wall," with weight increasing about 6 lb in the last inch. The bow is stacking badly. You feel certain the bow is about to blow. Your face automatically winces, anticipating a shower of splinters.

This is an almost universal reaction to serious stack. It is based on the common misconception that wood itself stacks, that wood approaching its breaking point becomes suddenly harder to bend.

In fact the opposite is true. As wood approaches its breaking point belly fibers begin to fail; poundage increase per inch begins to fall. You can easily demonstrate this using a pull scale and a stick of wood secured at one end.

Then what causes a bow to stack? Given equal early draw weight, *stack is purely the result of increasing string angle during the draw.* The approximate 20-degree string angle of a normally-braced bow provides great mechanical advantage in the early stages of draw. Each inch of draw advances limb tips only some fraction of an inch - a gear effect is at work. Later in the draw, as string angle increases, as the string is pulling more at a right angle to the bow tips, this gear effect is lost, and each inch of draw advances the bow tips a similar honest inch. The "wall" of hard stacking.

Pull a moderately short, full-draw bow using a pull scale. Note weight increase per inch of draw. For a 50 lb bow this will be about 2 lb at mid draw, but about 5 lb during the last inch of draw. Now replace the normal string with one half-again longer. This new string hangs far down below the bow.

Using the pull scale, again draw the limbs to the same degree of bend as at mid draw when strung normally. String angle is now about 90 degrees, as at full draw when strung normally. Each additional inch of draw now increases weight by almost 4 lb., almost the same as during the last inch of draw when strung normally, even though the limbs are now far less strained than at full draw.

If you're not yet convinced that stack is due to string angle alone, make a 56", 50 lb at 28", hard-stacking, "about-to-break" bow. Pull it to full draw, just to get that sensation in the pit of your stomach. Then lash on 6" long tips, retroflexed to a 45 degree angle, converting the bow to a makeshift recurve.

Note the substantially lower string angle during all stages of draw. As the bow limbs reach the degree of bend which once caused defensive wincing, you will feel a smooth, sweet draw, with no sensation of stack. The limbs are bending far more than before. They may be silently screaming from the abuse, but you hear nothing. If the wood does not break, it will have massive set. Stack is due to string angle alone. Almost.

Two bows of equal full-draw string angle, but having different early-draw weights will stack differently. A f-d curve's end-of-draw climb can not be as steep if it begins its ascent from a higher plane.

With the cause of stacking understood the effect of varying profiles can now make sense.

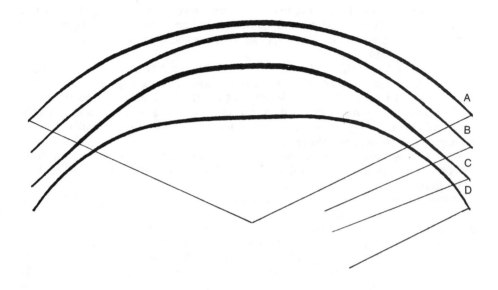

*Various tillering profiles.*

Note the variation in string angles in the illustration. A working-grip, round-in-the-handle bow (A) permits the lowest near-tip string angle. Therefore it is the least-stacking, highest energy-storage bow. Such bows must be tillered with insight and care: unlike other parts of the limb, handle and near-handle wood must not bend enough to take a set. Even small near-grip set causes large, permanent tip deflection, or string follow.

There are other benefits of working-grip bows: Eight to ten inches of wood is taken out of commission by thicker, non-working grips (even more on wide-limbed bows). A stiff-gripped bow is, in effect, a less severe example of a whip-ended bow. Up to 20% more total wood is available for storing energy in a working-grip bow. As a result, the rest of the bow need not bend as much, will therefore take less set, and is less likely to break. And because less mid-limb wood is needed limbs will have less mass.

Longer draws can be obtained from bend-in-the-handle bows, which is useful if full length staves are not available. Bows which work in the grip need not jolt the hand as reputed. When tillered as suggested above they shoot as sweet as any bow.

Well-made working-grip bows are highly efficient, but have some limits. Since the grip is part of the working limb, it cannot be narrowed. As a result, limb width is limited to a minimum of about 1-1/2". Above this width, arrows have difficulty **paradoxing,** or bending, around the handle, and gripping a bow wider than 1-1/2" is uncomfortable. This restricts wood choice to only the strongest, most elastic woods, or to draw weights in the 50 lb range. At 1-1/2" wide, most hardwoods will take too much set above this weight, canceling any benefit of the design.

*Built-up riser on a bow which works in the handle.*

Safe, efficient poundage can be raised by increasing bow length, but above 72" or so, too much energy is spent throwing such long limbs forward. Length can be extended anyway, raising bow weight, trading slightly lower efficiency for somewhat higher net cast, but a wider-limbed, 64" to 69" length would be a better choice.

Medieval English longbows chose the longer-limb option, with bows in the 120 lb range reaching 80". This choice may have been forced on them however, for two reasons: 1) The English required staves by the tens of thousands, and more staves can be taken from a tree if they are narrow, and 2) Cross-sections indicate these bows were sometimes made from relatively small diameter trees. Why safe, wide-limbed bows cannot be taken from small diameter stock will be covered farther on.

There is one style of working-grip bow whose limbs are wider than their grips. Ishi's bows, and North Pacific Coast bows in general, had working grips about 1-1/2" or wider, with mid-limbs often considerably wider. Tillering such bows require the highest levels of skill. Narrower grips must be thicker to hold their own against wider limbs. But they must be thin enough to bend only slightly less than wider, near-grip portions of the limb. If not perfectly crafted, such grips become overstrained, either breaking or taking a set in the worst place to take a set. A very delicate balance. Stiff handles would have been much quicker and easier to make. These superior bowyers were obviously aware of the benefits of working grips.

Average-weight bows which work in the handle will be too thin at the grip to hold comfortably. A built-up riser of leather, cloth, or such, remedies this problem. Wood risers can be used if wrapped or tied in place, not glued, so the handle can continue to bend.

Bows which bend too much in the handle also have high energy storage, but this potential cannot be exploited. Since most bending takes place in a relatively short area less total wood is asked to do all the work. A mid-section of horn/sinew could safely absorb this much energy but wood cannot: it will break or take a very large set. Bows which bend too much in the handle must be bending too little everywhere else. Mid-limbs are too thick to bend normally, which means that in addition to not storing energy their excess mass must be thrown forward at great energy expense.

A too-round-in-the-handle bow is in effect a very short bow with useless staves attached to each end. And all this on top of excessive tip deflexion due to inevitable grip set.

A hinged-near-the-handle bow (C) has near identical problems as a round-in-the-handle bow.

A too-flat-in-the-handle, or mildly **whip-ended** bow (D) also makes less total wood available for energy storage. Since only outer portions of the limbs are fully working they must bend more severely. This more severe curvature produces a higher string angle. Such limbs stack badly, storing considerably less energy. A whip-ended bow is effectively a stave with half of a short bow attached to each end. This is a bad situation, but not as bad as its F-D curve alone indicates. These overworked outer limbs are less massive. And hardly-working inner limbs take no set whatever. Still, such bows have poorer cast than if ideally tillered.

Whip-ended bows are, however, generally sweet to shoot, with little or no hand shock. In fact, the outer limbs of bows with severe hand shock can be retillered, slightly "whipping" their ends, then shortened sufficiently to maintain draw weight.

From all of the above, it's obvious why normal tillering was chosen to be normal. But there are subtleties to "normal" tiller worth examining. A bow limb should not bend in a perfect arc of a circle. To resist increasing leverage, a limb must be progressively thicker moving from tip to grip. But, thicker wood will not bend as far as thinner wood before breaking or taking a set. Each part of the limb should be strained to the same percentage of safe capacity. To achieve this, thicker sections must be tillered to bend less than thinner sections.

An ideally tillered limb will therefore be somewhat elliptical, with two additional refinements. 1) Near-handle sections should be tillered to bend even less,

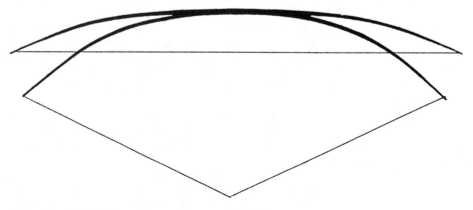

*This is the ideal tiller for working-grip, narrow-limbed bows.*

so as to take negligible or no set. 2) Straight tips yield lower string angles at full draw. Low string angles decrease stack, therefore increasing energy storage.

As limb tips progress from deflex to recurve, two thing happen. 1) early-draw weight increases; 2) late-draw stack decreases. Energy storage rises correspondingly. This is why the last few inches of a straight bow should normally be tillered for little or no bend.

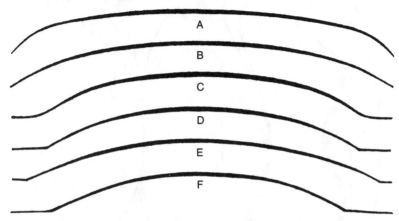

*Bows of equal draw weight and length, showing various profiles due to tillering and recurving.*

The bows shown have equal draw weight and length. Their f-d lines terminate at the same spot, but they store different amounts of energy:

A - Whip-ended tips, having steeper string angles, produce a steep f-d line the last inches of draw, therefore, fairly severe stack. The f-d line must therefore rise up from a lower level, which translates to low early and mid-draw weight. As a result, less energy is stored.

B - Straight tips, having moderate string angles, producing a near-straight f-d line the last inches of draw and stack moderately. The f-d line rises up from a higher base, which means higher early and mid-draw weight. More energy is stored than with whippy tips.

C, D - Recurved and retroflexed tips, having low string angles produces a slightly convex f-d line, therefore no stack. Early and mid-draw weight is higher still. Even more energy is stored than with "B".

This design receives added early-draw weight from another source: recurved and retroflex tips set some distance forward of straight tips. Recurved limbs are therefore under higher strain when braced, just as are reflexed limbs.

Picture, for example, a non string-contact, short-recurve bow whose tips rest three inches forward of the handle. To brace such a bow these tips must travel 4-1/2" farther than tips of a straight-stave bow having 1-1/2" string follow. This extra three inches of travel pre-strains the limbs exactly as if bracing a bow having three-inch of setback or reflex. Early draw weight rises considerably.

E, F, - The percentage of limb length devoted to recurve determines average string angle, therefore energy storage. A very low-percentage recurve has essentially no string-angle benefits.

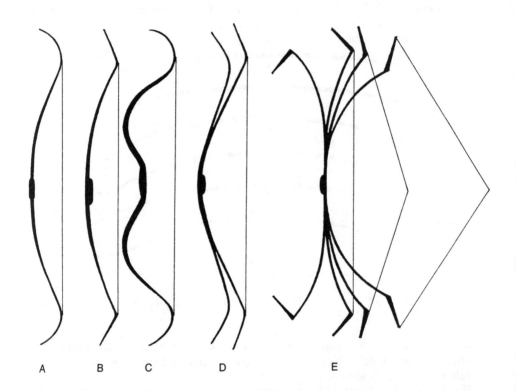

*Measured from point of string contact, recurved bows are shorter when braced, longer when fully drawn.*

If measured at point of string contact the illustrated bows are shorter when braced, longer when fully drawn. Early in the draw, when deprived of the leverage of longer limbs, such bows are very hard to pull. During mid-draw, when draw weight would normally become uncomfortably high, strings lift off their contact points, letting their retroverted tips work as levers, keeping final draw weight at tolerable levels. In effect, such tips work as cams.

Because such two-stage designs are harder to pull during early inches of draw, total energy stored is very high.

The energy storage capacity of each of the above two-stage profiles varies due to:

A: Early and mid-draw weight, as determined by:

    1) Degree of pre-braced limb reflex.

    2) Percentage of limb length each side of string contact point.

    3) Angle of after-contact setback.

B: Late-draw stack, as determined by string angle during latter stages of draw.

Based on these considerations, primitive technologist John McPherson has developed a very efficient design which can be made in primitive conditions using only stone tools. Is is similar to "B", about 60" long, wide-limbed, heavily sinewed, with Asiatic composite-type static retroflexed tips. He makes the tips just the correct length and angle to yield maximum energy storage short of causing limb failure. Asiatic-style string bridges permit normal brace height with less limb strain.

The most energy-storing design illustrated is "E", the highly reflexed and retro-tipped 46" long Turkish flight bow. Four-hundred years ago such bows cast flight arrows up to one half-mile. Energy storage is high because early and mid-draw weight is high, largely due to the great strain involved in bracing such severely reflexed limbs. Tension and compression work is done by sinew and horn on such highly strained limbs.

Many explanations have been offered to account for the speed of Turkish-style bows. A common one notes that because of very high early draw weight, syiahs (retroflexed tips) suddenly slam home on their return, snapping the string taut with greater than ordinary force and speed. But that's putting the cart before the horse. A bow's profile only determines how much energy is stored, not how it is expended. Syiahs simply make the bow store more energy. After that, arrow speed is inevitable.

*The author draws an Asiatic-style composite bow.*

Imagine an unbraced bow with a reverse-coiled clock spring profile. Enormous energy would be imparted to such limb as it is straightened and braced. As a result, total energy stored could be made to match that of a syiahed composite. Assuming equal mass, length, and draw, both bows would have equal cast.

The deflex-recurve, "D" is probably the most efficient design for a wood-based bow. Because of its deflex little of its ability to do work is used up bracing the bow. Since little before-the-draw work is being done by the limbs, more during-the-draw work can be done.

Being under little strain when braced, a deflex design would normally have very low early-draw weight. This is overcome by using thicker, harder to bend limbs. Such thick limbs would normally result in intolerably heavy draw weight later in the draw, but after string lift-off this design's levers keep full-draw weight down. Such a thick limb would normally be overstrained when fully drawn, but these limbs do little work being braced, making this unused capacity available during the draw.

Let's say two bows are made with identical side-view, un-strung profiles. Both have equal draw weight and length. One is made of wood, the other horn/sinew. Which will shoot a given arrow farther?

Counter to expectation, wood out-performs horn/sinew in this case. But why? Horn/sinew is far more elastic than wood, and can therefore store far more energy. How can wood possibly out-perform horn/sinew?

If both have equal side-view profiles both require equal work of the arm, therefore store equal energy. But horn/sinew has about twice the mass of wood. More energy is used to throw its heavier limbs forward.

Highly recurved, reflexed profiles with short bow length to arrow length ratios are needed to exploit horn/sinew's energy storing potential.

Short, plains-style, set-back-in-the-handle bows seem to shoot no faster than

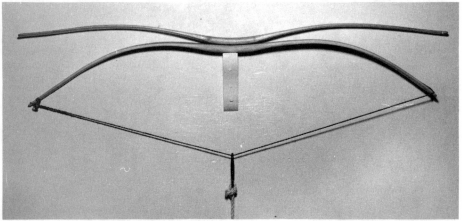

*If set-back limbs bend throughout their entire length, as do straight-stave bows, string angle will be very high. Such limbs will stack, and store less energy. As with these set-back Plains-style bows, string angle can be kept fairly low if limbs are tillered to bend very little, it at all, near the tips.*

same-width straight-stave versions. Such limbs, having started from farther forward to be braced or drawn, must approach the string at a greater angle, a formula for increased stack and lower energy storage. This becomes progressively less true with increased bow length, because string angle is progressively lower. For set-back bows of 66" or so, the advantages of counter-acting string follow overcome the disadvantages of increased string angle.

Set, or string follow, degrades efficiency on a straight-stave bow, but not on a recurved bow. By adjusting the percentage of limb devoted to recurve or syiah, the cast-robbing effects of set can be easily canceled. There is an advantage to overstraining such limbs: more energy is stored per ounce of material. This is true to a lesser degree with straight bows: Limbs could be widened and thinned to take no set whatever, but mass would rise too high. Some set is tollerated so that limbs can be narrower and lighter.

A bow's profile at rest, braced, and drawn – all three matter to energy storage. If recurves straightened completely when braced, for example, a bow would have some slight advantage of pre-stressed energy storage, but none from string angle during the draw. If recurves uncoil and straighten as the bow is drawn, string angles rise, lowering energy storage due to stack. This is why a **static recurve,** or one with tips stiff enough not to bend during the draw, is more efficient than a **working recurve,** or one which uncoils as the bow is drawn.

We've all read that draw length cannot exceed half of bow length. This rule of thumb is accepted widely. Yet limbs of very light bows, or very wide-limbed bows, are so thin they can be bent nearly in circles. Especially if made from highly elastic materials.

On the other hand, a very narrow, heavy bow made of brittle wood might break if drawn only one-third its length.

Where did this rule come from, and how did it manage to survive?

A possible explanation is that straight-stave bows pulled beyond half their length stack severely. Hard-stacking bows are inefficient, and uncomfortable to draw. String angles on 48" bows, for example, reach 90 degrees at about 24" of draw (if drawn beyond 90 degrees strings slip off of their nocks unless restrained).

Pictured is a 48" bow, 2" wide at mid limb. It draws 57 lb at 28". Limbs are

*This 48" hickory bow pulls 57 lb at 28". It is far overdrawn by conventional standards, so far that its tips are reflexed to keep the string from slipping off of the nocks. Yet it shows little set. An important lesson can be learned from this bow: If limbs are perfectly rectangular in cross section, the edges do just as much work as the center. Since more wood is working, the limb can be thinner, allowing the limb to bend into a smaller circle at the same draw weight. This translates to longer draws, or more severe recurves, both of which store more energy.*

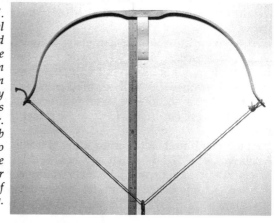

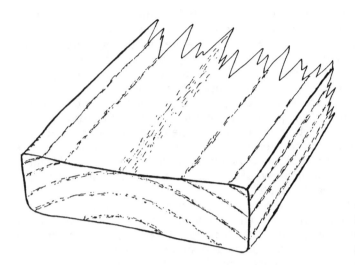

*Cross section of hickory bow's limb, showing orientation of yearly growth rings.*

1/4" thick at mid-limb. It is made from a kiln-dried hickory board and the tips are slightly curved to retain the string. A perfectly rectangular section insures equal work load across section width. A 2" limb in more than name. Rings are orientated as illustrated.

This bow is set back slightly in the handle, and slightly recurved, both of which causes more strain than if made from a straight stave. In addition, a stiff handle section renders 8.5" of its center inert. All intuition says this little bow is being horribly overstrained. Its limbs, however, take only a moderate set. Again our intuition must be wrong.

Energy can only be stored by straining wood. Set must develop if limbs are over-strained. If limbs have less set than expected they must somehow be strained less than we assume.

A glance at this bow's f/d curve tells the story. At equal draw weight and length, a long bow stores more energy than a short bow. This very short bow stores much less energy, straining its wood less than draw weight alone implies.

The draw weight of full-draw, very short, straight bows is largely stack weight or artificial weight, which fools the fingers and the scale, but not the arrow.

At a given limb width, same draw-length bows must be longer as draw-weight increases. A 56" X 1-1/4" wide ash bow will break if pulled to 28" and 50 lb. At 64" it may not break, but will take a very large set. At 72", surface wood is much less strained. Set will be small, and the chances of breakage even smaller.

Various cross sections have an indirect effect on mass placement. But *different cross sections are important chiefly to the extent they permit a given side-view profile to exist.*

At a given limb length, limbs must be wider as design draw-weight increases. As above, A 56" X 1-1/4" ash bow will break if pulled to 28" and 50 lb. At 1-1/2" it may not break, but will take a very large set. At 2", surface wood is much less strained. Set will be small, and its chances of breaking even smaller.

Some woods are weak in tension relative to compression strength. Limbs from these woods, such as red cedar, must be wider in order to bring enough tension wood into play. If backed, however, a narrower, lighter limb can be safely made.

A flat belly brings more wood into play, to resist compression. High stacked "D" bellies are more likely to fail by taking an excessive set than by breaking. A "D" belly first **chrysals**, or fractures from excessive compression, on its very narrow surface. Narrow chrysals on "D" bellies, affecting only a small percentage of the limb's width, are not as fatal as chrysals on a flat belly, which usually lay across the entire belly. If observed early enough in their formation on a "D" belly, a strong safe bow can still be delivered. These early chrysals become an emergency tillering guide, indicating wood should be removed everywhere else.

Most woods are two or three times stronger in tension than compression. Limb set is due to compression failure only. A simple experiment can demonstrate this.

Rough out a flat-backed, flat-bellied bow blank. Mark a small ink dot near each end, on both back and belly. Measure the distance between dots with precision. Tiller this test bow to an even bend. Then over-strain it to induce a large set. Cut the bow in half along its neutral plane, separating the back from the belly. The back half will spring straight again. The belly half will keep its large set. Carefully measure dot distance again. Back dot distance will not have changed. But as a result of belly compaction belly dots will be measurably closer.

Staves from smaller trees will have a more rounded back, and the effect of a crowned, or rounded, back is too often overlooked in bow design. Wood's bending resistance is proportional to the cube of thickness, in other words, a piece of wood twice as thick will be eight times as strong. Accordingly, thicker central portions of a high-crowned cross section do much more work than the thinner edges. Such a limb may measure two inches in width, but functionally, because of the crown, it is a much narrower bow asked to do the work of a 2" bow. For visible evidence of this, note that chrysals on such bows are restricted to a narrow central strip of belly lying opposite the crown. Chrysals on flat-backed and bellied bows run almost edge to edge. Highly crowned limbs are actually narrower limbs with dead weight at their sides. Since narrow limbs must be made longer to prevent set or breaking, highly crowned limbs must be longer and narrower.

When making light bows from crowned staves, limbs should be narrowed, as in "B". Thin, hardly-working edges are only dead weight. Since light bows are understrained, limbs can be thicker relative to width.

*Illustration "A" depicts a typical cross section when a wide-limbed bow is made from a small diameter tree.*

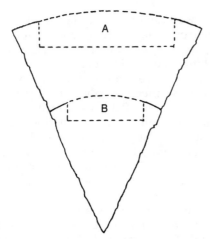

*Note the flatter cross section when limbs are taken from larger diameter logs. Even the edges of "A" are thick enough to do real work. This means the center section will be relatively thinner, therefore less strained. This cross section is less likely to break or take excessive set than if more highly crowned. The piggy-back stave from lower in the log, "B," does not share these benefits.*

With a wide belly to resist compression, a high-crowned bow will have minimal set. But its narrow back will be dangerously overworked. Small diameter trees, and inner splits of trees, should make only low-weight bows, or longer bows. Of course there are shades of exception. Some woods are stronger in tension than others. To the degree this is true such woods can stand up to high-crown strains. Two woods which handle tension well are hickory and elm.

Shorter, wider limbs accentuate back crown. Larger diameter logs are needed for wide bows. Piggy-back staves, staves split from deeper in the tree, were formed when the tree was smaller. Their higher crowns must be worked down to a single growth ring, but the fact they are "free" justifies the effort.

There is one way to make strong, safe, wide bows from small diameter stock: remove the crown! Decrowned, small diameter stock then takes on a rectangular, evenly-strained cross section. De-crowned limbs are evenly strained at every point across their width.

Decrowning is a delicate operation: Wood must be removed so that exposed growth rings run in straight parallel lines the length of the bow when viewed from the back. Wood must also be removed so that the new back perfectly parallels the original tree surface. This insures that wood fibers will be kept intact, not cut across. Such limbs will be almost as strong as if made from large diameter,

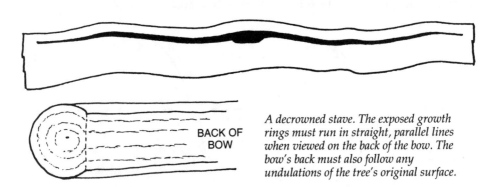

BACK OF BOW

*A decrowned stave. The exposed growth rings must run in straight, parallel lines when viewed on the back of the bow. The bow's back must also follow any undulations of the tree's original surface.*

naturally flat-backed stock. They will be much stronger than if left high-crowned. Staves which are weaker in tension especially benefit.

If, for whatever reason, de-crowned back rings are not perfectly parallel for the limb's entire length, a thin backing will insure full safety. Sinew or pre-stressed silk are especially effective on thinner, wider, rectangular, decrowned cross sections, pulling such limbs into greater reflex.

### Limb Dimension Overview

To maintain an efficient degree of set and safety:

Shorter bows must be wider, or have lower draw weight, or be made of stronger or flatter-crowned wood, or have shorter draw length than longer bows.

Narrower bows must be longer, or have lighter draw weight, or be made of stronger wood, or have a shorter draw than wider bows.

A longer draw length requires that a bow be longer, or wider, or have lower draw weight, or be made from stronger wood.

Heavier bows must be wider, or longer, or have shorter draw, or be made of stronger wood or flatter-crowned wood than lighter bows.

Weak-wood bows must be longer or wider, or have a lighter draw weight, or have a shorter draw, or a flatter crown than bows made from stronger woods.

Crowned cross-sections must be narrower and longer or have lower draw weight, or shorter draw length, or be made of higher tension-strength wood than flat cross-section bows.

The fastest wood bow I've yet tested was made by Jay Massey. Just 56" in length, this bow pulls 66 pounds at 27" and shoots a 500 grain arrow 184 fps. The secret of its speed lies, of course, in its profile. It is a bow-profile lesson in itself: it is short for low inertia, recurved for low stack and high energy storage, and reflexed for high early-draw weight. In order to hold its high energy-storage profile, it is 2" wide and sinew-backed.

All of the factors outlined so far affecting arrow speed- draw weight, draw length, string height, and bow profile - determine the amount of energy stored in a bow's limbs. But at release, as this energy begins to flow to the arrow, the following obstructions come into play.

### Limb Mass

Medium length, straight-stave, 50 lb bows weigh about 23 oz. For bows of this length, weight, and mass, *a difference of one ounce in limb mass, on average, affects arrow speed by about one foot per second.* For mid-weight bows a difference in *one pound of draw weight also equals about one fps of arrow speed.* Lowering limb mass allows a lighter draw-weight bow to equal the cast of a heavier draw-weight bow.

Heavier woods are generally stronger and more elastic, therefore, less wood is needed to do the same amount of work. Lighter woods are generally weaker and less elastic, requiring more wood to do equal work. But, mass ends up about equal for same-weight bows made of light or heavy woods.

Some woods store fractionally more energy per ounce than others. But, in this regard, greater variety exists between staves of the same species than between staves of different species.

When wood width doubles, strength, stiffness, and bend resistance doubles. But when wood thickness doubles, strength increases eight times, meaning eight times more energy can be stored per inch of bend. Narrow limbs of equal bend strength therefore have considerably less mass per amount of stored energy than wide, thin limbs.

But there are no free lunches in nature. Eight times as much work is being done by only twice as much wood. Something has to give. If narrow, thick limbs are bent as far as their thinner cousins they will break, or take a very large set. Narrow, thick limbs must be made longer to reduce strain. And longer limbs, as seen below, have their own mass-related drawbacks.

For a given length, limbs should be as narrow as possible while 1) maintaining a margin of safety against breaking, and 2) not taking an excessive, cast-robbing set.

This width is different for each species of wood, and different for each stave within a species. To determine optimum widths for different species and staves see "A Standard Wood Bending Test" later in this chapter.

### Mass Placement

Long, heavy limbs have slower cast. But why? Even if lead weights were attached, shouldn't a limb's kinetic energy transfer to the string as limbs slam home, snapping the string taut?

This is like asking which will propel a golf ball faster, a 10 mph freight train or a 100 mph golf club. Vastly more energy is stored in the freight train, but 10 mph is 10 mph. Too-long and too-heavy limbs come home too slowly. They can only snap the string slowly.

Much of the energy stored in long and heavy limbs remains in the limbs after release, becoming hand shock, string twang, and limb vibration. This is why slower moving, very heavy arrows leave the bow quietly. Heavy arrows make bows more energy efficient because more of the bow's energy has time to leave with them.

This is why flight bows are golf club-like: short, low mass, fast-reacting limbs. Flight arrows, arrows light enough not to impede these fast limbs, can be shot much faster than normal weight arrows. The same flight arrow shot from an English war bow of equal weight would be considerably slower.

It matters a great deal how mass is distributed on a bow limb. Weight placed near limb tips slows cast considerably. The same weight has progressively less effect when placed closer to the handle.

On bows of average length and strength, 65 grains of weight at each tip effects arrow speed by about 1 fps. More than one ounce must be placed mid-limb to slow cast by this same 1 fps. (437 grains equal one oz.). One ounce added to each tip slows cast by about 7 fps. One ounce placed near the grip has virtually no effect on cast.

Cast can be increased by shifting mass toward the handle, allowing more work to be performed by wider, heavier, near-handle wood.

If a given weight bow is tillered to bend excessively near the handle, mid-limb and tipward areas have obviously been tillered too wide or thick, and are therefore too massive. And they are massive where mass is most costly to cast. One of the benefits of perfect tiller is that limb mass is not only reduced, but IDEALLY distributed.

Imperfectly tillered bows often shock the hand at release. Energy is required to jar the hand. If the bow had been designed and tillered correctly that energy would have gone into the arrow.

Narrow, thick limb tips have less mass than if wide and thin. An average piece of bow wood 1/2" square by 1-1/4" long weighs about 65 grains. In worst-case/best-case comparisons, several fps of cast may be gained by narrowing tipward portions of a limb.

Tip width and weight are less important on shorter bows.

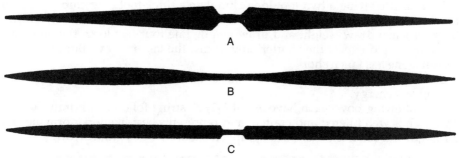

*Front-view shapes.*

The three illustrated designs represent the principle reasonable variations of front-view limb shape. Each affects mass placement, therefore performance.

"A" – Pyramid limbs have a much higher percentage of working wood near the handle. Such limbs are fairly uniform in thickness their entire length. Near-handle wood is therefore free to bend farther than otherwise. Being wider, near-handle wood now stores a larger percentage of total energy. This means "less bow" is needed from mid limb outward. Several ounces of limb mass are therefore shifted toward the handle. Upper limbs are now lighter where lightness is most important. This bend-near-the-handle design also has high energy storage due to its favorable string angle. Normally such round-in-the-handle bows shock the hand, but lighter mid limbs and nearly mass-less tips prevent such shock.

This is an efficient design, but often impractical: unless taken from an unusually large diameter tree the very wide near-handle area would have excessive crown. Flattening the crown would solve this problem, but this has its dangers. Decrowning and backing the limb safely solves the problem. The question then becomes: is the four or five fps gain over limb "C" worth the extra work.

"B" – As opposed to "A", narrow near-handle wood cannot bend far without taking a set or breaking. Therefore more "bow" is needed at mid limb. As a result mid-limb and near-nock mass rises at some cost to arrow speed. Most of the energy storage is confined to a fairly short section of limb, which will be overstrained if not widened. If widened, mass rises even more. This bend-at-mid-limb design has reduced energy storage due to its steeper string angle.

"C" – This design lies between "A" and "B" in the amount of wood put to work near the handle and at mid limb. Mass placement adjusts accordingly. Energy storage lies between these two designs also. Appropriate log diameters are the same for both "B" and "C".

At first, it may seem pointless to worry about a couple of fps difference in arrow cast. But each fps equals the effect of about one pound of draw weight. There are several areas within a given design where cast can be altered by one to five fps. The accumulated effect can be substantial. Two straight-stave bows of 40 lb and 60 lb can easily have the same cast.

## Bow Length

It's easier to swing a two-foot long club than a three-foot long club. It's easier for a bow to swing a two-foot long limb than a three-foot long limb. Given two bows of equal draw weight and draw length, one four-feet long, the other six-feet long, you'd expect the shorter bow to cast the faster arrow. But once again reason alone has fallen short.

Short bows shoot same-weight arrows slower because short limbs stack badly, storing less energy.

The following bows each have about 1-1/2" string follow, and draw 50 lb at 28". Each is well tillered and crafted, and represents best-likely performance for its length and set. Each was chronographed shooting a 500 grain arrow.

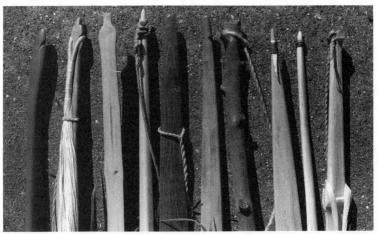

*Nock design can affect performance. From left to right: Raised nock, giving the effect of a slight reflex. Double nock, one for the string, the other for the cable back – not as weight efficient as the cable-backed bow at far right. Pin nock, which requires slightly wider, heavier tips. No nock – the string is secured with half-hitches and the limb taper keeps it from sliding- permitting very narrow, light tips. Two conventional nocks – the English-style on the right permitting slighly narrower tips. Small branch nock. Two wrapped-on nocks – on the left a sliver of rawhide is tied in place for the string to rest upon; on the right sinew or other fiber is wrapped and glued or tied in place. A small loop or half-hitch rests on the shoulder. Both designs permit very light tips.*

These results are an approximation. Tens of bows of each length would need testing for complete dependability. But it's unlikely these figures would shift substantially either way.

| Length | fps | mid-limb width | mass |
|---|---|---|---|
| 48" hickory | 135 | 2-3/4 | 17 oz. |
| 52" ash | 144 | 2-3/8 | 18 |
| 56" yew | 150 | 1-5/8 | 19 |
| 59" hickory | 151 | 2-1/4 | 22 |
| 65" Osage | 151 | 1-1/2 | 24 |
| 66" hickory | 153 | 2 | 23 |
| 67" maple | 153 | 2 | 23 |
| 69" birch | 151 | 1-3/4 | 21 |
| 70" yew | 150 | 1-1/8 | 21 |
| 78" cherry | 148 | 1-1/2 | 24 |
| 88" maple | 142 | 1-1/4 | 30 |
| 94" maple | 136 | 1-1/4 | 35 |

For different-length bows to assume equal sets, longer bows must be narrower and thicker, shorter bows wider and thinner. Strong and elastic woods, of course, are made narrower than weaker woods.

The 94" bow was a pleasure to draw – absolutely no stack. As expected with such a low string angle, this bow had the plumpest f/d curve, storing more energy than any other. But 94" is a lot of lumber to haul forward. As a result, its cast equaled that of an average 40 lb bow.

At the other extreme, the 48" bow stacked abruptly and uncomfortably, and it, too, had a cast like that of a 40 lb bow. In practice, shorter self bows usually perform even worse than in this test. These shorter bows were made especially wide to avoid excessive limb set. For the test to be valid, string follow had to be equal for all. Shorter bows usually follow the string more than longer bows, and therefore have even slower cast than shown.

Based upon a starting point of 66" to 67" for a 28" draw length, the ideal bow length rises and falls with draw length, and an adjustment of two inches of bow length for every inch of arrow length will be very close to correct. Depending on

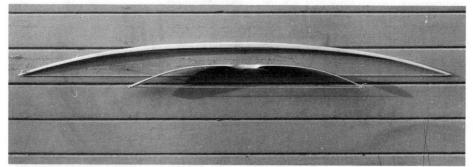

*48" and 88" bows used in the test. The 88" was remade from the 94" bow, picking up six feet per second in the process.*

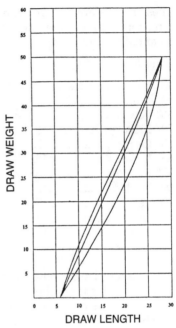

DRAW WEIGHT

DRAW LENGTH

*F-d curves for the 94" maple, 67" maple (center), and 48" hickory bows from the test. Speed was almost identical for the longest and shortest bows. 67" bow was faster than either, providing the best compromise between low mass and high energy storage.*

*Both bows drawn, illustrating the different string angles.*

how a bow will be used, an archer might wisely trade a few pounds of efficiency for a short bow's maneuverability or a long bow's smoothness of draw and accuracy.

As was discussed under "Limb Profile", recurved limbs give short bows the low-stacking characteristics of longbows. This, combined with the low inertia and mass of a short bow yields very fast-shooting bows.

As an example, here is the "winning" 50 lb maple bow from above, compared to two same-weight, sinewed, yew recurves, and a hickory recurve. Notice how arrow speed rises as limb length and mass fall.

| Length | fps | mid-limb width | mass |
|---|---|---|---|
| 67" straight maple | 153 | 2" | 23 oz |
| 60.5" yew sinew recurve | 162 | 1-3/4 | 21 oz |
| 59" hickory recurve | 160 | 2 | 22 oz |
| 51.5" yew sinew recurve | 168 | 1-3/4 | 18 oz |

The recurves are FAST! But for center-of-the-target accuracy longer, straight-tipped bows are more consistent.

*The hickory bow (at top) is from a board stave, its milled surface becoming the bow's back. Its perfectly rectangular cross section kept mass and set low. The two sinew-backed yew recurves (below) had slight crowns. With a rectangular cross section their performance would have risen a few fps.*

Note the heroic performance of the kiln-dried, decrowned, unbacked, $3.50 lumberyard hickory bow. With a less severe recurve, and unaided by sinew, it shot within 2 fps of the sinew-backed, recurved yew beside it. This bow's absolutely flat back and belly account for its performance.

### Hysterisis ("Internal Friction")

For an example of hysterisis in action drop a plain rubber ball and a superball from the same height. The plain rubber ball does not bounce as high as the superball because internal friction dampened recovery. This is the case with rubber balls, but, contrary to long-held archery lore, has only a minimal effect in regard to wooden bow limbs. Some wood species have greater average hysterisis than others, but, as with mass, strength, and elasticity, variability is greater within species than between.

Paul Klopsteg wrote many ground-breaking articles on the physics of bows. In the August, 1943, edition of the *American Journal of Physics*, he wrote THE word on this subject. He plotted f/d curves of various bows, noting weight at each inch of draw, and at each inch during return. Return weight was some amount lower. When both f-d curves were plotted on a graph, under-curve squares were counted. Squares between the two f-d curves were divided into total squares, the difference equaling percentage of energy loss through hysterisis.

Klopsteg got figures of between 1% and 20% energy loss. A bow with 20%, or even 10%, loss would shoot sluggishly.

Klopsteg's technique and conclusions, since reported by Elmer and other writers of influence, have become widely accepted. As a result, woods with higher laboratory-measured hysterisis, such as hickory, have been given a black eye.

After testing scores of bows, I was unable to duplicate these results, regardless of wood species. There was simply no room for significant hysterisis in the arithmetic.

Duplicating Klopsteg's figures requires measuring just-braced, non worked-in, "cold" bows. Hysterisis in the range he reported immediately appeared. But this method is incorrect for archery.

If bows are measured under conditions of routine use – if they are pulled once or twice before being measured or shot – hysterisis usually shrinks to insignificance. (F-d measurements should also be made in a worked-in state. This discloses a bow's true weight and true behavior).

Here, a typical 58 lb maple bow was braced and drawn cold. Using a short-hand method, weight was noted at 20" during the draw, then at 28", then again at 20" on the return. Measured weights were 36 lb., 59 lb., 34 lb. A two-pound drop, or, after squares are counted, about 7% hysterisis.

This procedure was repeated immediately, yielding weights of 34 lb., 58 lb., 33.8 lb., a level of hysterisis too small to bother computing. Arrow speed would be effected by too small an amount to measure.

Many tested bows have lower cold and worked-in hysterisis percentages, many have higher. A bad-case example is a 52.5 lb hickory bow yielding 15% cold hysterisis, dropping to 3% when measured on the second drawing. This bad-case example shoots about 151 fps instead of an average-hysterisis bow's 154 fps.

Here are figures from twelve near-50 lb bows selected at random. Column one shows the difference in cold weight at 20" when weighed during the draw, then again on the return. Column two gives the same figures when drawn the third time:

| | | |
|---|---|---|
| Hop hornbeam | 1.8 lb | – .7 lb |
| Yew | 1.5 lb | – .2 lb |
| Ash | 2.4 lb | – .5 lb |
| Osage | 1.9 lb | – .7 lb |
| Hickory | 2.9 lb | – .6 lb |
| Cherry | 1.0 lb | – .0 lb |
| Maple/sinew | 3.4 lb | – .9 lb |
| Yew/sinew | 2.6 lb | – .9 lb |
| Hickory | 4.0 lb | – .7 lb |
| Yew | 2.0 lb | – .7 lb |
| Maple | 2.2 lb | – .2 lb |
| Osage | 2.0 lb | – .2 lb |

A different set of bows would give slightly different figures, but would lead to the same conclusion: an average bow, regardless of wood type, looses a very small percentage of stored energy to hysterisis. So small that for all practical purposes it can be ignored.

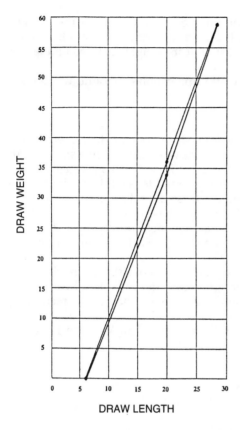

*Hysterisis curves for 58 lb maple bow. The area between the curves represents energy lost to hysterisis when measured "cold." However, 36/59 lb was not this bow's true weight. At its true, "worked-in" weight of 35/58, hysterisis is too small to illustrate.*

The above bows which were sinew-backed produced the highest cold and worked-in hysterisis. This is typical of sinewed bows. On the face of it such bows should loose about four fps of cast. But in fact these two straight-stave bows shoot about seven fps faster than similar unbacked bows. You could say that through reduced string follow sinew increased potential cast by eleven fps, lost four to hysterisis, and is still ahead by seven.

By the same token, hickory's performance can be raised, as well as that of other high tension-strength woods. Hickory, on average, shoots fractionally slower than other common bow woods, but is harder to break. Steam-bending a low-angle recurve or retroflex into the limb's last tipward inches will raise hickory's cast at no cost to safety.

### String Weight

For bows of average weight and length each 20-grain increase in TOTAL string weight slows cast by about one fps. A string weighing 250 grains instead of 150 grains will slow arrow speed by about 5 fps, or to about the speed of a 5 lb lighter bow.

At release, string near the nocks accelerates at nock speed. Near-nock string weight lowers cast as if its weight had been added to the bow's tips, costing about one fps per 65 grains of weight on an average length and draw-weight bow when shooting a 500 grain arrow. Near-arrow string, on the other hand, accelerates at arrow speed, and lowers cast as if its weight had been added to the arrow, the most costly place to add weight.

Thick, reinforced loops slow a bow by an imperceptible amount, while horn nocks cost less than one-half fps.

### String Stretch

Intuitively it would seem that an elastic bow string should store energy during the draw and surrender that energy to the arrow at release – like shooting an arrow from a harp string. A bow string, however, is under greatest tension not at full draw, but as it slams home and abruptly straightens – this is where bowstrings most often break. At this instant an elastic string acts, literally, as a shock absorber, effectively diverting energy intended for the arrow.

Dacron, linen, and most plant fibers are relatively inelastic. Nylon, silk, sinew, gut, and rawhide are highly elastic. Some of a string's elasticity can be removed by severe stretching.

For the same reason a coil stretches more than a bar, a bowstring stretches least when twisted least. Only twist strings enough to lock in component fibers. Minimally twisted strings are also stronger and can therefore be lighter, increasing arrow speed.

String properties and construction will be covered in Volume II of *The Traditional Bowyer's Bible*.

### Arrow Speed Reviewed

The speed of a given arrow is determined by:

1) The amount of work which goes into drawing the bow, as determined by:
- Draw weight
- Draw length
- String height
- Side-view profile.

2) Minus the slowing effects of
- Mass
- Mass placement
- Hysterisis
- String weight
- String stretch

All of the factors discussed to this point affect arrow speed, but there are nine additional factors which must be considered when designing a bow.

### ACCURACY

Regardless of a bow's length, a long-draw bow is more accurate than a short-draw bow, for several reasons. On average, such bows have faster cast. Full-draw bows are easier to hold and aim. Short-draw bows tend to spray arrows right and left: it is harder to pull a short-draw exactly the same distance every shot, and resulting variance in poundage changes effective arrow spine. Short-draw bows also spray arrows high and low, varying draw weight from shot to shot causing erratic cast.

When shooting short-draw bows, long arrows are more accurate than short arrows. Most of the arrow, and its mass, are already heading straight for the target by the time the arrow's caboose begins deflecting around the grip. Like a caboose, the arrow's rear must follow obediently along.

Long bows are more accurate than short bows. Longer limbs possibly work as stabilizers, making a bow steadier to aim and shoot. And with straight-limbed bows, a longer bow will stack less, contributing to a smoother, cleaner release.

Short bows stack harder than long bows, so small variations in draw length changes draw weight more than on a non-stacking bow, as a result, arrow speed varies from shot to shot.

Long-draw bows are usually strung, or braced higher, and high-stringing favors accuracy. Nock two arrows on two bows, one strung 4" high, the other 8". Notice how much farther left the 4" arrow points. Upon release this arrow has a much tougher time bending around the grip and getting true to the target line.

For a similar reason, narrow handles are more accurate than wide handles. Stiff handles should be narrower on the belly side, so the arrow will then behave as if the entire handle is narrower.

Unintentional grip torque, or twisting of the bow, causes successive arrows to spray left and right. Reverse risers, as on many Asiatic designs, have lower pivot points, so less leverage is brought to bear on the handle. This, of course, shortens draw length by the amount of riser added to the back of the bow. Bows which work in the handle automatically have this stability advantage. Shooting with a loose grip largely solves torque problems.

A small amount of string follow contributes to accuracy. Weaker early draw translates to a gentler send-off during the last critical inches of acceleration, as arrows struggle to paradox around the grip.

The most accurate natural-material bow shooting is consistently done using longbows having moderate string follow.

## COMFORT OF DRAW AND RELEASE

Because of low string angle at full draw, longbows and recurves have little stack. Such bows are "sweet" to draw. Due to both lower string angle and higher early-draw weight, recurves generally stack less than longbows.

Longbows are sweet on release, if tillered properly - here sweetness refers to lack of hand shock. But, again, recurves are generally even softer. Physicist Jeff Schmidt, who replicates the highly recurved Turkish bow, attributes recurves' soft release to their more vertical limb movement. Reinforcing this idea to some extent is the fact that high-strung bows, full-draw short bows, and deflex-recurve bows have less hand shock, and such limbs also move more vertically than a straight stave bow.

Jim Hamm reports that cutting 3/4" from each limb tip can help decrease above-average hand-shock. We've both noticed handshock in bows having unbalanced tiller and had independently decided that harmonics (Jim's word) and wave action (my words) may somehow be involved. Robert Elmer, in *Target Archery* (1946), wrote that a Japanese bow which kicked in the hand became docile when gripped a few inches from the handle. There are clues here which need to be pursued. Moving a given weight up and down the limb, searching for dampening positions, might shed some light on the harmonics aspect of hand shock.

One reason very short bows have little hand shock may be that these hard-stacking bows store less energy to begin with. Very long bows, exemplified by the 94" maple bow discussed earlier, store more energy, but their slow cast leaves much of this energy behind in the bow where it is available to shock the hand.

During limb-tip weight tests, hand shock increased as more lead weight was added to the tips. This increase might be due partly to mass placement, and partly to the extra energy available for mischief in the now less energy-efficient bow. No matter what the reason, this makes a case for narrower, thicker, therefore lighter limb tips.

A bullwhip channels a given amount of energy into an ever-smaller, less massive cross-section. When this wave of energy reaches the whip's end, the near mass-less tip accelerates beyond the speed of sound. A cracking whip is a little sonic boom. A reverse bullwhip effect might dampen handshock in a bow; very small, low mass tips progressing to very wide, high mass inner limbs.

Almost any bow design can be tillered to shoot without severe shock. Bows with stiff, or only slightly bending mid-sections (not just handle sections) tend to release with less hand shock. Poorly tillered, too-round-in-the-handle bows can shake fillings loose, even if stiff-handled. Thick handle risers, with "Buchanan dips," are often reported to eliminate hand shock. But risers alone diminish hand shock by an insignificant amount. Both working-grip and stiff-grip bows have unpleasant hand shock if tillered too round in the handle. Handle risers were more likely developed for grip comfort on low draw-weight, thinner limbs, and for greater gluing surface with spliced billets. Light-weight bows for the genteel archer and spliced grips were both becoming popular during Buchanan's time, in the middle of the last century. A properly tillered bow seldom has objectionable hand shock.

Hand shock is as much a rattle of vibration as a solid thump, so a loose grip tames most offenders. Covering a grip section with different materials can also affect hand shock, and is explained by John Strunk in the chapter on Finishes and Handles later in this volume.

## DURABILITY

The full-function life of a wooden bow is measured in decades in many cases. Horn-sinew bows may shoot strongly for a century or more.

Softer woods, such as yew, juniper and cedar scratch and dent easily. These woods need coddling. Medium-weight hardwoods, such as ash, elm, maple, and birch endure dings and scrapes fairly well, while hard, heavy woods, such as Osage, locust, hornbeam, and hickory can be handled roughly without a second thought.

Yew has the reputation of breaking in freezing weather and losing weight in hot weather. But, arctic conditions aside, there is no reason to believe any particular wood will shoot more arrows over more years than any other wood, though palm may be an exception. Dr. Charles Grayson reports that it disintegrates over time. Palm, however, is a monocot, more closely related to bamboo than the common trees.

Most bows break not because of abuse but because some part of a limb is overworked due to poor design or tillering. No bow type is immune. All should be designed with the same margin of safety. Very overbuilt, highly under-strained bows necessarily hold up better against all causes of failure; the only cost being very slightly reduced arrow speed.

An overbuilt, all horn or horn/sinew bow would be the most durable. But wooden bows last as long per unit of construction time and material cost.

*This gemsbok-horn bow pulls 80 lb at 24", which projects out to well above 100 lb at 28".*

But the easiest to make, most durable, and most awesomely primordal-looking bow of all time is likely the gemsbok take-down. This bow is made of two gemsbok horns shoved onto a whittled stick.

Total construction time: ten minutes.

Estimated life-span: 400 years.

A very hot item of conversation down at the bowmakers' bar.

**The Reasons a Bow Breaks:**
- Too narrow
- Excessive crown
- Back rings or fibers cut through
- Overstrained during tillering
- Overdrawn during use
- Poor thickness taper or low spots on belly
- Damaged wood – drying checks, bacterial decay, insect damage, cell collapse while drying, laminar separation between growth rings (very rare)
- Knots incorrectly worked
- Premature handle dip
- String breaks during shot

## SUITABILITY FOR ITS USE ENVIRONMENT

Short bows are easier to move through brush and maneuver on horseback. Unless recurved, short bows shoot slower than longer bows. Long bows are more accurate. Choose the longest design compatible with ground cover and stealth requirements.

Historically, and by inference, prehistorically, large, powerful bows have almost exclusively been used to kill men from a distance (distance because this prey was fighting back).

American Indians of the Eastern Woodlands used long, heavy, full draw bows, similar to neolithic European designs. Two principle factors may have shaped this longer, stronger bow. First, vertical forests instead of Western brush. Second, the Eastern tribes practiced agriculture, which inevitably means larger populations competing for limited resources, which in turn inevitably meant periodic war.

Al Herrin, author of *Cherokee Bows and Arrows*, reports bows of two weights used by his ancestors: 50 lb for hunting, and 70 lb for war.

Bow design in pre-firearm, agricultural cultures must somehow have been influenced by the occasional perceived need to kill, or defend against, other men. Design disparity between pre- and post-agricultural bows is most obvious when comparing Bushman bows of southern Africa to medieval English longbows. Both are straight-stave bows, both round bellied, both work in the handle. They are very similar bows. But one is three feet long and about 25 pounds of draw weight, while the other is twice as long and four times as strong.

A well-made 50 lb straight-stave bow will shoot a 500 grain normal-fletched arrow about 166 yards. At 70 lb., cast rises to about 210 yards. But an arrow from a 70 lb bow shot from 75 yards arrives at about the same speed as if shot from a 50 lb bow at 25 yards. At somewhere around 125 yards a 100 lb war bow would be equally tamed. These are very rough figures, derived from penetration tests, but the principle holds true: Light bows at 25 yards, or typical hunting distances, have equal penetration to massive bows at military distances.

True hunters, stealthful, patient, and crafty, do very well with 50 lb weapons. American Indians of the West fed themselves quite adequately using low weight bows that cast light arrows, commonly shooting from within 15 yards.

Steve Allely has no difficulty taking deer with his Western Indian bow replications. Kills with a 44", 43 lb Hupa bow replica were made from 17 yards to as close as 10 feet. Arrows were 30" long, weighed 300 grains, and tipped with small "bird points." To shoot from these distances Steve first learned deer movement patterns then fashioned a brush blind.

A 43", 48 lb Shasta replica, shooting 465 grain arrows from a distance of 12 feet, passed through both lungs of a deer and shattered #6 rib on the far side. Forty-eight pounds was more than enough bow at this distance. Steve says he is confident a 30 lb bow would have been adequate, though he doesn't advocate hunting with such a light weapon.

A bow of Steve's Shasta design, of the same weight and 22" draw length, shoots a 465 grain arrow about 140 fps, or about the same speed as a full-length, full-draw 38 lb bow shooting this weight arrow.

Howard Hill claimed that a 450 grain arrow, "...and a 40 lb bow is an adequate weapon for not only deer but elk and moose." Hill's envisioned 40 lb bow would have been a full-draw longbow, which would shoot his suggested 450 grain arrow just over 140 fps.

Art Young believed, quoting Pope, "...he can kill the largest bear in Alaska with a fifty pound weapon and proportionately adjusted arrows."

Paul Comstock, hunting in the Eastern Woodlands, recently took a 300 lb black bear from 15 yards shooting a 53 lb elm, Neolithic European replica. Comstock made this bow in four hours from half-green wood:

"I knew better, but made the bow on a whim. I wanted a spare bow for this hunting trip. I had a bad piece of wood, not good enough to sell or give away. I knocked the bow out quickly. It was ugly, crooked, covered with tool marks, but it was good enough for a spare. Not seeing anything for four nights, I picked up my new bow for luck. And the bear came right in. This bow followed the string by nearly 3" so it shot about like a 48 pounder." The broadhead passed through 20" of bear, bringing the animal down within 60 yards.

Pope wrote that Ishi's favorite hunting bow weighed 40 lb. For bows of this weight, Hill and Young in the old days, and Comstock and Allely today, advocate narrow, more penetrating points (or "bird points", as stone heads of this type are sometimes inaccurately called).

It is clear that a well-placed shot from a fairly light bow can bring a deer-sized animal down in short order. The best weight for a hunting bow is the weight which results in the most accurate shooting at 25 yards. For the majority of hunters this will be between 45 lb and 55 lb. A bowhunter's success rate might best be improved by answering the following question: "What is the highest weight bow I can shoot before my accuracy at 25 yards begins to fall off?"

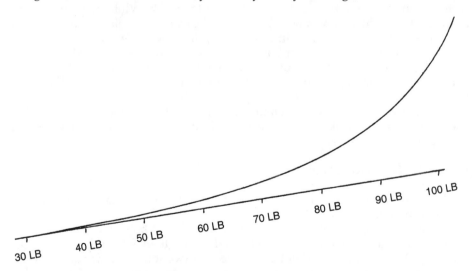

*This drawing is meant only to put an idea into visual form. The straight line represents the increase in penetrating power as draw weight rises. The curved line represents the increase in difficulty and decrease in accuracy as draw weight rises.*

When shooting an uncomfortably high weight bow, archers tend to shorten their draw. Less energy is stored because both draw weight and draw length are reduced. Which leads to a surprising reduction in arrow speed.

A 58 lb bow and the same 500 grain arrow shot the following speeds at the following draw lengths:

    28" – 162 fps
    27" – 154 fps
    26" – 146 fps
    25" – 139 fps

Just one inch reduction in draw length dropped this 58 lb bow's performance to that of a 51 lb bow.

## BEAUTY

It's hard to make a wooden bow which isn't beautiful, even if it's ugly. Don't be so quickly won over by the easy beauty of recurves and Cupid's-bow shapes. There is hardly a more appealing design than a simple, straight-stave bow drawn to the shape of a new crescent moon.

Some woods are conspicuously beautiful. Osage, yew, red cedar, purpleheart, goncalo alves... But even the plainest wood has special character and charm. The apparent bland whiteness of elm, hickory, and ash is like that very ordinary girl you once met. With familiarity, peculiarities of face and form slowly appear to enlightened eyes as unique and valuable, in the end becoming objects of most sincere desire.

Each bow design has its own appeal, largely determined by taste, but within each design there is room for the artist to do his work. While never departing from function, John Strunk's bows, for example, stand on their own as works of art. Pipe-straight staves have little appeal. John relishes working with more visually interesting staves, then with the innovative use of bark, fish skin, and snake skin backings creates beautiful and completely unique bows.

Wooden bowmaking seems to attract people who are competent in the gritty material world, but who also have a sense of subterranean magic. The existence of this quality could not be proven in court. It's displayed subtly, by tone rather than words, and in the bows they make. This is, no doubt, why they have rejected the soul-less, uniform factory bow.

## EASE OF CONSTRUCTION

Making Asiatic composite bows of sinew, wood and horn require the highest levels of knowledge and skill, and from 50 to 100 hours of labor spread over weeks or months.

The various sinewed, recurved, setback, and reflexed bows take about 8 to 20 total hours to make. But drying time is needed for glue joints and steam bends. This 8 to 20 hours can spread out over a week or two if done in dry air, a month or so in more humid air. These bows require intermediate levels of knowledge and skill.

An Eastern Woodland, or Neolithic European straight-stave bow, made of a

*Two plum-branch bows, each made in less than an hour. One is 66", drawing 50 lb at 28". It shoots a 500 grain arrow 146 fps, about 4 fps below average. The smaller bow is 50", drawing 42 lb at 22". At close range, this bow is well able to take deer-sized game.*

North American white wood, can be finished by a relative novice in less than a day. Unlike Osage, locust, mulberry, and sometimes yew, the under-bark sapwood surface of the white-woods is the bow's back. The bow is "half made" before starting.

Surprisingly strong and efficient bows, comparable in performance to other straight-bow designs, can be made from 1-1/4" to 1-1/2" branches or saplings. No splitting, no roughing out. Back and sides are left as is. Only the belly needs tillering. As little as one hour's work will yield a well-tillered, character-laden, smooth-drawing, fast-shooting bow.

Branches and saplings are tapered. Sometimes imperceptibly, sometimes very noticeably. The first bow ever made might have been such a naturally well-tapered branch. Select a six-foot long branch which, when cut to bow length, will be about 1/2" in diameter at one end, about 1-1/4" at the other. Brace and draw the untillered stave, gripping it well below center. It will have a marked asymmetrical profile, but wood will be bending, which means energy is being stored. Draw weight is determined by wood type, limb diameter, and limb length.

This design can be more effective than might be expected. The thick bottom limb is massive – you'd think its weight would smother cast. But the thick bottom limb hardly bends, therefore hardly travels at all, therefore expends little energy. Most of the energy storage and limb travel is done by the tapered (naturally-tillered), efficient upper limb.

As with any bow, arrow speed results from energy stored, minus energy retained. What kind of arrow speed can be expected from this unorthodox design? To know this answer in principle simply answer two questions: 1) How much work is the arm made to do drawing this bow? 2) What are the impediments to the transfer of this energy to the arrow?

If the bow takes a moderate set, if 50 lb of force is needed to draw 28", if the bow is long enough not to stack, then identical energy will be stored in this unlikely bow as in any other having the same if's. This bow can only be slower than others to the degree its length and mass produce greater inertia. Such bows generally must be longer, to prevent excessive set, but perform almost as well as conventional bows which are too long. This bow's length and profile is reminiscent of the Japanese bow, which also bends primarily above its below-center grip.

Asymmetrical bows are not highly efficient, but if "tillered" correctly, can be effective weapons. "Tillering" is done by selecting a branch or sapling with the proper taper, length, width, strength, and elasticity. Such a bow could be made in literally a couple of minutes, using green wood. If debarked and left in the sun and wind for a few days a fully adequate hunting weapon would emerge.

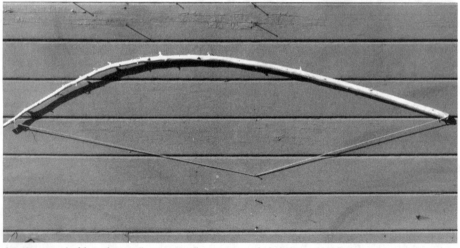

*An asymmetrical bow from a "worst-case" stave: a weak, brittle wood (black acacia), riddled with branches (which were broken off). The bow is used completely untillered. It draws 30 lb at 28", shooting a 500 grain arrow 87 yards, making it adequate for small game only. Draw weight and cast is low due to this weak wood's 4 1/2" string follow. A stronger more elastic wood would have higher draw weight, less string follow, and far greater cast.*

The following "quickie" bow has average efficiency and is traditionally shaped. It can be made in five minutes using a hand saw, or in less than an hour with stone tools. And it has the advantage of being a takedown. I haven't seen or read of this design, but it's so obvious and simple it must have been made at some time in the past.

Cut two branches whose cut dimensions are about 40" long, 1/2" in diameter at one end, and 1-1/8" or so at the other. Make an 8" long bias cut at the base of each, then lash the limbs together. Overlap the tapered faces to thicken the handle. Pictured is an example of worst-case stave selection. Still, this bow is quite serviceable. Straight, knot-less branches yield safer and more efficient limbs. Debarked and wind-dried, a durable take-down bow will be ready for service in three or four days after being cut from the tree.

Bow weight and tiller is determined by wood type, diameter, and bow length. Steeply tapered branches will permit 59" to 70" bows, an efficient length range.

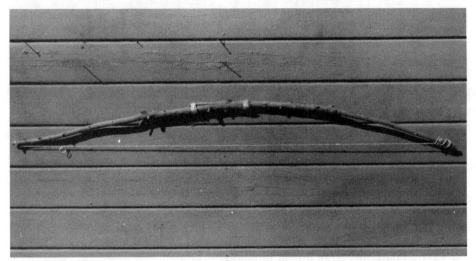

*When made with knotless, strong, well-tapered branches a two-branch takedown is competely serviceable. The limbs can be carried in a quiver, then strapped together when needed.*

Less-tapered branches must be longer in order to "tiller" properly. Short low-tapered limbs are too round in the handle, and too nock heavy, so efficiency suffers.

But efficiency isn't everything. There is satisfaction in coaxing a decent bow from unwilling material. Of course there is is no rule against doing a little touch-up tillering on this two-limb takedown. Far less work will still be needed than if made by conventional methods.

Less character-laden, but none-the-less elegant bows can be made from lumberyard hardwood boards. A fine Sudbury-style hunting bow, for example, can be had for less than a $5 investment. 1" by 2" (actually 7/8" by 1-5/8") ash, hickory, birch, oak and etc., will yield a safe, efficient 50 lb bow. Use wider boards for higher weights.

*This 6' by 1-3/4" by 5" maple lumberyard board cost $24. It yielded six high-efficiency, low set longbows. About one in forty boards will have straight enough grain to be so completely useable.*

With bandsaw and spokeshave an un-sanded but ready-to-shoot, dependable bow can be made from 1" by 2" boards in less than an hour. Three hours with hand tools, five hours including smoothing and sanding. Double these times for novices.

Board staves are sometimes thought of as unnatural, processed, somehow artificial material. But boards are simply trees which have been treated in a rather undignified manner. When making a bow from board staves you are freeing a thing of dignity from the humiliation of static servitude.

Ring orientation on board staves is less critical if a backing is used. Backing a bow isn't always an admission of inexpertise. Wood will often come your way which could not be prudently used if unbacked. Backing such staves allows them to become bows instead of firewood.

The word "grain" has dozens of meanings, many of which are confusing or misleading. Ron Hardcastle has recently done archery a service by coining three new, long-overdue words referring to the orientation of yearly growth rings in a board stave: edge-ringed, flat-ringed, and bias-ringed. He fully describes the making of bows from lumber in Volume II of *The Traditional Bowyer's Bible*.

## EASE OF MAINTENCE

Green wood loses water until a certain percentage moisture content is reached, ranging from about 5% to about 14%, depending on local average relative humidity. Before being tillered, staves should be dried to local equilibrium, or to equilibrium with conditions in which they will be stored and used.

Equilibrium moisture content at various relative humidities:
Moisture content – Relative humidity

6% – 30%
8% – 43%
10% – 55%
12% – 65%
14% – 75%

In many areas of the western U.S., the relative humidity is so low that air-dried wood is dangerously low in moisture content. There are two ways to deal with this. One is to maintain the humidity during manufacture of the bow at about 40 – 50%, then seal it completely with one of the new urathane finishes. The completed weapon must be stored in a higher than ambient relative humidity, or it will eventually dry out. The second method for dealing with this problem, and probably the easiest, is to make the bow's limbs a bit wider than usual. Then, when properly tillered for weight, they will also be thinner, which places less strain on the wood since more wood is working.

A bow made in 50% humidity air, but used in 75% humidity air will lose much weight over time, have limp cast, and take excessive set. A bow made to correct weight in 75% humidity but used in 50% humidity will gain weight over time. A bow which was dried, made and used in 75% humidity must have wider, more massive limbs for a given amount of set. This bow will have more sluggish cast. Wood strength falls about 6% for each 1% rise in moisture content. Damp, weaker limbs take much more set, thereby robbing cast. Forever.

Wood absorbs moisture in reverse order of drying speed, but any wood, if exposed to rain or extended periods of high relative humidity, will take on water, so it is clear that bows need protection. This can be accomplished by sealing the limbs, keeping them unstrung during sustained humid conditions, and storing them in conditions of moderate temperature and humidity when not in use.

Archers living in muggy climes may choose to make, store, and use their bows in conditions of lower humidity. A bow can be made and stored at 9% moisture content, sealed with a moisture-resistant finish, and used in very damp conditions for some time before going soft, though even the most moisture-proof finishes only slow the passage of moisture, not stop it entirely.

When visiting much damper areas, bowyers can carry their home humidity with them. Sinewed bows especially benefit. When not in use bows can be kept in sealed bags or tubes containing packets of silica jell, or "Damp-Gone" type products sold in large hardware stores.

More information on wood sealing finishes, and their application and relative merits, will be found in the chapter on Finishes and Handles later in this volume.

Though moisture protection is the primary concern, other factors also enter into maintenance.

Fenceposts of yew, Osage, cedar, or juniper may last for decades, even centuries, while those of ash, oak, hickory, or elm may decay very quickly as they are digested by bacteria. The difference in lifespans of various fenceposts may be an accelerated example of the fate of unsealed bow limbs.

A one-hundred year old wooden bow will likely break if drawn. Wood weakens with time, but not because it dries out - wood's moisture content quickly reaches equilibrium and remains relatively constant over time. Bacteria feed on wood sugars and starches - this could shorten the life of a bow. Perhaps, due to oxygen infiltration, cellulose and lignin polymerise over time, losing elasticity just as skin and windshield wipers do. Denser woods would be less permeable to bacteria and oxygen. Horn's density may contribute to its longevity. Apart from acting as a moisture barrier, an efficient surface coating will also slow the movement of bacteria and oxygen.

All chemical/organic processes slow when cooled. Whatever the cause of wood's aging, it would no doubt be accelerated by hot-attic storage, and slowed by storage at the coolest feasible temperatures. Most bows shoot safely in below freezing weather, so storing them at such low temperature should do no harm. A bow's useable lifespan might be extended by many decades, although the moisture content of a bow stored in this manner should be allowed to reach ambient equilibrium before being strung and shot.

Dr. Errett Callahan's Eskimo replica performed well in the arctic. Made of white ash and braided sinew cable, this bow was shot hundreds of times in near 50-below weather. A 4,000-plus year old archer was recently discovered in an Alpine glacier in Europe. Archer, bow, and arrows were well preserved.

Asiatic composites must be kept warm and dry, or else elaborately warmed before bracing. Composite-armed warriors typically slept with their bows while on campaign. Once braced, these bows performed well at either cold or warm temperatures.

Sinew-backed bows, composite bows, and bows using animal glue are more sensitive to moisture than self bows. Unless hermetically sealed, sinew will take up moisture quickly in damp air, causing draw weight and accuracy to plummet. Weight rises again when dried.

Mice, dogs, raccoons and insects – especially moths – eat sinew. Moths eat horn too.

## COST, OR AVAILABILITY OF MATERIALS

Yew and Osage are not rare, but bow-quality wood from these gnarley trees is far from common. A pair of top-quality yew billets sell for $90 or more. Equal quality Osage billets sell for near that. Perfect, full-length hickory, locust, elm, and ash staves sell for from $25 to $60.

In one sense, Osage and yew are underpriced: Set out some morning intending to cut and split as many bow-quality yew or Osage staves as you can. You might come back very late that night with nothing at all to show for your effort. Next morning set out again, this time targeting white woods. About ten in the morning you'll have to come back for a larger truck. North America is awash with bow wood.

Commercial lumber for use in bows is easily accessible and inexpensive. A bow made from lumber will cost $3 - $10.

When making bows in the fifty pound range, hundreds of tree and bush species become reasonable stave sources.

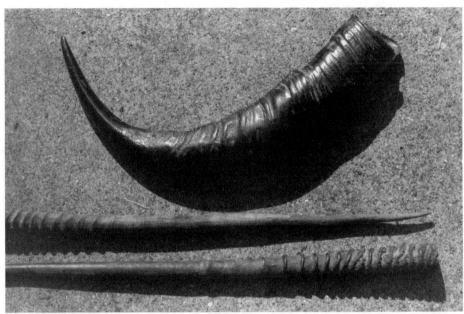

*For centuries, water buffalo horn has been the material of choice for Asiatic composite bow bellies, but their $60 to $100 cost inhibits experimentation. The straighter, longer gemsbok horns seem to work as well, are cheaper (about $25 a pair), and require less work to prepare. Cut in half, each horn supplies sufficient horn for one limb.*

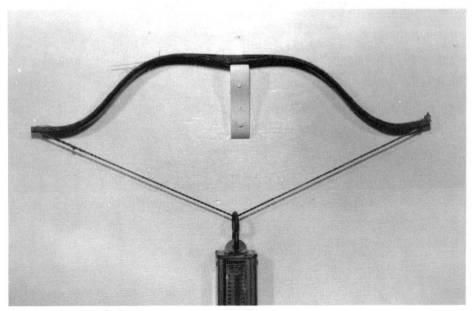

*Asiatic-style composite bow.*

Sinew is potentially quite abundant. Presently most game backstrap sinew is destroyed during butchering, and legs discarded. But this can easily change. Market forces will no doubt prod supply to keep even with demand.

Hide glue is cheap ($3 - $15 per pound, depending on quantities and grade), though not always easy to find. It is, however, easy to make.

Domestic Southeastern Asian water buffalo are raised by the millions. Tractors may replace them in time, but the foreseeable supply of this superior bowmaking horn is secure. A set of large horns cost from $60 to $100.

For strings and backing, sinew, rawhide, gut, silk, linen, and bamboo are in good supply. They are fairly accessible and inexpensive.

## UNOBTRUSIVENESS

Many game animals, notably deer, "jump the string" at the slightest sound.

Jim Hamm: "Most experienced bowhunters can tell stories of making a good shot, but the deer, hearing the release of the arrow, is gone when it arrives. Deer have such quick reflexes (from tens of thousands of years spent dodging wolves, mountain lions, bears, and humans with rumbling bellies), that the unusual sound of a bowstring is enough to send them instantly dodging from harm, and the arrow's, way. For a target shooter, the noise a bow makes when an arrow is released is insignificant and scarcely noticed. But for any hunter trying to provide sustenance for his family, at any time throughout history, a noisy shot could be the difference between an abundance of food and watching his children whimper with hunger. This is why hunters, both ancient and modern, wrap strips of fur or attach bundles of feathers to the bowstring, to dampen the twang. And wrap the grip with leather to muffle the passing of the arrow. For a hunter, a very quiet bow may be more of an advantage than a very fast bow."

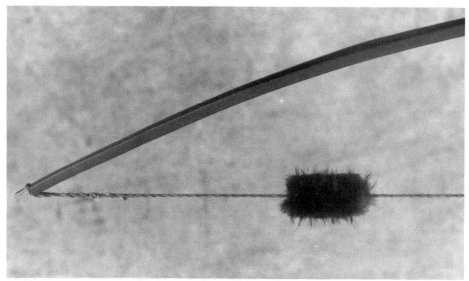

*Narrow strips of fur wrapped around the bowstring act as string silencers.*

Low-strung bows have quieter string twang.

Straight bows are quieter than recurves.

Low-weight bows are quieter than strong bows.

Thick strings are quieter than thin strings.

Energy-efficient bows are quieter because less energy remains behind to vibrate bow limbs and string.

Heavy arrows shoot quieter than light arrows – less string twang because more energy is drained from the bow.

Shiny surfaces attract any eye. As do light colored surfaces. White-wood bows, if intended for hunting, should be darkened or camouflaged with stain, snake skins, or some such. By the same reasoning, the sealer or finish on a bow should not be shiny or reflective.

Becoming familiar with the preceding ten bow qualities will make you fluent in bow design, in all its dialects, both present and past. Once you might have stood mystified at the hidden logic of some strange, ancient design. Now you can share the thoughts of its distant designer.

For example...

A bow has only so much bend in it. It can store only so much energy and no more. Much of its bending capacity is used up in the process of being braced. When an arrow is released that brace-energy stays in the bow, it is not available to the arrow.

With a bow of very weak and inelastic wood, a large percentage of the bow's bending ability is used up before an arrow is drawn the first inch. Very little is left to propel an arrow. If forced to use very weak wood, a bowyer might try to get at the energy hiding in those braced limbs. To do this unconventional means would be needed.

Exactly such a problem confronted Indians of the Southwest, who were forced to use willow for bows. And a peculiar design appears among these bows: deflexed tips. Such a bow is under no strain when braced. Its full energy storing capacity is now available to the arrow. This is an inefficient design. It will not shoot as fast per pound of draw weight as a normal design, but its makers traded efficiency for net arrow speed. And in the process gained a couple of other benefits: a hunter could leave his bow braced and at the ready indefinitely, with no loss of cast. And because little energy is left in this bow, string twang should be almost non-existant.

Similar deflex-tip designs were used in ancient Egypt. Such bows were reportedly made of accacia. The only accacia I've tested rated somewhere between willow and ash. Both an early Egyptian and a Southwest Indian may have come across identical solutions to a common problem.

You have to trust a theory that has such symmetry. Sinew/wood, or sinew/horn represent the polar extremes of willow-like materials. And the profiles of such bows are precisely opposite.

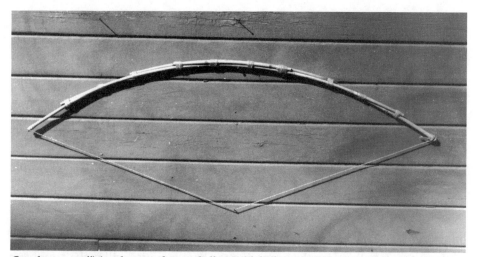

*Cane bows are efficient because they are hollow, with little mass. But in an emergency, any assemblage of twigs will work. Mass will be high but sufficient arrow speed can be achieved with high enough draw weight. Even old warped and injured arrows can be given another life.*

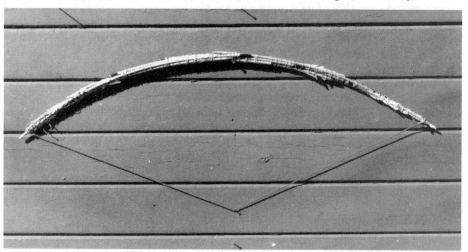

Being fluent in bow design will also let you solve unusual problems. For example... You've been dropped into a swamp. You need a bow. But no trees grow in this swamp, only small-diameter cane. A six-foot length draws about 10 lb., and, of course, bends only in the handle. How can a decent bow be made from such material?

Two problems must be solved right off: 1) Draw weight can be raised by bundling canes together. 2) Even curvature can be affected by imitating normal tillering: using more canes mid bow, fewer canes toward the tips.

Unlike a normal bow, each cane is strained independently. Strain on a single cane is the same whether bent alone or incorporated in a multi-cane bundle. Draw weight can be raised simply by adding canes.

What diameter and length cane to choose? You know that about 67" is the most efficient length. You know that 1.5" is the most efficient set, from straight stock. So pick a cane diameter which will take a low set when bent. One-half to five-eight's inch diameter turns out to be about right. If available canes take too much set at 67", lengthen canes in compromise to set and length. Wrap the bundle tightly with cord, concentrating where cane lengths end.

My best cane bow so far was made of four, 1/2" diameter, bamboo, garden-supply bean poles. Lengths were 23", 36", 54.5" and 70". Thick ends staggered. Wrapped every five inches. At 28" this bow drew 58 lb., took a 2-1/2" set. and weighed 20 ounces. It shot 157.5 fps, just about average for a straight-stave bow. Its slightly high set canceled its slightly low mass. Thinner canes would have taken less set, but mass would have risen with additional canes. Slightly shorter limbs would normally shoot faster, but narrow canes would be needed to keep set low, and mass would rise farther.

I left the "55 cents" price sticker on each cane. Great fun when shooting in a line beside $400 factory jobs.

One more example...

You're at the hardware store looking for two matched-grain hickory pick handles to splice together for a bow stave. You notice a cluster of 1" diameter push-broom handles. Ramin wood, $2.60 each. You've been promising some neighborhood kids you'd make them a bow.

The grain isn't perfectly parallel, but you're only going for 30 lb. The belly is worked down flat for the first version, but at 30 lb splinters rise on the narrow crown of the back, and the bow fails.

On the next bow, the back is worked flat, the belly left round. With more wood fibers doing tension work this bow now pulls safely to 30 lb., but the very narrow-arched belly takes too much set.

Bow three is worked down at both back and belly. The wider belly succeeds in reducing string follow, and sufficient width remains on the back to resist splintering. Success.

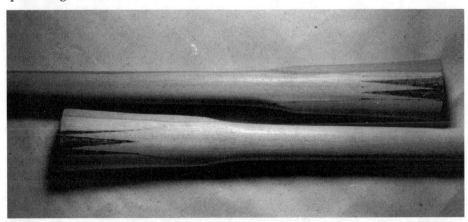

*If there are no trees in your town, and no hardwood lumberyards, pick up a rake, broom, or hoe handle at the hardware store. The longer, thicker, and more straight-grained the better. The larger diameter handles make up to 40 lb bows. Hickory pick handles, pictured, can be spliced together to make a first-class, high-weight longbow or flatbow.*

# Additional Design Considerations

## BUILDING THE PERFECT BOW

If an experienced bowhunter had to feed his family with a bow, day-in and day-out, which design would he choose? What mix of design qualities would he settle on? Assuming, of course, he had full knowledge of the options.

Paul Comstock, Jim Hamm, and I have pondered this question. And in full appreciation of the irony involved decided he would likely choose the most ancient bow, the Neolithic European/ Eastern Woodlands bow. No recurves, no setback, no sinew, no tricks. 65 to 70 inches long. About 1-1/2" of string follow. He would choose this design for the simple reason that he likes to eat. It is an un-fidgety, durable, straight-shooting design. "A bow that makes meat," as Jim puts it.

I believe such a hunter would use easy-to-get and easy-to-work white wood because life is tough enough already. Paul feels the same. Jim leans toward Osage because of its "drag through the bushes durability."

Stepping back in time might yield new insight. With only stone tools in his kit, our hunter would probably choose the strongest and most elastic woods available, because good bows can be made from small diameter limbs and saplings. The white woods, though more easily worked, require bigger trees to construct their wider, thinner limbs. Felling, splitting, and reducing staves from large diameter trees is daunting work with stone tools. Paradoxically, this means he would likely choose yew and Osage where available. These hardest-to-work woods become the easiest to work under primitive conditions.

As for the bow design, I have two favorites, one for up to 50 lb., the other for over 50 lb.

The first is 64" to 70" long. Length depends on bow weight, wood strength and elasticity, and severity of back crown. This is an efficient, easy to make

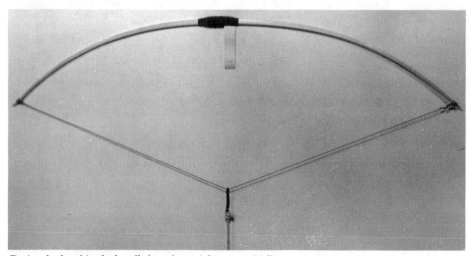

*Design for bend in the handle bow for weights up to 50 lb.*

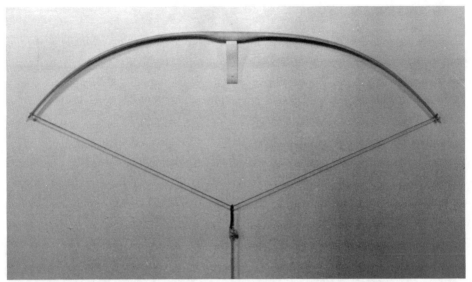

*Design with narrow, thicker handle-section and wide limbs, for weights above 50 lb.*

design. The center two-feet of length is 1-1/2" wide, tapering in curved graceful lines to 1/2" nocks. This is a flat-bellied, bend-in-the-handle, unbacked bow. It is tillered so that handle and near-handle wood bends just enough to take no visible set. Bend increases moving tipward, but the last eight inches have almost no bend. Since these tips do not work they are made narrow and deep, thereby reducing mass.

Fifty pounds is about this design's white-wood weight limit. Higher weights cause undue set unless woods of greater strength and elasticity are used.

For above 50 lb., limbs widen according to draw weight, wood used, and degree of back crown. This bow is 64" to 68" long, unbacked white wood. Length adjusts according to severity of back crown. Its 4" X 1-1/4" X 1-1/4" grip flares abruptly to a full width of 2", then runs parallel to mid limb. From there it curves gently to 1/2" nocks. Except for a stiff handle this bow is tillered just like its 50 lb mate above: near-handle wood bends just enough to take no visible set. Bend increases moving tipward, the last eight inches have almost no bend, tips are narrow and deep, reducing mass. Its grip is fairly wide and short so that near-grip wood can start working almost immediately. To insure low back-crown, logs above 6" in diameter are preferred.

Wayne Simpson, a bowmaking friend from Tracy, California, recently brought three longbows over for testing. One each of Osage, yew, and hickory-backed lemonwood. All of classic English longbow design. The lemonwood bow, in fact, had just been imported from England.

He was interested in determining how these three traditional bow woods and the English design compared to his white-wood longbows. We had earlier test-ed a similarly designed hickory of Wayne's, now included here. Also tested was a maple bow of my favorite design, as described above.

Here are some of the stats:

|  | Yew | Osage | Lemonwood | Hickory | Maple |
|---|---|---|---|---|---|
| Weight | 51 lb | 65-1/4 | 55 | 55 | 58-1/2 |
| Length | 72-1/2 | 67-1/4 | 75-3/4 | 69 | 67 |
| Near grip | 15/16 | 1-5/16 | 1-1/16 | 1-1/4 | 2-1/16 |
| Mid limb | 15/16 | 1-1/8 | 15/16 | 15/16 | 2-1/16 |
| Mass | 22 oz | 31.9 | 26 | 22 | 25 |
| Belly | D | flat | D | flat | flat |
| Dried | air | air | ? | kiln | kiln |
| Set | 2 | 2-3/8 | 1-7/8 | 1-3/4 | 1-1/2 |
| String ht. | 7-1/2 | 7-1/2 | 6-3/4 | 7 | 6-1/4 |
| Speed | 145 fps | 159 | 145 | 152 | 164 |
| Efficiency | -4 | -7 | -8 | +1 | +4 |

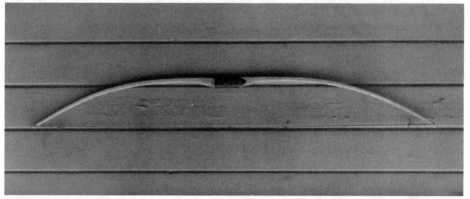

*Wayne's hickory longbow. Perfect tiller for a stiff handle: near-handle wood barely bending, near-tip wood barely bending, even curvature at mid-limb.*

"Efficiency" represents the number of fps over or under average straight-stave bows of equal weight, as described later in this chapter.

Why did each of these bows shoot the way it did?

YEW: 4 fps under average. This bow is 4-1/2" too long. If 68" long, and if strung a bit lower, performance would rise to near average. If shorter, limbs would have to be 1-1/8" wide at mid limb to prevent excessive set. A flat belly might take it over average.

OSAGE: 7 fps under average. About five or six ounces overweight at 32 oz. This costs several fps. About one inch too much set. This costs three or four fps at this set and weight. This bow originally weighed 80 lb. It took the set an 80 lb bow of this width would take, then was tillered to its present weight. This accounts for its excessive set, and some of its mass.

LEMONWOOD: 8 fps under average. This bow is eight inches longer than it should be, too narrow near the grip, and about three ounces too heavy. A flat belly or wider limbs would lower its set. If shorter, as with the yew, limbs should be wider. The core of this bow was a dark, heavy tropical hardwood.

Since the center of a bow does virtually no work, a lighter, weaker wood would have been a better choice here, saving a couple of ounces.

HICKORY: 1 fps over average. Good mass. Good set. Only an inch or so longer than needed. Hickory is less elastic than yew. This hickory bow is 4 lb heavier than the yew. It is 3-1/2" shorter. Both bows have identical mid-limb widths. Despite all this, the hickory bow's flat belly yielded lower set.

MAPLE: 4 fps over average. Length is good, set is good, mass is good for a wide bow of this draw weight. Lower string height added one fps or so.

The maple bow won hands down, or more accurately, its design won. Trade designs with any of the other woods, and the performance results would change accordingly.

Oregon bowyer Wally Miles has been using a moderately flat-bellied English design for over forty years. Like Wayne's, his bows have less set, and are among the fastest-per-pound straight stave self bows I've tested.

From one point of view, the above yew and lemonwood bows are too long and too narrow for their weight and design. But their slightly lower cast may buy slightly increased accuracy. Raw arrow speed is not always the most important requirement.

I once took a devil's-advocate stance in discussing this view with Paul Comstock. He finally erupted in exasperated eloquence:

"Look, I know a guy who makes nice Osage-sinew bows, he makes long, wide-limbed white-wood bows that shoot fast per pound, but what he likes best are long narrow bows made of white woods, and they all follow the string about 3", therefore the cast per pound is basically mediocre. But this man can take one of his bows and stand 90 ft. away from you and hit you right between the eyes, and the arrow is going to go in one side of your head and come out the other side, and this guy dearly loves these bows. And why shouldn't he?"

## BOWS FROM GREEN WOOD

Oregon primitive technologist and bowyer Jim Riggs makes hunting-strength bows from green wood. Jim has his students reduce just-cut, chokecherry saplings to bendable thickness (many other species will do). These very wet, very pliable saplings are then tied in place over a board or branch form.

The form is removed two days later. Limb tiller is touched up a bit, and the bows are braced and shot. Probing with an electronic moisture meter revealed surprisingly low readings of around 15%. Eleven percent on the third day. Similar temperature and humidity had always needed double these drying times in my shop. The fact that the bow were cured outside in the wind made the difference. My drying box now contains a small fan.

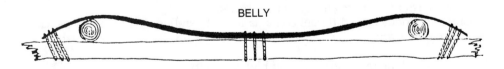

BELLY

*Recurving green wood.*

The dried-in-place recurves give these short bows surprising quickness, and sweetness of draw and release. Being somewhat green, these limbs took more set than normal, but the recurves more than compensated.

Two or three days may be too long for you to wait. If so, a hunting-strength bow can be made in an hour or so from dripping, green wood. Green wood is little more than half as strong as cured wood and will take a very large set, which would normally yield a very limp shooter. Normally.

Once a green blank is roughed out, bend the last six inches or so into recurved or retroflexed tips. These tips will want to pull out when braced and drawn – so tie them in place: cut side notches about 7" from each nock and run a cord from notch to nock.

This green bow's big set, and large retro tips take on a deflex-recurve profile. A highly efficient design. As the limbs lose moisture, draw weight will increase and the bow must be retillered to desired weight.

Another green-bow option is to make limbs much wider than if the wood was cured. Wider, therefore thinner, limbs will take less set. As the bow dries and draw weight rises, the limbs can be narrowed to maintain desired weight.

## BOARD STAVES
Properly cured, tree-split staves are more desirable than board staves.
But:

1) Many would-be bowmakers live in virtual tree deserts.

2) A beginner, on average, will break or maim a dozen staves before making an efficient, durable bow. Twelve times a cheap "natural" stave price of $50 is $600. Twelve times an average lumberyard stave price of $5 is $60.

3) At these prices a beginner, or a veteran, can afford to experiment, to make mistakes, to take chances, to learn things about bowmaking he would never learn otherwise.

4) At $5 each a lot of bows can be given to friends and neighborhood kids.

## COMPRESSION STRENGTH/ELASTICITY
Relative compression strengths of woods are often given to indicate bow wood quality. But these figures can be misleading. Compression strength is only important if accompanied by elasticity, which is the percentage of length a material will stretch or compress before taking a set.

In order for a bow limb to store energy it must have both strength and elasticity. One is useless without the other. Concrete, for example, has terrific compression strength, but since it won't compress very FAR it can't store much energy. Concrete would make a poor bow belly – even if sinew-backed!

A rubber-band and cotton string both stretch before breaking, and may break at equal pounds of pull, but rubber will stretch much farther before breaking, storing enormously more energy in the process.

Different woods have different combinations of bending strength and elasticity. Some examples are:

• Osage – high bending strength and high elasticity.
• Yew – medium bending strength and very high elasticity.

- Locust – high bending strength but medium elasticity.
- Ash – medium bending strength and medium elasticity.
- Willow – low bending strength and low elasticity.

Osage and black locust have about equal compression strength, but a same-thickness piece of Osage will bend farther than locust before taking a set. It is more rubber-band like; the locust is more cotton string-like. The high compression figures published for locust have led to many crysaled and overstrained locust bows.

Since Osage bends farther than locust, more energy is stored. But it's simple to cause a locust bow to store as much energy as an Osage bow of equal draw and weight – just add more locust. Let this extra locust be in the form of a wider, thinner, limb. It will then bend as far, and store the same energy as Osage. Even thought there is now more of it, locust is lighter wood, so mass remains about equal for both bows, therefore cast will be the same.

Ash will bend about the same distance as locust before taking a set, but has less bend strength. So same-dimension ash stores less energy than locust. Again, just add more ash. Since these two woods have about equal elasticity, thickness can remain the same. Ash need only be wider to store the same energy as locust. Again, since ash is lighter than locust, equal strength bows made from these woods will have about equal mass, equal set, and equal cast.

Willow, pine, poplar, basswood, and other light woods are weak and brittle. They store little energy. Such wood must be made into light bows, or very wide, thin-limbed bows. Usually so wide that crown height becomes too high, or limb width too ungainly.

Wide-limbed weaker-wood bows shoot as fast as "normal" bows, but why?

Make ten same-design, same-width bows from ten different woods, ranging in strength/elasticity from pine to Osage. Tiller each so that when broken-in, draw weight and length are equal for all. Each of the ten will have taken a different degree of set. Those made of the weakest, least elastic wood may even have broken.

Those that don't break will shoot faster or slower according to the amount of set taken. And set will vary according to the strength and elasticity of wood used. An Osage bow will have the least set and shoot the fastest. If the pine bow hasn't broken, its set will be highest, its cast lowest. It's not hard to see how the different woods got their reputation.

Again make ten same-design bows using the same woods as before. But this time make the weaker-wood bows with appropriately wider limbs. If the Osage is 1-1/5" wide the locust will be 1-5/8", the ash 1-3/4", the pine 3". Tiller each to the same weight. When broken in all bows will now have identical set, or side-view profiles. Which means they must drain identical amounts of energy from the arm when drawn. Because they are made from progressively lighter woods, wide and narrow limbs will have about the same mass. All ten bows will shoot at virtually identical speeds.

To restate: Tension and compression strength in bowmaking materials is important, but equally important is the percentage of length a material will stretch or compress before taking a set.

Horn, for example, has only about twice the compression strength of ash, but will compress about four times farther before taking a set. Horn is four times more rubber-like than wood, and can therefore store much more energy.

Some woods are stronger and have greater elasticity than others. Put another way, some woods are more horn-like than others. When made into bows, weaker, less elastic wood must have proportionately wider limbs.

Here is a convincing way to demonstrate this idea:

Make several 1" wide ash bows. Start at 20 lb., raising the weight of each successive bow by a couple of pounds. Shoot each and see how fast each shoots per pound of draw weight.

Each new bow will take slightly more set than the last, but be slightly more efficient due to its lower mass per pound of draw weight. Stop making heavier bows when the level of set becomes severe enough to produce diminishing cast returns. You will notice this ideal 1" wide ash bow is about 30 lb.

Now make another such bow, identical in every regard.

Grip both 30 lb bows together, side-by-side. Pull both strings as one, and draw both bows as one – presto, a 60 lb ash bow, 2" wide.

*To make efficient high-weight bows from weaker woods simply make them wider.*

To test this principle in the extreme I once made a 70 lb de-crowned pine sapwood bow. At 66", the mid-limbs were 4-1/4" wide. It performed well, but due to its enormous size behaved differently from other bows. With so much surface area it kicked up dust storms with each shot. But these wide limbs also had benefits: It worked well as a slalom ski when traversing the Sierra Mountains. With one end stuck in the ground it made a good wind screen while camping. And during desert crossings refreshing naps could be taken in its shade. Regrettably, this bow had to be retired. The U.S. Meteorological Service asked me to quit using it, due to its effect on local weather patterns. While wider limbs hold true in theory, there clearly are practical limits to their use.

Having taken a set, a material is said to have exceeded its elastic limit. Different materials reach their elastic limits at different percentages of stretch or compression.

Merely for perspective, different materials may be laid out on an elasticity spectrum: On a yardstick concrete would be at the 36" mark, horn on the 1" mark. Yew and Osage are at 20" and 21", locust, hickory, ash, etc., hover at 25". The least elastic wood tested so far is Sitka spruce. In A Standard Bend Test, to follow, spruce bent 2-3/8" at 18 lb before taking a standard set. Ash pulled to about 3-1/4". Put spruce at 30" on the spectrum. Willow tested 3" at 13.5 lb. Put it at 27".

Although hickory out-shines most others in the hard-to-break category, this is not a big advantage in a straight-stave design. If made correctly, that extreme ability will never come into play because hickory must take a large, cast-robbing set before breaking.

Yew without sapwood tests about the same as with sapwood, except samples break at an average of 6" instead of 7". This difference is relatively unimportant. Yew bows made with or without sap must be given massive sets before breaking.

*Jenny Comstock draws a heartwood-only yew bow, a prehistoric European replica. Growth rings are violated on the back, as on the originals. Jenny, by the way, is an actual descendant of Stone Age Europeans.*

Unless terribly mistillered or overstrained, heartwood yew bows shoot as fast and as durably as with sapwood.

## A STANDARD WOOD BENDING TEST

Wood does not stack. Wood gives no signal of any kind before failing. How can a bowmaker know the amount of strain a certain wood will take? How can he know how much bow can be obtained from a given stave of wood?

You'd think that once familiar with a few favorite woods, trial and error would show the correct limb widths for each wood. But the range of strength and elasticity within a species is far too great from stave to stave. Same-species staves picked at random and made into identical bows will have striking differences in cast. Cast differences, of course, will largely parallel the amount of set each bow has taken.

This test can tell a bowmaker everything he needs to know about a sample of wood, with far less work and more dependable results than making standard miniature bows.

It will let him know exactly how wide limbs must be for a given draw weight, how much set the limbs will take, and how much mass the limbs will have. From this he can know how fast the bow will shoot, within one or two fps. This test is reliable because, unlike static and linear laboratory tests, it makes wood samples do exactly what they would do in a bow.

For about three inches each side of its point of bend, the sample should have precisely the qualities you want tested. Normally, the sample will be flat-ringed, with wood fibers paralleling the back, but you can also learn the comparative bending characteristics of a sample having unconventional grain orientation. Junk wood will often yield a testable sample: only about six inches of the sample's length must have the qualities you want tested.

Sample size is 1/2" square X 18". Width, and especially thickness should be accurate to within 1/100". A 1% difference in thickness throws the reading off by 3%. 1/1000" layers can be removed with a spokeshave, and the cheapest hardware store dial calipers will measure finer than 1/100". A 1/2" end wrench can be used instead of calipers.

Make sample dimensions uniform their entire length so the weight comparisons will have value.

Dry all the samples to equilibrium moisture content for your area. A difference of 1% in moisture will throw the reading off by about 6%. I use 9%, and

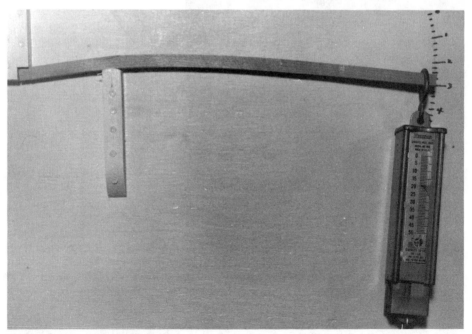

*Place the scale one-half inch from the sample's end. Always keep the scale at a ninety degree angle. Center of fulcrum is 4" from sample's secured end.*

keeping samples in 50% humidity air insures this moisture content.

Pull the sample one inch, then release and re-pull five times before taking a weight reading. This gives the wood its true new set and weight. Release and measure the amount of set taken. If there is fairly rapid return movement wait until the movement slows to a creep.

Continue as above, increasing pull length by one-half inch at a time until the sample breaks.

Make a special note of the pull length and weight needed to give the sample a 1/4" set. Also note pull length, pull weight and set at the time of failure, and when chrysals form.

A medium-performing sample will bend 3-1/4" and pull 25 lbs when taking a 1/4" set, and will break at 4". Its key, quick-glance figures are:

25 lb – 3-1/4" – 1/4" – 4"

A bow made from this sample will be the standard for comparison here. It is 66" long and pulls 50 lb at 28". In order to have optimum set, speed, and safety, this bow, made from such wood, will be 1-3/4" wide. This width was determined by extensive trial and error. Crown height is based on a 6" diameter log.

Another stave might test:

20 lb – 3-1/4" – 1/4" – 4"

Having taken its 1/4" set at 3-1/4" of bend, this sample has identical elasticity as the above standard, but has lower bend strength. To make a 50 lb., optimum-speed bow from this weaker wood, it must be a certain percentage wider. Divide 25 lb by 20 lb = 1.25", times 1.75" (limb width of standard bow) = 2.19". At 2.19" wide the weaker-wood bow will then have the same safety, set, and speed of cast as the stronger-wood bow.

A stronger but more brittle stave might test:

40 lb – 3" – 1/4" – 3"

Pull weight is above-standard at 1/4" set, but pull distance is below standard. The sample is stronger but less elastic, therefore capable of storing less energy than its high pull weight indicates. This wood would have to be thinner, and therefore have lower pull weight to take its 1/4" set at 3-1/4". Trial and error shows that for each 1/4" difference in pull length, at 1/4" set, pull weight shifts about 20%. If this sample was thinned enough to take its 1/4" set at 3-1/4" instead of 3", pull weight would drop about 20%, from 40 lb to 32 lb. Standard width and weight is 1-3/4" at 25 lb., so divide 25 by 32 = .781, times 1.75 = 1.36". A bow from this wood should be 1.36" wide instead of 1-3/4".

A stronger, more elastic stave might test:

30 lb – 3.5"– 1/4"– 6"

Pull weight is above-standard at 1/4" set, and pull distance is also above standard. This sample is stronger and more elastic, therefore capable of storing more energy than its moderate pull weight indicates. Such wood would have to be thicker, and therefore have higher pull weight to take its 1/4" set at 3-1/4". If this sample was thickened enough to take its 1/4" set at 3-1/4" instead of 3-1/2" pull weight would increase about 20%, from 30 lb to 36 lb. Again, divide 25 by 36 = .694, times 1.75" = 1.21". Limbs from this wood should be 1.21" instead of 1.75".

And so on.

The standard test bow was taken from a 6" diameter tree. For limb safety, and for these comparisons to be accurate, crown ratios must remain constant. Wider limbs must come from larger diameter trees – or else crowns must be flattened. Narrower limbs can come from narrower trees.

All the above figures are approximations. They will be fine tuned as time goes on. But they have proven to be satisfactory in practice.

A piece of old-growth fir heartwood once tested in the low-ash range. This was perplexing. Fir's published mechanical properties showed it to be a brittle, inferior bow wood. To resolve this dilemma an ash-wide, ash-weight bow was made from the fir stave: 66" long, 1-3/4" wide, 50 lb at 28". The test predictions were precisely correct. The fir bow has average set and average cast. This was an unusual piece of fir. Almost twice as heavy as average, it had an unusually dark latewood equaling about 40% of ring width instead of fir's normal 15% or so.

To determine the properties of a particular stave only its "key numbers" need be noted as in the stat sheet:

Test #3-7/11/91 Species: Ash Subspecies: Oregon Sex: ?
Test purpose: Effect of 6% Moisture Content
Pull -lb- Set" Natural or planed surface: Natural
1" -11.5 - 1 End, back, side view:
- - 1
2" -22.5 - 1/16
-27 - 1/8
3" -31 - 1/4 :Crysals formed
-35 - 3/8
4" -36.5 - 1/2 Key numbers: 3"—31'6
-38 - 3/8
5" - Broke - 1 Reason for failure:
- - 1 Sketch of failure:
6" - - 1 None clean, normal break:
- - 1
7" - - 1

SAMPLE:
-Weight in grains: 740
-Rings per inch: 13
-Early growth %: 20%
-Moisture content: 6%
-Tree diameter: 6"
-Kiln or air dried: Air
-Made into bow #: 163-91
Comments: At 9% m/c sister sample's key numbers were 3¼ — 27'6.
Where grown: S.W. Wash.
Month felled: 3/91
Growing conditions: Rich soil, good water, shade
Drying history: Debarked same day, cut to 2"x2" stave
Other: Dried at 70°, 50% Hum.

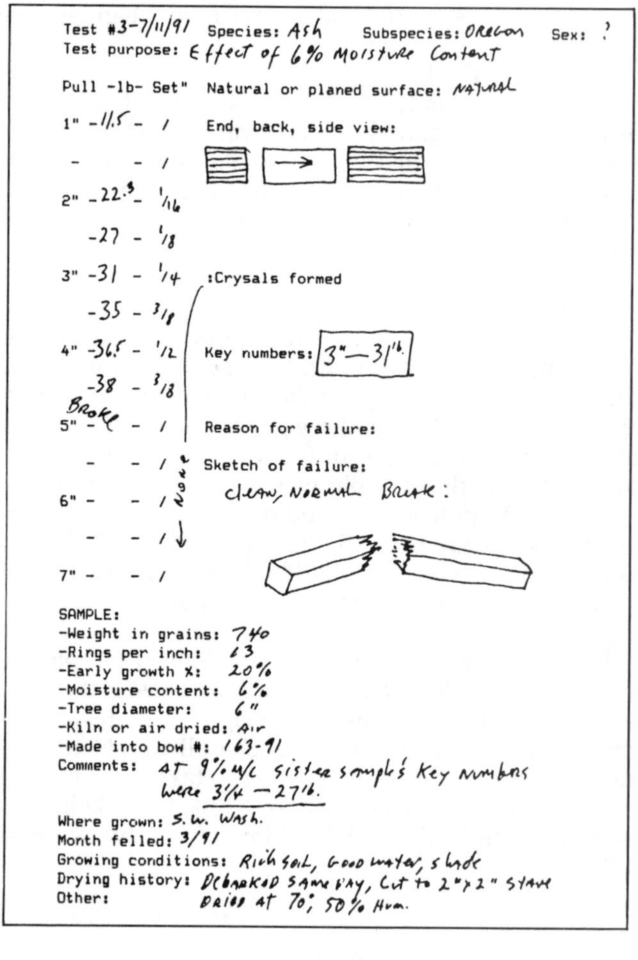

*The stat sheet I've evolved over time. I hope others will use it, and exchange results. By comparing data on different samples the variables which affect performance can be identified. Which species are stronger if grown in shade? Are male or female trees of a certain species stronger? Do acid soils produce more elastic wood? Are southern elms stronger than northern elms? Such questions are endless, and answering then can only lead to more satisfying bowmaking.*

To more comprehensively research the properties of wood, and how these properties affect bow design and performance, a more detailed stat card is useful. A standard test procedure and card will let experimenters exchange test results.

### LESSONS FROM THE BENDING TEST

Different types of breaks and failures are clues to wood properties.

Samples which bend a great deal before taking 1/4" set are more elastic in compression. Osage and yew are examples.

Samples which take an early set, but bend very far before breaking have low compression elasticity but high tension strength. Such wood can be reflexed and recurved with safety and will be more tolerant of tillering errors and hidden internal flaws. This tolerance is less valuable when working perfectly straight wood, but is especially valuable when working problem staves. Examples are hickory and elm.

Samples which break in tension before taking much set have low breaking strength in tension relative to compression strength and are good candidates for backing. If unbacked, limbs should be wider and thinner to safely bend farther. Examples are cedar, juniper, willow, cherry, and many of the conifers. Tension breaks can be recognized by the characteristic transverse crack across the back, often leaving the belly beneath it unbroken.

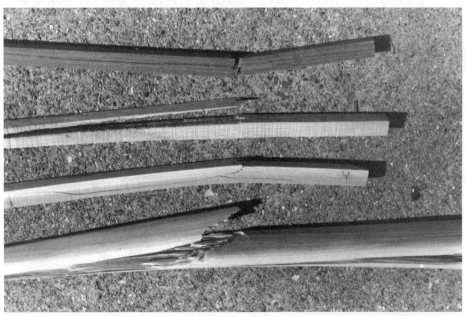

*The top sample is an example of a normal break. The bottom three broke in tension. Notice their bellies are still perfectly intact. These samples would not have broken had they been backed. The bottom sample is an actual bow made from the same stave as the sample above it. The bend test had given eloquent warning, and, indeed, the sample and bow failed in precisely the same manner. The bend test will tell you everything you need to know about a stave.*

Samples which break normally before taking much set are brittle in tension and compression. Bows from such wood must be wider than their key figures indicate. Such woods are rare. Teak and some conifers are examples.

Edge-ringed samples, on average, are 10% weaker, take a set 10% sooner, and break 10% earlier than flat-ringed samples of the same wood.

Some wood species take less set than others before breaking. Hickory, for example, takes a lot, red cedar very little, exploding with little warning. This is another reason to test stave samples.

There is a difference between bending strength and breaking strength. For example, Sitka spruce bent one inch when pulled with 10 lb of force. It broke at three inches and 20 lbs. A same-size sample of yellow birch also bent one inch at 10 lb., but pulled to 4-1/4" and 29 lb before breaking. Both woods have equal bending strength, but very different elasticities and breaking strengths. Bows made with identical widths and thicknesses from these woods would be equally hard to pull each additional inch, until the spruce broke. The birch would continue to a longer draw and higher weight, storing more energy in the process.

But before declaring birch the superior wood, note the birch sample's weight of 800 grains against spruce's 500. Spruce equals the bending strength of many heavier hardwoods at 5/8 of their weight. This is why Howard Hughes' aeroplane isn't called the Osage Goose.

When comparing species, heavier woods are generally stronger than lighter woods. Osage, locust, ash, and red cedar, for example, descend in both weight and strength. Within a species heavier wood is almost always stronger.

## SUGGESTED WIDTHS FOR SOME COMMON WOODS

The widths listed below cause bows of the same design in every other respect to take identical sets. These figures indicate average strength and elasticity. Keep in mind that variations within a species can be extreme, which is one of the values of testing an actual sample as outlined above.

These are approximate figures for 66" bows pulling 50 lb at 28". All have flat bellies and equally low-crowned backs, with wider limbs needing larger diameter trees. Note the approximate straight-line relationship between wood strength\elasticity and mass.

| Wood type | Suggested width | Specific gravity |
|---|---|---|
| Australian acacia | 2 | medium |
| ash, white | 1-3/4 | .60 |
| birch, yellow | 1-3/4 | .62 |
| black locust | 1-5/8 | .69 |
| black walnut | 1-3/4 | .55 |
| cherry | 1-3/4 | .50 |
| choke cherry | 1-3/4 | medium |
| dogwood, flowering | 1-5/8 | .73 |
| elm | 1-7/8 | 55 |
| eucalyptus, | 2-1/4 | medium |

| Wood type | Suggested width | Specific gravity |
|---|---|---|
| fir, douglas, heart | 2-1/2 | .45 |
| goncolo alves | 1-3/8 | .84 |
| hackberry | 1-7/8 | .50 |
| hickory | 1-3/4 | .72 |
| hop hornbeam | 1-1/2 | .70 |
| juniper | 1-3/4 | low to medium |
| lemonwood (degame) | 1-5/8 | .67 |
| maple, sugar | 1-3/4 | .63 |
| mulberry | 1-5/8 | .66 |
| Osage | 1-1/5 | .82 |
| pecan | 1-3/4 | .66 |
| persimmon | 1-3/4 | .74 |
| pine, heart | 2-1/2 | .45 |
| purpleheart | 1-5/8 | .67 |
| ramin | 1-7/8 | .52 |
| oak, red | 1-7/8 | .63 |
| oak, white | 1-3/4 | .68 |
| red cedar | 2 | .48 |
| red cedar | 1-3/8 | backed |
| rosewood, Braz. | 1-1/2 | .80 |
| sassafras | 2-1/4 | .45 |
| sycamore | 2-1/4 | .49 |
| Teak | 1-3/4 | .60 |
| willow | 3 | .39 |
| wenge | 1-5/8 | medium to heavy |
| yew | 1-3/8 | .69 |

If a stave is heavier or lighter than average, limbs should be proportionately narrower or wider. If the percentage of porous early growth is higher or lower limbs should be wider or narrower.

When in doubt always make limbs a bit wider. A bow which is 20% wider than ideal will gain only two or three ounces of mass on an average weight and length bow. This would normally cost two or three fps in cast, but the now-wider limbs will take slightly less set. This too-wide bow will shoot one or two fps slower than an ideal-width bow. A very cheap price to pay for durability.

## SINEW

Sinew is more rubber band-like than wood. Both have similar breaking strength, but since sinew can be stretched about ten times farther than wood, and only weighs about twice as much, it can store more energy per unit of mass.

The following may explain sinew's cast-improving behavior on short and recurved bows.

1) Wet sinew shrinks about 4% as it dries, pulling a bow into reflex. This gives a straight-stave bow the energy storing profile of a reflexed bow.

2) Like most backings, sinew holds splinters down. But this is hardly needed,

because:

3) Physicist Michael Bloxham worked out the following figures. Column one indicates percentage of limb depth, at either back or belly. Column two indicates percentage of tension or compression work done at these depths. These figures assume a homogeneous material.

| | |
|-----|-----|
| 1% | 6% |
| 5% | 27% |
| 10% | 49% |
| 20% | 78% |
| 30% | 94% |

Here we see that just 10% of a limb's thickness does half of the tension work. But sinew has less pull strength than wood, so a 10% backing would do less than 50% of the tension work, though such a backing would still relieve considerable strain from the underlying wood, diminishing its desire to crack or splinter. When 20% thick, sinew-backing assumes a substantial amount of the tension load. And at this thickness is more helpful in other ways also:

4) Sinew is easier to stretch than wood. Bending sinew-backed wood is like setting a heavy child and a light child on opposite ends of a see-saw; the pivot point must be adjusted for even balance. With easy-to-stretch sinew on one side, and hard-to-compress wood on the other, the bow's neutral plane must shift toward the stronger belly in order to maintain balance. Being farther from the neutral plane, the surface fibers of the sinew-back now prescribe a larger circumference when drawn, stretching farther than otherwise, storing more energy in the process.

5) The farther the surface of the wood is from the neutral plane, the more tension or compression it has to endure, and the closer it is, the less force to which it is subjected. With its neutral plane now closer to the belly surface, the wood of a sinew-backed bow is less stressed. This now-thinner, less-strained belly is able to bend farther, permitting the whole system to store more energy. This explains a short sinewed bow's ability to endure recurves and longer draws.

This neutral-plane shifting also explains the feasibility of sinew/ antler bows. Antler is stronger than wood, but more brittle. It has less elasticity than wood. It is more concrete-like, unable to store much energy in compression or tension. But if made thin enough, then thickly sinew-backed, the resulting neutral plane is very close to the belly surface, forcing sinew surfaces to stretch enormously more than the belly compresses. A sinew and caribou antler bow made by Dr. Charles Grayson required a 60/40 sinew to antler ratio. This is typical of museum specimens also.

A sinew-backed wooden bow is a less-severe example of this sinew/antler principle. A wood-based bow with a sinew back 30% or 40% thick (measured dry) would thrust its sinew working surface much farther above the neutral plane. Belly surfaces would move even closer to the neutral plane. This configuration could bend considerably farther than if 10% or 20% sinew. Such a limb could accept greater reflexing or recurving, profiles which plump up a f-d curve. But sinew is much heavier than wood. Total limb mass rises with increased sinew, causing diminishing returns at some point of sinew thickness.

Sinew works best on wider, flatter limbs; it is able to pull such limbs into greater reflex. Higher reflex equals higher early-draw weight.

Horn compresses about 4% before failure, wood about 1%. Horn's resistance in compression, and sinew's resistance in tension are similar. As a result, sinew/horn bows store closer to equal amounts of energy in their backs and bellies.

## OTHER BACKINGS

Linen and other vegarable fibers won't increase performance by shrinking into pre-tension or my nuetral-plane shifting as sinew will. But reflexing or recurving the bow when applying such backings causes the bow to store more energy. Limbs are now more strained, therefore take more set, but not enough to offset energy storage gains of their more efficient profiles.

The neutral plane in most about-to-break all-wooden bows rises progressively closer to the back surface. If strain continues to build, insufficient back thickness remains to counter compression forces, and the back breaks.

But the boundary between a flax backing and the wood beneath is a barrier to a neutral plane's upward travel. Flax can not go into compression, thereby forcing belly wood to remain in place and take the punishment. With sufficient flax thickness, bows are almost impossible to break. They may take a large set, but will hold together until strained far beyond normal capacity.

A 3" wide pine sapwood bow was backed with raw flax. Comparable

*The three forms of flax; still in the stalk, combed, and spun.*

unbacked pine sapwood bows had been breaking at 55 lb. This pine/flax bow was drawn to ever higher weight, searching for its breaking weight in order to assess the value of flax as a backing. But at 70 lb sentiment overcame science. The poor bow's wide belly was laced with catastrophic networks of chrysals. The tortured bow had tried to break at every spot and in every way it knew, but its flax backing would not let it go. The bow had earned its right to live.

For pure brute protection a thin flax backing is more effective than a thin back of sinew. At comparable degrees of stretch sinew has a much lower pull strength than flax and is able to stretch much farther; when weak-in-tension bows are lightly sinewed, the wood beneath can still stretch beyond its limit.

*Back view of the 3" wide combed flax-backed pine bow. Also a combed flax-backed fir bow and a flax string-backed ash longbow.*

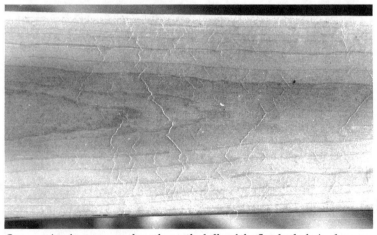

*Compression fractures, or chrysals, on the belly of the flax-backed pine bow.*

A peculiarity of most fiber backings is that they stack, or become progressively harder to stretch. A 1/10" diameter flax sample pulled 37 lb at 1% stretch, 98 lb at 2%, and 182 lb at 3%, its breaking point. By my preliminary tests, sinew does not begin stacking until stretched about 10%.

Bows often break because of an isolated point of weakness. A longitudinal flax patch, like a patch on an inner-tube, will keep such localized areas sound. Here is a possible benefit of backing with stacking fibers: If one small limb area is bending too much and about to break, the fiber back above that one spot will be forced to stretch farther. The backing will stack at this one point, becoming much harder to bend and creating something of an automatic splint.

Often new or old limbs will develop potentially fatal flaws which can be remedied if caught early. Transverse tension cracks, lifting back fibers, hinged limbs, grip sections which work too much, and so on. Flax is better than sinew in these cases for two reasons. It's much stronger at the degrees of stretch involved. And flax is not affected by moisture. Mixed with glue, flax fiber, and other vegetable fibers, can be molded into recurves, handle risers, string bridges, form-fitting grips, and so on.

Using high-stretch and high-strength backings on weak wood would have the opposite effect of sinew-backing: to balance forces, the neutral plane must rise, placing belly fibers under more strain. Such backing would prevent the back from breaking, but string follow would be excessive. Better to use low-

*A graphic illustration of the capabilities of a linen-backing. Despite the catastrophic break in the wood, this bow was still shootable (the backing was removed only to photograph the break).*

stretch/low-strength backings, such as sinew, rawhide, gut, or silk.

Other vegetable fibers, such as jute and sisal, are almost as strong as flax. Cotton might be worth investigating for use as a backing. Preliminary tests show it stretching about 7%, more than twice as elastic as linen.

In the spring, '91 edition of *The Bulletin of Primitive Technology*, Dr. Errett Callahan described replicating and using an Eskimo sinew cable-backed bow. Inspired by this article, Dick Baugh made a nylon cable-backed bow, describing the physics of its design in the spring, '92 edition of the Bulletin. Their work has opened the door to interesting design possibilities.

Silk has similar stretch strength and elasticity to sinew and nylon. Like sinew,

Bamboo bow with silk cable backing.

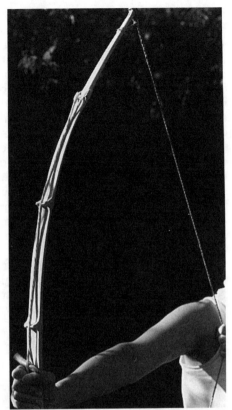

Bamboo bow with nodes left intact and elevated for silk cable channel. Elevated cable is farther from the nuetral plane and therefore does much more work with this design.

it enhances performance both by neutral-plane shifting and by assuming part of the tension load. Unlike nylon, silk is a natural material; unlike sinew, silk is unaffected by moisture.

Silk cable backs are simple to make, using unbleached silk string, not thread. It can simply be wound from nock to nock until the desired thickness is reached. For best performance, silk should be stretched, or pre-stressed, about 6 to 8% of its length. This pulls a bow into reflex, and lets less silk do more work, saving both mass and silk. Use an amount of silk equal in cross section to about one-fifth that of the mid limb.

Unlike glue-on sinew or silk, a cable back is uniform in cross section its entire length. The ratio of backing to wood becomes higher near the nocks. This causes normally-tillered limbs to become stiff-ended and appear round-in-the-handle. Cable backed bows should therefore be tillered whip-ended. When the cable is added, near-nock tiller will then stiffen to normal curvature, as with the short bamboo/silk bow at left.

The last few inches of limb need not work, and can therefore be narrow, deep, and rigid - or even retroflexed. A silk cable need not stretch from string nock to string nock; it can have its own nocks as at left. Cables can be twisted to desired tension, permitting bows of variable poundage!

## BOW TESTING

There is only one way to learn the secrets of bow performance with certainty: Make bows of every possible design, of every possible material. Shoot each for distance, or through a chronograph, and note which shoot the fastest per pound of draw weight, or shoots the smoothest, or the quietest, and so on.

Write down, and study, all the information from the stave's bend-test stat card, and the bow-test stat card.

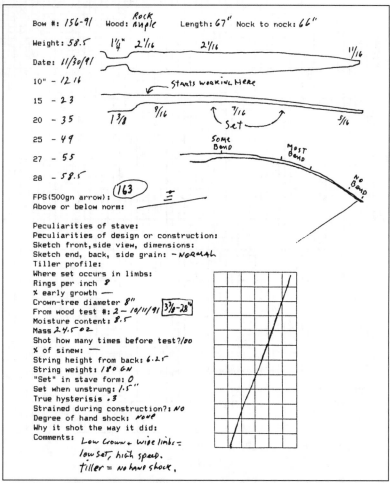

*This stat sheet lists most of the variables affecting bow performance. A quick glance reveals how well this bow shoots relative to the norm. By comparing variables of different bows the qualities that produce poor and excellent performance quickly become apparent.*

Soon it will become apparent which design and material ingredients yield which performance features. This is a weak-back rather than a strong-mind approach. But much more is learned of a territory by walking through instead of flying over it.

It's not necessary to make same-weight bows in order to compare performance features.

To begin with, indicate the performance of different-weight, average-length, average-set bows, as above. Once sufficient dots have been plotted draw an average-line through them.

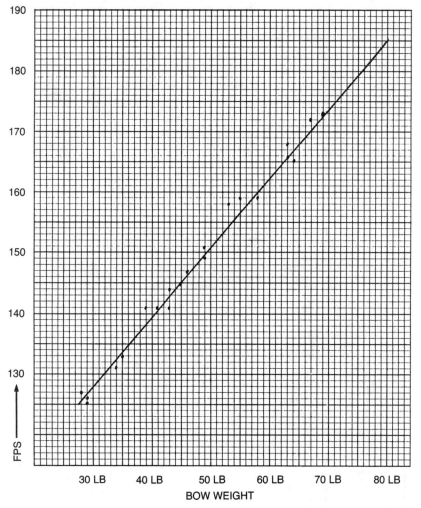

*The average-line should be laid down over dots representing average-performance bows. Separate lines, representing, say, short bows, sinew-backed recurves, setback bows, etc., can be on the same graph. Just use different symbols for each type: squares for recurves, triangles for sinew-backing, etc.*

From then on, every time you make and test a bow you can immediately determine if its performance is above or below average. And then look for reasons why.

Bows can be modified, new design ideas tried, and even if poundage changes, relative efficiency of the new design can still be judged by its placement relative to the line. This is a powerful investigative tool.

You will soon be able to estimate the speed of a bow within a couple of fps, before shooting it, even before making it. This means, of course, that you will have learned exactly which design features produce which effects. You will have become design-fluent.

A bow's set should be measured immediately after unstringing. Different woods have different rates and degrees of recovery.

In the same vein, it doesn't matter how far sinew has managed to reflex a bow in a day, or a year. Its reflex, its side-view profile immediately after being unstrung is the best clue to knowing its behavior when drawn.

## WHY THE CHRONOGRAPH?

An arrow doesn't know it's been shot through a chronograph. If we choose to place a chronograph between the bow and the target there is no complicity or expedience on the arrow's part. The arrow's behavior remains pure.

By eliminating the variables of wind, air density, and release angle, one minute spent with a chronograph is worth hours on a flight range. It puts a hard dot on the graph instead of a blur. It tells the quick, hard truth.

## THE OTHER ARCHER'S PARADOX

You've just finished a nicely-tillered, smooth-shooting 50 lb bow. You've shot it for distance, pacing off 165 yards. You're happy.

Then a bowmaking acquaintance calls and tells you about a bow he's just made. Also 50 lb., he says it shot 225 yards. You're devastated. You wonder what in the world you're doing wrong.

You inquire and learn that his bow, like yours, was made from a straight stave of normal length, width, and tiller. It has about the same worked-in set as your bow, and his arrow matches the weight and fletching of your arrow. He accounts for his bow's cast by some extraordinary property of the wood.

Over time you will hear many such accounts, claiming performances outside the realm of natural law. The paradox is that these callers are honest men. They believe what they're saying.

The source of this paradox is a drug called bias. Bias, and the artificial satisfaction it generates, can decimate a bowmaker's hope of progress. Bias can't be weighed or carved but it's as real as wood itself. And unless consciously taken charge of it will affect bow performance more than any material or design ingredient.

None of us is immune.

Once, I was explaining a new bow theory to Dick Baugh (Dick invented the Bow Scraper). The theory involved the "fact" that wood becomes suddenly harder to bend before breaking. Dick is an engineer, well-schooled in the behavior or materials. He asked why I thought wood stacked. "Because you can feel it," I said. "And everyone knows bows stack because wood becomes harder to pull before it breaks." He suggested, mildly, that I might be in error on that point.

I turned to the stress and strain curve in Bruce Hoadley's *Understanding Wood*. Here was the proof: wood deformed in a straight line all the way to its proportional limit, after which the line curved gently to its apex, then fell. I took this proof along the next time I visited Dick. I simply couldn't have been more sure of anything.

Triumphantly, I showed Dick the curve. Then he explained, patiently, that for wood to stack the curve would have to bend upward, not downward, that wood doesn't stack before breaking, that in fact it does the opposite.

I sputtered for several minutes in disbelief, but finally the unavoidable truth of it settled in. I can't remember ever being more deflated.

Bias had kept me from seeing the simple black-and-white facts. I sat myself down that night and gave myself a good talking to.

Yet another example:

I once proved beyond all doubt that bows shoot farther as nock weight rises. Progressively larger amounts of lead wire was wrapped around the nocks of a bow. Each added ounce yielded a couple of additional yards of cast. I was elated at this discovery, and wrote several bowmaking friends about it, enclosing an elaborate theoretical explanation for the effect.

Months later, after the Dick Baugh trauma and self-lecture, this test was repeated using a chronograph. To prevent overdrawing, a stop was taped to the arrow shaft. Surprise, surprise. I was 180 degrees in error; additional nock weight slows, rather than speeds, an arrow.

In the original experiment I obvious hadn't measured distance accurately, or had progressively overdrawn the arrow, or had unconsciously adjusted release elevation. But the main thing I hadn't done was have a decisive, critical, skeptical overview.

A trick I use now is to imagine explaining test results to a reasonable, knowledgeable, but skeptical second party.

You'll forever be hearing of someone's new bow shooting supernatural speeds and distances, far beyond those of your bow's. Such reports are bias-generated delusions.

Below are listed the farthest distances various weight and design bows can be expected to cast an arrow. Wind resistance due to arrow length, diameter, and fletching size affect distances somewhat. But for "normal" arrows, give or take a few yards, THESE ARE THE ONLY DISTANCES SUCH A BOW CAN SHOOT.

A 28"-draw, 67" length, medium-set, straight-stave bow will shoot a 500 grain, normal-fletched arrow about as follows:

| | | |
|---|---|---|
| 40 lb | 138 fps | 148 yards |
| 50 lb | 150 fps | 166 yards |
| 60 lb | 163 fps | 186 yards |
| 70 lb | 177 fps | 210 yards |

Such a 50 lb bow with severe string follow will shoot about: ...............140 fps – 151 yards

With 3" string follow: ..............................145 fps – 159 yards

With 1-1/2" string follow ..........................150 fps – 166 yards

If very slightly reflexed: ..........................155 fps – 174 yards

If moderately recurved: ..........................160 fps – 185 yards

If severely recurved: ..............................170 fps – 200 yards

After 10,000-plus years of rasping and scraping, archery knowledge has barely reached a rough-tillered state. And in places it is out of tiller.

Among the contributions of each writer and researcher of the past are inevitable oversights and errors. In future hindsight this will be true of this chapter also. It is unavoidable.

The task is to set a decisive, tillerer's eye on the store of archery knowledge and scrape off what doesn't belong.

Discovering the truth of a matter is analogous to hunting. Both require cunning, energy, ingenuity, and most importantly, the willingness to discard preconceptions, false leads and easy paths – the willingness to be wrong.

No one has all the answers, and no one is always correct. Therefore, be skeptical of every claim you hear, including any of mine.

Pope, Hickman, Nagler, and Klopsteg produced a large, valuable body of knowledge in the first half of this century. If we see some gap or flaw in this work now, we must also note that they didn't have Pope, Hickman, Nagler, and Klopsteg's shoulders to stand on. They didn't have the sweep of knowledge that exists today, or the present network of cooperative researchers freely exchanging information, ideas, and most importantly, positive criticism. And they didn't have casual use of the Unmerciful Extractor of Truth, the modern chronograph.

It's enjoyable theorizing about principles of bow design, but also dangerous. Theorizing only has value if results are submitted to rigorous tests. Simply figuring something out isn't good enough. Whatever certainty you feel for your new conclusion is identical to the certainty you felt just before seeing the flaw in you last conclusion.

There is only one proper judge in these matters:

Let the measured speed of an arrow weigh the merits of your conjecturing. The arrow, by the speed it chooses to fly, displays wisdom beyond Solomon's.

# YEW LONGBOW

*John Strunk*

Much has been said of the longbow and its place in the history of warfare. The fear and respect it commanded in the hands of an experienced archer could be likened to the artillery weapons of modern times. When one thinks of the longbow, he usually pictures a bow as tall as the archer, about six feet in length and deep and narrow of core. These standards have remained throughout history. Many people today say a longbow is one which has straight ends whose string reaches nock to nock without touching any portion of the bow limb. To me, this is too loose a definition. Others say the longbow must equal the height of the man, and this seems a more acceptable standard.

With this in mind, some materials make a finer longbow than others. Therefore, we would be accurate in saying that the longbow design is influenced by the nature of the materials used. As an example, many bow woods can better withstand the compression and tension forces when left long. With ancient war bows drawing 100+ pounds at 30" of draw, it is easy to understand why it was safer and more durable to make a longer bow. Also, a bow of this type better casts a heavy arrow accurately over great distances, as has been detailed in the previous chapter on Bow Design and Performance.

As a guide when making a longbow, I like to fit the bow to the nature of the wood and the archer. This is the most logical way to make decisions about the style, length, and dimensions of the bow. You must compromise between smoothness, bow weight, draw lengths, etc., to obtain the best efficiency from the bow. As a rule of thumb, a 26" draw works well in a 66" bow, 28"/68" bow, 30"/70+" length bow. Woods having good compression strengths and light physical weight, such as yew, cedar, or juniper, make the best longbows. This is why yew is my favorite choice of all bow woods. As Earl Ullrich once told me, "Yew wood was a gift from God to the bowmaker."

The yew tree is one of Nature's most perfect bow materials. It has great compression strength and resiliency, as well as being lightweight and smooth of draw. As many have said, "It makes a sweet shooting bow." Its only drawbacks are that it can be scratched and dented from hard use. This fault usually only causes a "memory" mark and does not damage the bow's integrity. Yew is also affected more by temperature changes than some woods. However, I find that when it's exceedingly hot or cold, I am also affected! At least, that must be the reason my arrow missed its mark!

Most yew trees will provide enough material for at least one bow, though I rarely cut down a tree which will not provide several staves. Its creamy colored sapwood is a perfect bow backing. The orangish-colored heartwood withstands the compression forces and springs back quickly to provide good cast.

Usually, the best yew comes from the higher elevations in the Cascade Mountains of Oregon, Washington, and British Columbia. In some areas, the yew stands are quite thick under the canopy of old growth Douglas fir timber. Because of the limited exposure to sunlight, the tree grows very slowly – on an

*Yew with "snakes" in the grain can make very fine bows loaded with character.*

average of 40-60 growth years per inch of wood. Yew is also found at lower elevations; but as a rule, it grows too fast to produce good bows. The denser the growth lines, the smaller the bow's dimensions for a given draw weight, meaning that such wood is stronger. As is true with most things in Nature, there are exceptions. Gilman Keasey, an old-time bowmaker from Corvallis, Oregon, said that some of his best materials came from wood found along the Willamette River of Western Oregon. However, these may have been target-weight bows rather than heavy hunting bows.

The yew tree is rather unique because there are male trees and female trees. The male tree produces cones and the female tree small red berries. In the past, there has been some discussion as to which will make the best bow, though I have not been able to discern a difference. The tree is easily recognized by its short, flat reddish-green needles and thin, scaly red bark. Two kinds of yew trees exist: ones which are straight and true without knots and suitable for bowmaking, and those that won't make a bow.

To begin your bowmaking experience with yew or any other wood, you must find a useable piece of material. You can either purchase it from an experienced bowmaker or try cutting your own. I would recommend buying a piece so you can immediately begin work. Don't expect to make your first bow out of the best piece in the woods. Expect to make some mistakes and have some failures. Therefore, it is best to learn on less than perfect materials, though wood that possesses some humps and bumps will make a very fine bow.

The mistake we make most often is to build the bow in our mind's eye and not let the wood give us the direction to follow. The grain and character of each piece should dictate the style and shape of the bow. Don't make the piece of wood fit your pattern without considering these important facts. If you do, you usually haven't a chance of producing a suitable bow. A bow must do two things: draw evenly and not break. How the bow looks has very little to do with this.

After a few attempts at making a bow, you will have gained valuable experience that will be useful later if you decide to cut your own material. Not only will you be able to see where in the trees lie the good pieces, but your knowledge of bow styles, seasoning methods, and so forth will have been greatly expanded. I have a lot of yew wood fence posts around my yard that were cut by people looking for bow staves. Experience is a great teacher, so be patient and have fun learning all you can. You can read about bowmaking, but sooner or later you must make some shavings! The only way to fail is never to start.

Here are some tips on seasoning yew. There are as many theories about seasoning bow stock as building a bow. The amount of drying time necessary is certainly related to the climatic conditions of one's area. I have been able to season some woods in as little as six months, but on an average it's at least a year. The best procedure is to split the yew wood into halves or quarters depending on the size of the tree. This is done as soon as the tree is cut. Then store the wood outdoors in a covered area to keep the wood dry. After about six months, cut or split the wood into 1 1/2" x 1 1/2" or 2" x 2" billets or staves. This will allow the wood to dry quickly to around 10 percent moisture content. These pieces can be stored in an unheated room having a much lower humidity than

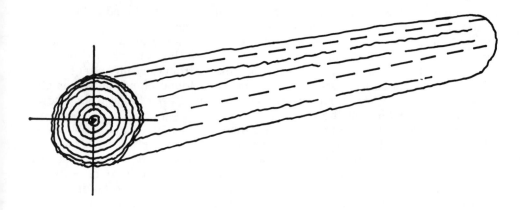

*Split logs into halves or quarters.*

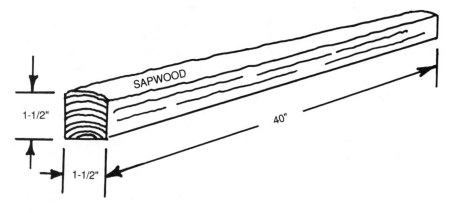

*Dimensions of a yew billet.*

outdoors. After three to four months of air drying the bow material, I like to quickly reduce the moisture content of the wood by using a heat box. To accomplish this, I have an 18" x 24" x 80" plywood box that uses light bulbs as a heat source, which controls the temperature at 85-95 degrees. Wood left in the heat box for three to four weeks will cure out to 6-7% moisture content. CAUTION: Too much heat, or wood left too long, may lower the moisture content of the wood to a point which causes brittleness.

There are many others ways of quick-curing woods, but the one explained above is what has worked well for me. Always experiment on your lesser-quality pieces of wood, whether it be seasoning processes or bowmaking.

Now that your wood is ready, let's proceed with the actual making of a yew wood longbow. The best type of bow for the beginning bowmaker is one that can be laid out using a pattern. As you gain more experience, you will want to try pieces that are crooked and twisted. They are a challenge to make and totally unique. Contrary to most beliefs, these pieces of wood make very fine bows.

Those things in Nature which struggle to survive have great inherent qualities which produce the toughness and resiliency necessary to making a bow.

## STARTING THE BOW

By now, you should be truly committed to the task of building a bow. This enthusiasm, apprehension, and desire to do it right should be channeled by simply going at the task. Don't feel that you need more information or experience. You are going to get that as you build the bow. Everyone who is known for his bowmaking skills had the same feelings of inadequacy when they started. Soon people will be coming to you for information on how to make a bow!

The methods and techniques given here will allow you to make your bow by using basic hand woodworking tools. Start by removing the bark from your stave or billets using a drawknife, rasp, or by scraping with a knife. Be careful not to cut into the white sapwood at this time, we will decide later if it is necessary or desirable to thin it.

If using billets, it will be necessary to splice them before proceeding further. Refer to the chapter on Splices, later in this volume, for more information.

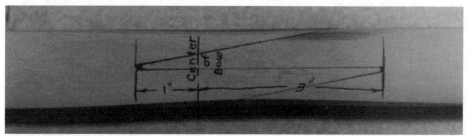

*Handle section, showing layout in relationship to center of bow. Note "Z" splice used to join billets.*

## LAYING OUT THE BOW

If using a splice, when the glue is dry clean off the excess using a wood rasp, and also scrape off the center lines originally drawn on the billets. This is done to lay out a new centerline for drawing the bow pattern. This center line can either be drawn using a long, straight edge or by stretching a small thread between two tacks placed into the ends of the bow stave. Tape down the thread in the middle of the handle to prevent it from moving as the pattern is drawn. Sight down the line to insure it is straight.

Next, measure and locate the center of the bow. Now select the end of the stave to be the top limb of the bow. To do this, choose the end which is naturally bending more toward the archer. Draw a line 1" above the center point of the splice joint as shown in the illustration. Later you will find this line is located an equal distance from each string nock. This will make the top limb 1" longer, thus enabling you to tiller the bow properly.

Now you are ready to draw the bow outline. The bow at this time will fit the following illustration. The midsection of the bow, for 12", will be 1-1/4" wide, then taper to 5/8" at each tip. This 12" section will later be reduced to a handle

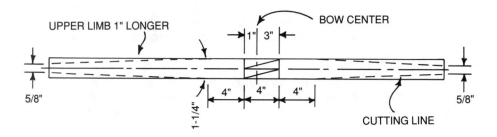

*Bow dimensions laid out on stave or spliced billets.*

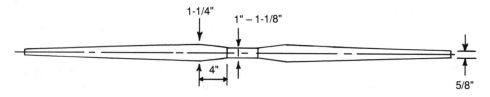

*Bow cut out.*

of about 1-1/16" wide as shown in the sketch. Bow design is a personal preference so these dimensions are only guidelines.

## CUTTING OUT THE BOW

Once the outline is established, you can bandsaw just outside this line and then plane, sand, or file down to it. If a bandsaw isn't available, shape with a hatchet and hand plane or other hand woodworking tools. Sand the contour with coarse 80-grit garnet paper using a sanding block. Now turn the stave on its side and draw a new line representing the rough profile or thickness of the bow. This line must follow the grain of the wood. Even though the thickness of the bow limb tapers from the handle to the tip, its profile must parallel the back surface of the bow. In others words, if the stave dips on the backside, you must allow for a corresponding "bump" on the belly side. You must always be aware of this. Don't flatten out the bumps in the stave's back or belly. These irregular places will serve to give each bow its own individual character.

## SHAPING THE BOW

I reduce the bow's thickness with a bandsaw. A drawknife will also work here, although it may tear wood grain around a knot or where the grain dips towards the back of the stave. Be careful to taper the bow limb following the contour as the back dips or rises. I recommend that you use a large 12" wood rasp and later smooth with a scraper. When doing this, be sure to proceed slowly and allow the belly to begin taking on a contour that is parallel in shape to the back. Again, if the stave dips on the backside, you must allow for a corresponding "bump" on the belly side. Also, the grain will look like that shown in the photo. I use an outside caliper and match thickness every 6".

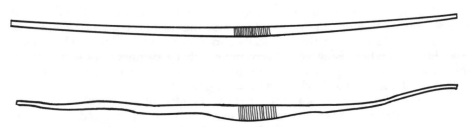

*The natural shape of the wood should be faithfully followed.*

The bow's cross section will gradually become a flat "D" or rectangle. Maintain this cross-section throughout the tillering process until you reach the final bow weight. The measurements given in the illustration are only approximate and refer to the rough dimensions of the bow. Work the stave down slowly to arrive at the final draw weight. This is done to teach the stave to bend properly. Be aware of taper of the grain as you shape the belly. The grain should always point toward the bow tips. The only exception would be to leave some extra layers around a knot or in a sharp dip.

*Optional cross sections.*

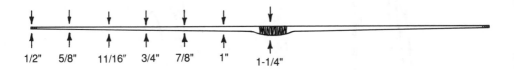

| 1/2" | 5/8" | 11/16" | 3/4" | 7/8" | 1" | 1-1/4" |

*Thickness of longbow along the limbs.*

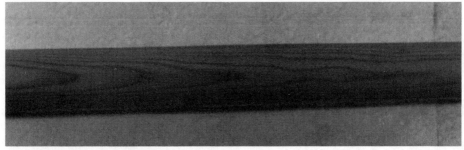

*Yearly growth rings feathering out on belly of bow.*

At this time, you need to decide whether to thin the sapwood. If so, it is best to do it now, as thinning the sapwood later during the tillering process will most likely reduce the bow weight drastically and alter the tiller of the limbs. This is risky business when using yew. I recommend that a beginner not worry about the thickness of the sapwood, as the only advantage is cosmetic, and tinkering with it greatly increases the chances of ruining the stave.

Continue working the stave until it can be strung. To check the stave's strength, I place the lower end into the instep of my right foot and pull on the handle, while pushing away on the top limb. When the stave bends about 4" to 5", you will be ready to file temporary string grooves using a 1/8" round file.

To this point, I refer to the piece of wood as a "stave" and not a "bow." Even though the piece of wood looks like a bow, it must be strung and taught to withstand the stresses necessary to allow it to bend to the archer's draw length before it should be called a "bow."

SIDE VIEW

BELLY OF BOW

*Self nocks.*

To locate the string grooves, measure from the stave's center an equal distance to each end. The distance should be one-half the length between the nocks you want when the bow is finished. Example: 34" for a 68" nock-to-nock bow. Shape the nocks as shown in the illustration. Buy or make a string that is about 2" shorter than the nock-to-nock measurement and string the stave using a bow stringer which fits over the ends.

The cross-section at the nock area of the stave is approximately 1/2"x 1/2" now. Beginning at the tip, shape the sapwood for approximately 3" so the stave's cross section is almost round at the nock location. This allows for the proper fit of the horn tips.

The stave should be **braced** about 4" now; if less, twist the string to shorten and restring the stave. The brace is the distance from the bow string to the handle.

Study the stave to see if it lies straight or wants to twist. Sometimes, it may be necessary to thin the edge on the opposite side of the twist. (The limb will twist toward the weaker side.) This will cause the stave to roll back into line. It may also be necessary to steam the stave to accomplish this task if the problem is severe. The steaming is done by placing a kettle of water on the stove and holding the affected area over it. Cover it with a lid or towel to trap the steam. About ten minutes is usually enough time to place sufficient heat and moisture into the wood so it will bend. Place the stave tip on the floor and push the tip in the direction necessary to straighten it, making a judgment about the amount of bend necessary. Allow the stave to dry a couple days before re-stringing.

You can also use this method to bend a stave tip and affect tiller. Sometimes a limb is so weak it won't tiller properly, and reflexing it will increase the resistance to bending and match it to the other limb.

Slowly and carefully, exercise the stave by pulling it gently and letting it get used to bending. To do this, hook a bow stringer over the ends of the stave and place your foot on the stringer. Begin pulling up on the handle; have a friend study the stave's bend for stiff places. (Stiff areas will cause your stave to have flat areas rather than a graceful arc.) These areas need more wood removal. This method works well with very heavy bows.

These are alternative ways to exercise a stave. You can string the stave to a brace height of 4", and slowly begin drawing it a short distance while studying its bend in a mirror. Another way is to mount a yoke or bracket on the wall which cradles the stave's handle. Attach a rope and pulley to the floor and use one end of the rope to hook the bow string. This will allow you to stand back a short distance and view the stave while you exercise it.

Rough-sand the stave without a sanding block to remove all file marks. Use 80-grit garnet paper and again be sure that you follow the grain of the wood on the belly surface. Now begin pulling the stave to about 12-15", and look to see how the stave limbs flex. File and sand any stiff areas very slowly to tune limbs for bending.

As you sand the stave, you should exercise it and watch its arc to see how much sanding is necessary. Go slowly because the stave hasn't yet "come to the string." This term refers the wood weakening and becoming used to bending. When this happens, the stave will lose draw weight quickly. If you oversand an area, the stave will bend too much at that point, or hinge, causing the wood to fail, thus ruining the stave. Draw the stave 20 times for a distance of 15", checking its arc to be sure that the stave is bending equally throughout its length.

The correct tiller or measurement between the string and the belly surface of the stave should be as follows: the distance from the string to the belly surface of the upper limb should be approximately 1/4" GREATER than the measurement

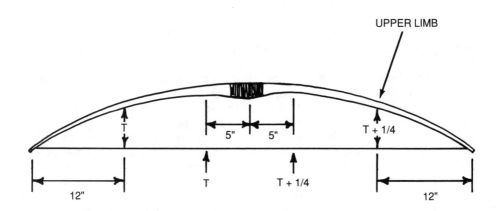

*Tiller of longbow, showing how lower, shorter limb will be slightly stiffer.*

at the same location on the lower limb because the lower limb is slightly shorter. This will allow both limbs to bend equally as you draw the bow while shooting.

Further information is available in the Tillering chapter in this volume, but remember to allow from two to five extra pounds for final sanding and final tuning of your bow as you shoot it.

GO SLOWLY! Haste can cause a **chrysal** or **fret** of the wood. This will appear as a small, light-colored line on the belly of the bow running across the grain. This occurs when the wood has been weakened more than in another area, causing the bow to fold or collapse at the weakest point. All is not necessarily lost if this happens near the handle. I have planed down the belly beyond the chrysal and glued on a new piece, then worked the belly down again before stringing the bow. A chrysal in this area was possibly caused by weakening the handle area too much.

Chrysals will also occur around a knot which has crumbled and weakened the wood. Leave extra layers of wood around the knot to compensate. Small knots usually are no problem unless near the edge of the limb. The knot can be drilled out with a 1/8" drill, and a small peg or "dutchman" glued in the hole. This is only recommended if the knot is loose or soft. I prefer digging out the loose knot material and replacing it with wood shavings and glue, though leaving the knot alone and reinforcing it with extra wood grain is usually best.

Once the tiller and weight are correct, the bow is ready to be shot. It is best to find any unseen flaws that may cause the bow to fail now rather than after further time has been spent.

If, after shooting 40 to 50 times, you still find the bend satisfactory, the bow is ready to be backed with rawhide. This isn't absolutely necessary on lighter bows under 50#, but I would recommend it on all bows because of the additional protection it gives the back.

1/16" THICKNESS

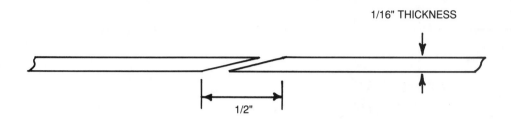

1/2"

*Splice for rawhide backing.*

To do this, take two pieces of rawhide measuring 1" longer than half the bow's length. Bevel the ends which will overlap in the middle of the bow's handle; this will make the handle area smooth, without a bump. Cut the rawhide about 1/8" wider than the bow limbs and scrape or sand the flesh side to remove fat which will inhibit glue absorption. Soak the rawhide for half an hour in warm water (water that is just comfortable to touch, not hot). Dry with a towel, then spread a thin layer of Elmer's™ white glue or Elmer's™ carpenter's glue on the sapwood of the bow. Avoid using too much glue as it just squeezes out and makes it difficult to unwrap the bindings.

Clamp the bow in a vise or have someone hold the bow firmly while you place the rawhide flesh side down. Using an Ace™ bandage, bind the first piece of rawhide at the handle and continue wrapping, working toward the tips of the bow. Don't wrap the bindings very tight, just firmly, or you will leave marks in the rawhide. Next, rub the surface of the bindings, stroking toward the outside edges to eliminate air bubbles under the rawhide. Apply the second piece of rawhide in the same manner.

Allow to dry one to two days, then unwrap. Use a cabinet scraper or file to trim the excess rawhide from the sides of the bow. The bow is now ready for further shooting. After shooting a dozen or more arrows, check the tiller to be sure it has remained the same. Also, have someone else draw the bow to your drawlength so you can be sure all areas are working properly. If the tiller needs slight adjustments, they can be made now.

When the tiller is correct, sand the rawhide to clean and smooth it. I use 180-grit garnet paper. The bow can now be fitted with horn or antler tips if you wish. This is optional; the original nocks can be left in place for your first bow. Horn or antler tips can always be added later.

I prefer using tips because they dress the bow properly and really set your bow off as being special. I use elk, deer, or cow horn for this. Choose a slightly curved antler tip, about 2-3" long, and 9/16" to 5/8" thick. It must also be round to allow you to shape it without entering the cellular area near the center of the antler. Cow horn doesn't have the porous interior and allows more shaping freedom. Cow horn is tough and elastic, more so than antler; but I have not had any problems with antler tips. An antler tip is really special if you took the deer yourself.

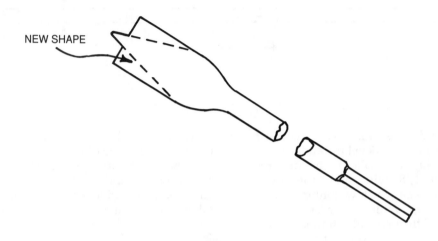

NEW SHAPE

*Bit for drilling horn nocks.*

Grind a 1/2" Stanley™ speed bore bit to the contour shown in the illustration. This bit will drill a tapered hole in the antler or horn tip about 1" deep. To fit this to your bow, file the bow tip (removing old string grooves) until the bow tip fits perfectly into the horn or antler. Rotate the tip until the curve points toward the back of the bow. Glue this in place with Elmer's™ white or carpenter's glue and allow to dry two to three hours. Shape the horn and wood into a perfect fit where the two meet. New string grooves can now be filed in the horn 3/8" from where the bow tip meets the wood.

The grip of the bow needs to be rounded by gluing a 3-1/2" x 3/16" thick block of wood to the back (over the rawhide) of the bow handle. This can be filed and sanded to its final shape. Bind this in place with heavy 25-45# braided fishing line and saturate the line with Elmer's™ glue to hold in place.

After final sanding, select a finish which gives the bow protection from moisture. I recommend gloss #90 varathane in an aerosol can, because it dries well without runs or bubbles. Five to seven coats of finish will be adequate. I rub down the last coat with 400 wet or dry silicon carbide paper, then with steel wool. After these two steps, I polish the finish using pumice and oil as a rubbing compound. This will produce a fine satin finish for the bow. How you finish the bow handle is a personal choice. For further information, see the chapter on Finishes and Handles.

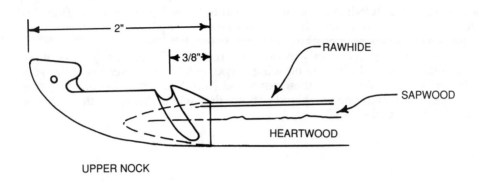

2"

3/8"

RAWHIDE

SAPWOOD

HEARTWOOD

UPPER NOCK

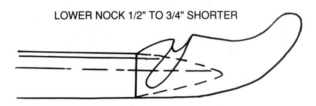

LOWER NOCK 1/2" TO 3/4" SHORTER

*Dimensions of horn nocks.*

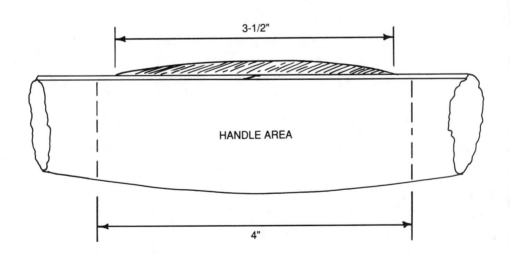

3-1/2"

HANDLE AREA

4"

*Detail of handle area for longbow.*

With a new string which will brace your bow at 6", you are ready to enjoy shooting. CAUTION!! If someone else wants to look at your bow...fine...but don't allow them to draw it. If I let someone shoot my bow, they must use my arrows so they cannot overdraw and possibly break it.

A bow of this type, properly made and cared for, will give many years of service, with the added pleasure of doing it yourself. I have never known anyone who could just make one of these bows and stop! You will begin noticing various trees and wondering what kind of bows they will make. When this happens, you'll know you are hooked!

# OSAGE FLAT BOW

*Ron Hardcastle*

Earl Ullrich of Roseburg, Oregon, was selling yew staves and bows in 1922 (you can read about him in some of the old archery magazines and books). In the early 1980's, shortly before he died, he sent me a letter in which he sadly wrote, "self bowyery will never return. Its days are gone." How I wish he could have lived to witness what has happened in the last five years. Archers in legions are coming back to wooden bows, as the "pendulum," which is the perfect metaphor for most human endeavor, has swung for many people back to simplicity, grace, beauty, and nature, and away from contrived, artificial, mass-production.

The recent course of archery history, with all of its so-called progress, necessitates that everyone reacquaint themselves with a fundamental definition of the Traditional Wooden Bow: a bow made of wood, sinew, rawhide, horn or other natural products, but containing no modern materials such as fiberglass or graphite.

It is common to hear a statement such as, "I have a lovely traditional yew bow with clear glass on the back." This constitutes an enormous contradiction in terms, the fiberglass making a definitive difference no matter what wooden cores and bow designs are used. I have never denigrated fiberglass or those who use fiberglass-laminate bows, and even though fiberglass can be made into traditional *style* longbows and recurves, it must be recognized that fiberglass is a man-made material which only came into existence forty years ago, while wooden bows have been around for something like ten thousand years. Fiberglass is a miraculous material, and it did nothing less than revolutionize archery. With its introduction in the late 1940's, an average chap could at last easily afford a warrantable, high-performance, dependable, inexpensive bow because the fiberglass lent itself to mass production. That was its appeal, and it's remarkable how inexpensive a good fiberglass bow can be. I own and shoot several, both longbow and recurve, and though I've never made one, I appreciate the skill of a truly knowledgeable fiberglass bowyer. The only hang-up comes when archers state, "I shoot orthodox traditional bows of yew, Osage, or maple," when, in truth, the bows are made from fiberglass, with the wood cores serving little purpose other than providing a gluing surface. Using fiberglass and wood laminations ground to 1/1000th of an inch tolerances, a bow can be made with a "recipe," and the results are virtually assured.

Not so in the "real" world of traditional wooden weapons, where the nonpredictability and surprises one encounters are the delicious reinforcements that keep us cheerfully engaged in our craft.

When six years old, I stalked and slew my first beast, a bird perched on the branch of a thorny "horse-apple" tree (Horse apple, bois d'arc, and hedge are all synonyms for Osage orange, whose formal botanical name is *Maclura Pomifera*). It has often struck me as "strong medicine" that my first kill took place in the same species of tree that was to become my art medium and my favorite bow wood.

I've experimented with many woods over the years, and discovered that some "unheralded" woods make fine bows, among them ash and hickory. Conversely, some of the seductive woods like purpleheart and padouk are beautiful, but with no substance, and are destined to break your heart with their fickle behaviors (such as splintering, chrysalling, and exploding, to name a few). But after all of the experiments, I always return to the old stand-by, Osage. It is an excellent bow wood for several reasons. Relative to other woods, it is:

1. Hard – Thus it resists damage from physical trauma and use, and also resists belly chrysalling from excessive compression.

2. Plentiful – While we fear for the future of yew, Osage can and does grow quickly and in many climates across the country.

3. Durable – Most of the old wooden bows which are still shooting, some of them decades old, are made of Osage.

4. Stable – Osage is minimally affected by temperature, losing little cast in throat-clawing heat, and stiffening very little in zero degree cold. This is one of the acid field tests of a bow.

In order to make a bow from Osage, or any other wood, you can take one of two approaches. You can say, "I want to make a bow with a given set of dimensions, and will look until I find just the right tree for the job." Or, you can say, "From this particular piece of wood I want to make the best bow I can." Obviously, the first approach will involve more searching for wood, but once it is found, the bow-making will be easier. With the latter approach, the true creativity and resourcefulness of the bowyer can move into high gear as he examines the strengths, weaknesses, and potential problems of a piece of wood and designs a bow to accommodate them.

*An Osage bowyer's dream, or nightmare, depending upon your current level of skill.*

As smitten as I am with Osage, even a cursory glance will show that it is far from perfect, often growing with treacherous twists and snakes and loaded with knots and thorns. But herein, for many bowyers, lies the interest and excitement of wood bowyery: to take a "fast" piece of wood with roller coaster humps, snaky twists, pins, and knots and by proper design and craftsmanship lure a fine bow from it. It is the ultimate compliment to have someone look at a bow with raised eyebrows and ask, "where did you find *that*?", but, upon seeing the bow shoot, change the question to, "where can I get one?"

If this type of bow appeals to you, then you will love Osage (Yew is another excellent bow wood which frequently grows with a great deal of personality).

Bows made of Osage (and any other dense wood), should have limbs which are comparatively wider, thinner, and shorter than the historical longbows. Ancient Europeans and American Indians knew this well, and Hickman, Klopsteg, and Nagler "rediscovered" this during the 1920's and 30's, when they announced the **flatbow** (with a rectangular cross section and flat back and belly) to a public brought up on English yew longbow traditions. A lighter wood such as yew, with narrow limbs, stacked belly, and long design is a pleasure to shoot: light in the hand, excellent cast, and with little jar or hand-shock. An Osage bow made to the same configuration, as most were in the first part of this century, will be physically heavy, have disappointing cast, and will blur your vision with extreme hand-shock.

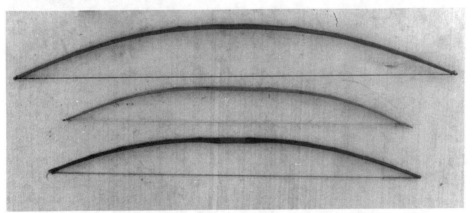

*The top one is a "D" bow, while the bottom two have semi-rigid handle sections.*

There are essentially three styles of flatbow which are suited to the unique characteristics of Osage.

The first is a "D" bow, which bends throughout its length in a continuous arc and has its widest point at the handle. It is easy and quick to make. This bow can shoot well, but is more difficult to aim and control, and does not lend itself to higher draw weights.

The second style (58-62") has a semi-rigid, somewhat narrowed handle section which appears flat when the bow is strung but which bends (you can *feel* it) as the bow is drawn. As Tim Baker has outlined in the Performance chapter earlier, this is one of the most efficient designs, though it is difficult to tiller properly.

The most stable, accurate, and comfortable to shoot is the third style of flatbow. This one has a rigid, 4" long handle which is oval in cross section and about 1-3/4" deep, and limbs about 1-3/4" at their widest point. Made in 67" length (for a 28" draw), this makes a serious, durable hunting weapon. You can decrease the overall length of this design 2" for each one inch decrease in draw

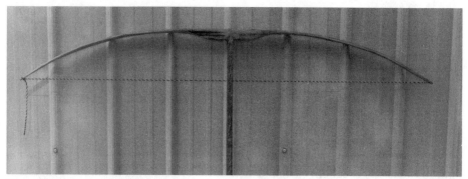

*Bow with narrow, deep handle section.*

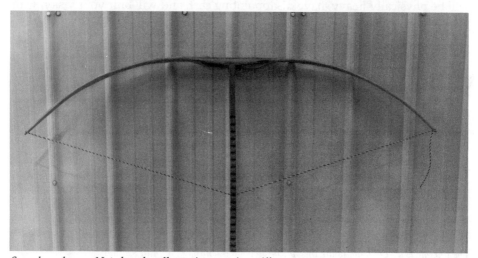

*Same bow drawn. Note how handle section remains stiff.*

length. For example, if your draw length is 26", the bow can be 63", though the stiff riser section should remain the same.

The instructions to follow will guide you in making a symmetrical Osage bow of the third type listed. We'll assume, for now, that the piece of wood is straight and relatively clear (free from erratic grain, **knots** – areas where a branch existed on the trunk, or **pins** – where a thorn or tiny stem grew from the tree). Not only will this provide you with a fine selfbow, but your skills – perceptive, analytical, and motor – will sharpen in the process, preparing you for advanced levels on more difficult pieces of wood.

Most of time, the denser, stronger, more desirable Osage comes from young trees, or the innermost wood from older trees, laid down when the tree was young. It has long been my observation that a tree from age fifteen to forty years (approx. 5" to 15" in diameter), will yield the densest, and therefore fastest bows, which is ironically the approximate age range of maximum athleticism in humans. An attendant complication with young wood is that it is often filled

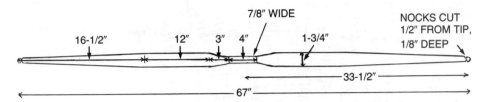

*Osage flat bow, top view.*

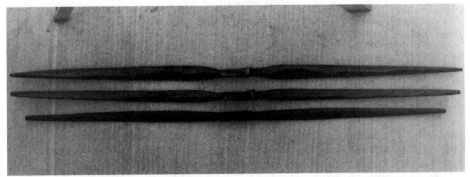

*Osage bows with variations on the illustrated design. All have a narrow, non-bending handle.*

with knots, pins, and other irregularities which require judgement and skill from the bowyer.

Jim Hamm has noted, and I concur, that the latewood color of Osage heartwood is a general indicator as to its strength. It seems a tree with darker, "oranger" wood is the densest, and therefore strongest, while the lighter-colored pale-yellow wood is comparatively lighter and weaker. It is almost as if the wood contains a certain amount of color, and the more condensed the color the more condensed the wood. This test is probably not infallible, but if a piece of Osage is light in color it may be well to make the bow a bit wider to compensate (it should be noted that even "weak" Osage is still stronger than almost any other wood). Osage is very photosensitive, that is, it turns dark in sunlight. So a valid color comparison between two logs would require they both be split at the same time (the darkening of Osage continues indefinitely, very old bows being purple-black).

The bow we will make comes from a quarter split log, 8" to 12" in diameter, as straight as possible, with no spiral showing in the bark, and no stems or limbs protruding. Begin by turning the split log into a stave. The easiest and quickest way to do this is with a bandsaw. If you plan to buy a bandsaw, make it a full-size 14" version (this refers to the depth of the cut it will make), with a strong motor and wide blade. The three-wheel table-top hobby bandsaws have not, in my experience, been up to the rugged task of making bows. If you have no bandsaw, shape your quarter log into a stave with a sharp hatchet by using short, controlled strokes, or with a coarse wood rasp, or a drill-type disc sander with coarse sanding wheel. I occasionally hear whispers that power tools are not

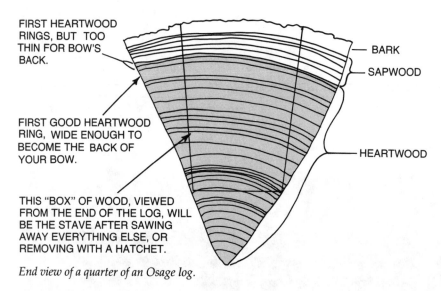

FIRST HEARTWOOD RINGS, BUT TOO THIN FOR BOW'S BACK.

BARK

SAPWOOD

FIRST GOOD HEARTWOOD RING, WIDE ENOUGH TO BECOME THE BACK OF YOUR BOW.

HEARTWOOD

THIS "BOX" OF WOOD, VIEWED FROM THE END OF THE LOG, WILL BE THE STAVE AFTER SAWING AWAY EVERYTHING ELSE, OR REMOVING WITH A HATCHET.

*End view of a quarter of an Osage log.*

primitive, or traditional enough. But the line must be drawn somewhere, and since few of us are capable, much less inclined, to walk into an Osage grove stark naked with only a stone ax for a tool (which is the only purely primitive way to do it), then the power tools are a reasonable alternative. The way I look at it, if a bandsaw was good enough for the master bowyers of the 1920's and 30's, then they are good enough for me.

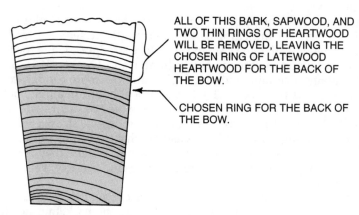

ALL OF THIS BARK, SAPWOOD, AND TWO THIN RINGS OF HEARTWOOD WILL BE REMOVED, LEAVING THE CHOSEN RING OF LATEWOOD HEARTWOOD FOR THE BACK OF THE BOW.

CHOSEN RING FOR THE BACK OF THE BOW.

*Stave after bandsawing away excess wood from quarter log.*

Whatever tools you use, reduce the quarter log until, for this bow, it is approximately 67" long, 2" wide on the bark side, and 2" deep, back to belly. A stave which becomes narrower or thinner toward the ends creates no problem as long as the intended bow can still be laid out.

Next, in order to obtain a better view of the wood, remove the bark with a trusty drawknife. The process of bowmaking will be easier if you have a solid vise of some sort to hold the stave, though it can be worked by simply standing it against the wall in a corner, or coercing a strong, dull-witted accomplice to hold it. But all of bow-making will be simpler if a secure vise is used.

Once the bark is removed down to the all-white sapwood, scrutinize the wood for grain trends, grubworm holes, cracks, knots, and pins. Circle any such potential problems boldly so as to be acutely aware of their location. Sometimes a slight change in a bow's design or layout will be dictated. For example: if there is an extremely snaky grain in one or both bow limbs, the sides of the bow should follow it, all the while tapering to a normal tip. Such work cannot be hurried with power tools, it must be carefully sculpted with a hand rasp. Or it could be that knots or other problems can be avoided by the way a bow is placed on the stave; it is better to avoid a problem than to be forced to deal with it in the bow.

*Any major "snakes" in the grain of the wood must be followed when the bow design is laid out. They do not effect the shooting qualities of the bow, but do add character. (courtesy Scooter Cheatham)*

You may well find upon exposing the sapwood that there are worm holes present. Often, the living grubs will be found, and battle-hardened bowyers generally squash them without mercy. Most of the time their ravages are confined to the sapwood, which is removed from a stave anyway. Occasionally, a grub takes a wrong turn into the heartwood, though he generally only travels into one or two yearly growth rings, and this is easy enough to compensate for by simply choosing a ring below the damage to be the back of the bow. If a stave from a smaller tree is shot full of worm holes, another piece of wood may be called for.

Assuming the wood looks satisfactory, draw the bow design on the sapwood (or on the heartwood if you've already removed the sapwood in your storage/curing procedure). One technique involves using a straight edge to draw a center line, and measuring out from it to draw the design as close as possible to the intended dimensions. Jay Massey initiated the simplest and most useful technique for drawing a center line, even on wood with undulations too severe for the use of a straight-edge. He marks where the center of each tip will be, then uses the shadow from a straight object, such as the side of a building, to connect them. The line will be straight in spite of humps or dips, and the bow's outline can be drawn using it as a starting point.

After laying out the bow, use first the bandsaw, then a rasp, to reduce dimensions to the drawn lines. Now, the wood will look like a bow from the back or belly, but will still appear as a stave from the sides.

Examine both ends of the stave to determine which specific latewood ring will become the back of the bow. If the rings are difficult to see, sand the ends with 100 grit sandpaper. The ring you select for the back should be as close as possible to the sapwood and for ease of working should be at least 3/16" thick. If thicker, so much the better.

To make absolutely certain you are looking at the same ring on both ends of the log, simply count rings down from the top, marking the one you want. Often, I polish the sides of the stave with a disc sander or some type of scraper, until the rings are visible all the way around the stave. With a dark, fine pencil, I draw a line on the earlywood ring directly above the latewood ring I've chosen, around the entire stave. If the line ends on the same ring it began on, then I'm in business and on target. A correct pencil line is an absolute reference point to prevent cutting through the chosen back ring.

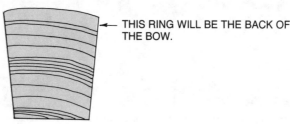

THIS RING WILL BE THE BACK OF THE BOW.

*Fully prepared stave, complete with a well-prepared ring of heartwood latewood for the back of the bow.*

As for tools, many Osage bowyers from the old days (most of whom have now passed away) spoke of using a heavy scraper, such as a large knife or squared-off power hacksaw blade to work the back of a bow. I have made scores of bows with this method, and long thought that it was the fastest way with a non-power tool. This is hard on the hands and wrists, but think of it as a character-builder.

Two rasps, a coarse one in conjunction with a fine one, make another effective method for working Osage backs. If you choose these, use the finer one the most, especially as you get closer to the desired ring.

An electric drill with a sanding pad and 100 grit discs is a very useful method, especially if the wood is somewhat green. This tool automatically keeps the back smooth, making it relatively easy to see the ring being worked. In order to use a power sander, the desired back ring should be at least 1/4" thick.

Malcom Smith, whom I introduced to wooden bows several years ago, has developed his own technique which works beautifully. He uses a small, sharp hatchet, gripped close to the head, utilizing a series of short, judicious chopping motions to remove wood above the ring he wants for the back. It's a bit scary to watch, but Malcom works the back flawlessly with just a hatchet.

All of the above tools and procedures can work well, but the best and fastest method is using a drawknife. Four years ago I was convinced Osage could not be worked this way; I either scraped or sanded to prepare a back. Every time I tried drawkniving, the blade dug into the wood, gouged out disastrous splits, and ruined the stave. Most old bowyers and literature corroborated my negative experience. But, after first watching Jim Hamm drawknife the back of an Osage stave in less than twenty minutes, it was clear the method worked well, though no one else had much success with it. His technique (revealed under my relentless third-degree questioning), boils down to three factors: 1) he uses well seasoned wood, 2) his drawknife has a slightly curved blade, and 3) most

*Drawkniving a stave.*

importantly, he NEVER sharpens it, even after 600 plus bows, which explains my earlier difficulties; I had an edge on my drawknife which would shave. At his invitation, I tried his tool on dried wood, and instantly became a drawkniving fool. The method is fast, precise, and leaves a smooth surface for the back of the bow. Jim's dull, curved blade acts more like a wedge than a knife, seeking and finding the weak, crumbly earlywood just above the chosen ring and wedging away the unwanted wood above it. If your drawknife does not work well, try dulling it.

On one end of your stave, use the drawknife to cut down to the ring chosen for the back, exposing it for about two inches. You have three sensory allies working for you as you remove the unwanted wood above the bow's back: sight, sound, and feel. The drawknife behaves differently when cutting through earlywood as opposed to late wood, it looks, sounds, and feels different. The earlywood is usually a thinner, lighter colored layer of soft material which contains many tiny open "air" pockets that make it look like Swiss cheese. It sounds and feels crunchy as you pull the drawknife through it, sort of like crushing a few fresh cornflakes in your hand. But as the drawknife passes through the soft earlywood and contacts the hard, dense latewood, the sound changes to a smooth, musical resonance – like rubbing a stainless steel rod across a marble table top. Thus the "crunch, crunch" of earlywood becomes a "hiss" as the blade contacts and glides along the latewood which will be the back of the bow. Go no farther into the layer of earlywood, but continue toward the other end of the stave.

Here is a basic concept which underlies all of the self-bowyer's efforts: you must be able to discern different growth rings as you work the wood, especially on the top of the stave, which is destined to be the bow's back. It may be difficult, at times, to judge where a particular growth ring begins or ends on the back, but two things will help you. The first is light. With the stave in a vise, move it relative to the sun, window light, fluorescent lights, or whatever may be the light source. There will be a specific placing of the work (usually between the light source and your eyes) where the earlywood rings will "jump out" visually. If the rings still aren't visible, try the second trick, which involves smoothing the back with a scraper (I use a stainless steel knife held at right angles to the wood). If rasp or sander are being used to work the back, this smoothing will be very useful, but a drawknife leaves a smooth surface, so this polishing will not be needed.

Continue removing wood above the chosen layer until the back is one beautiful, contiguous latewood ring. Be aware that the single layer will probably not be perfectly flat and straight; it may have humps, dips, or minor propeller twists – marks of beauty and character – but no matter what its shape it must be followed exactly. The back of the stave is now ready to slay an elk, and nothing further will be done to it beyond minor cosmetic sanding.

More often than not there are at least a few knots and pins in a stave. They must be dealt with, because their presence constitutes a weakness in their area of the limb. Simply put, you must leave more wood on the back around a knot to compensate for weakness. Because of the additional wood, it usually also means that the bow's bend in the area of a knot or pins will be correspondingly

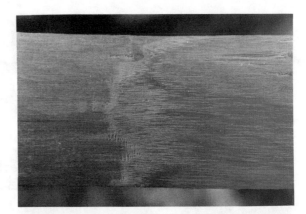

*The back of an Osage stave as it will appear while drawkniving.*

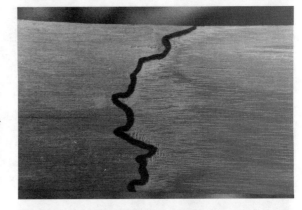

*Same stave with earlywood between two layers of latewood outlined for clarity. The back of the bow has been established as the solid latewood at left, and is the lowest, while the wood at right is higher and must be removed with the drawknife.*

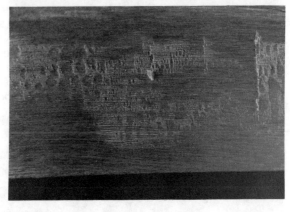

*Back of the bow as one continuous latewood layer. The spongy remnants of the earlywood layer just above it remain, showing that the latewood layer is pristine and intact. The spongy material is removed with gentle scraping and sandpaper.*

less, to protect the area. Mom Nature does most of the work for us by depositing more wood tissue in the latewood rings around a knot, i.e., the rings are thicker. By merely following the chosen growth ring, the "bump" around a knot will automatically be left intact.

*L - R; clean Osage stave, single pin (or thorn), multiple pins, and large knot.*

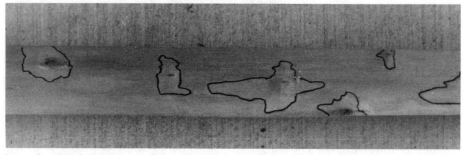

*Back of a stave as it appears while drawkniving. Single ring has been established for back at left. Note "islands" of extra wood left around pins.*

Earlier, it was mentioned that it is a good idea, long before any wood is removed, to mark knots on the back of the stave so you can keep track of where they are and work them properly. Proper treatment of pins is considerably more touchy, as they are usually tight clusters of three to five stemlets or thorns, and the tree normally doesn't accommodate them by much strengthening of the rings. Therefore, you must do the accommodating by leaving at least one and possibly two growth ring layers around the pin clusters, about 1/4" to 5/16" diameter.

*Stave after drawkniving is complete, with islands of extra wood left around knots and pins outlined for clarity.*

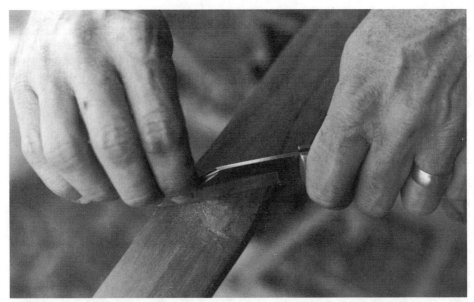

The extra wood around knots is reduced and made symmetrical with a scraper, such as a pocketknife.

Knot in an Osage bow limb.

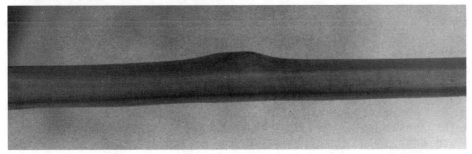

Side view of knot, showing extra wood built into the ring by the tree and followed by the bowyer.

At all costs, the bump around a knot must not be cut across with the drawknife. This gouges into an underlying layer of wood and jeopardizes the back of the bow. Leaving the desired fortifying wood requires that you stop wood removal with the drawknife sufficiently short of the pins, an inch or two, and continue following the established growth ring around one side or the other of the cluster, then continue working across the entire stave with the drawknife once the pins are passed. Traditionally called "raising the knots," the procedure leaves "islands" of extra wood around the knots. The delicate operation of working around the pins will require a finer tool than the drawknife, so with a scraper, such as a sharp pocket knife, held at right angles to the wood, reduce the islands in size and make them symmetrical. Later, as you make more bows and gain experience, you can scrape away the additional wood left on top of knots and pins and leave only the established back grain. But, early in a bowyer's career, it is far better to leave too much than not quite enough.

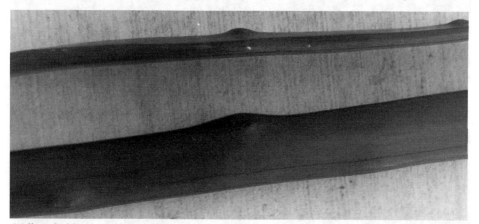

*Well worked knots and pins in Osage bows. Two things are noteworthy about the lower bow. First, extra wood was left around a knot which fell on the edge of the limb, and secondly, radial cracks normally do no harm as long as they stay within the limb and do not run out the side.*

If at any time, in any area of potential weakness, you feel that nature's thickenings on your raised plateaus are inadequate for protecting the limb's integrity, you always have an ace in the hole; leave a bit more wood on the belly side so the limb will bend less in that area. This is really a tillering technique, and is covered in a later chapter on that subject, but keep in mind there is rarely a knot or pin which cannot be adequately compensated for in some fashion.

A word about cracks in Osage self bows. Radial cracks of the hairline variety may be in the stave initially, or may develop during or even after a bow's manufacture. Radial cracks are oriented through the back to belly axis (the radial axis) and can vary greatly in length and depth. They may be only on the belly, only on the back, or may run entirely through a limb or riser section. Radial cracks are not threatening to a bow's health, IF they stay within the bow and do not run off of the side in a working section of a limb. Filling a crack with one of the "super glues" is good insurance, as the glue is thin enough to penetrate the deepest recesses of a crack and make it stronger. If the crack comes close, or runs off of, the side of a limb, then use super glue and wrap the area with sinew or silk thread.

Though rare with Osage, diagonal cracks on the belly of a bow which appear after tillering or shooting are usually compression fractures, or chrysals. These are indications that the bow is too stacked, or rounded on the belly (which is not a good design for Osage), narrow, overdrawn, or bends too much in that one area (i.e. is hinged). Re-tillering to a lighter weight usually allows such a bow to continue functioning, though deep chrysals can be fatal.

Another type of crack which shows itself on rare occasion is found running through the limb from side to side, separating the latewood rings. This laminar separation is actually a disintegration of an early wood ring, which allows the wood to come apart. This sometimes doesn't become evident until you pull a bow and subject it to tension and compression. This lethal flaw is usually caused by a log or stave which was left outdoors in sun and rain.

Another potential problem is transverse cracks (running from side to side) across the limb on the back of the bow. They are most likely to develop if you allow sapwood to be a working part of the bow, or if a knot or pin has been improperly accommodated. Remember, a latewood ring of Osage heartwood is exceptionally strong in tension and makes a redoubtable back, unless there is a weak area in it. If such cracks develop, a possible remedy is to wrap it with sinew, or better yet, sinew-back the entire bow.

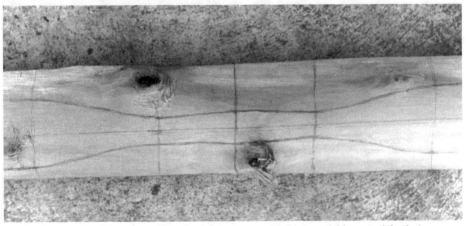

*Two big knots in an Osage stave. Note how they were avoided by careful layout of the design.*

If a stem goes through a limb from back to belly, and happens to be rotten, the pith can be cleared away, leaving a "bullethole" right through the limb. Compensate for this weaker area with more thickness on the belly side, or possibly some additional width in the limb at the knot.

Now that the stave's back is fully prepared, the next step is to reduce the thickness from the belly side. In the old days, I used a hand rasp for this, and on bigger staves this sometimes took days. A bandsaw can accomplish this reduction in minutes, and I can only attribute my early reluctance to buying a bandsaw to compulsive dumbness, with oak leaf clusters. Reduce the coarse stave by taking off belly wood with long bandsaw cuts until it is 3/4" thick at the nocks, 7/8" thick at mid-limb, and the full depth of the stave at the handle. Just make sure there is more than enough wood left for a bow, once you start shaping and tillering in earnest with a rasp.

*Drawing the limb's thickness on a stave with the back of the bow established. The pencil is held steady, and the fingers run along the back of the bow, thus the line exactly follows any undulations in the wood.*

The bow is now ready for tillering. Refer to that chapter, while keeping in mind that the bow we've laid out has a rigid riser, or handle section, which means that a section of about ten to twelve inches in the center of the bow will not bend.

After nocks are cut and the bow tillered, the handle can be shaped to your preference. Most find some type of oval cross-section the most comfortable. When the bow has proven itself to be well-tillered and stable, and the handle shaped, it can be smoothed by using successive grits of sandpaper (120, 220, 320, 400, 600), then by "boning" with a spoon or test tube. I finish my bows with linseed oil, usually, applied in five treatments with light sanding after each coat dries. Sanding can reduce a bow's weight a pound or two after perfect tiller is attained, so don't get carried away.

I usually rest an arrow on the first knuckle of my bow hand, which works fine as long as the feathers are perfectly smooth where they are attached to the shaft. Some prefer an arrow shelf, and the best, easiest kind is made from layers of thick craft leather glued with contact cement to the clean, finished handle. A cut leather handle cover can be glued in place over the shelf. These kinds of adaptions are personal touches; take leather, razor-blade knife, cement and start experimenting.

*Nock areas of Osage bows can be smaller and more delicate than with other woods, due to its strength.*

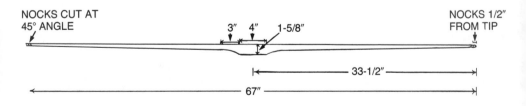

NOCKS CUT AT
45° ANGLE

3"  4"  1-5/8"

NOCKS 1/2"
FROM TIP

33-1/2"

67"

*Side view of Osage flat bow.*

After you have looked at and shot your bow enough to get a feel for its individuality, you might get a kick out of giving it a name. I've named many bows and heard many good ones: "Little Egypt," "Dennis Hopper," "Little John," "Beast," "Scrub," "Bodacious," "Sleeping Beauty," "Old Ugly," and "Slabsides," to name just a few.

You might make the ideal bow on the first try, but it is far more likely that it will take several attempts to get exactly what you want. Keep after it, for it takes some experience through reading, asking questions, and, most importantly, making wood shavings. Be comforted in the knowledge that your reward will be a bow which can shoot for a lifetime.

# OTHER BOW WOODS

*Paul Comstock*

In 1927, James Duff wrote his book, *Bows and Arrows,* on manufacturing archery tackle. At the time, Duff was a mature bowyer of many experiences. He immigrated from Great Britain and had worked in some of the legendary British archery houses of the late 19th and early 20th centuries – among them Highfield, Buchanan, and Muir.

Duff told his readers a bow of ash, elm, oak, or a similar wood would shoot in a soft and unsatisfactory manner as long as it remained green. When these woods dry out, they nearly always break, he said.

Hickory, Duff wrote, will stand a lot of hard use, but "cast is not in the wood."

"These are not bow woods," the Briton warned!

For generations many other old-time archery writers echoed Duff's remarks, sometimes nearly verbatim. Others would concede a bow can be made of these woods, but would say such bows would be far inferior to yew, Osage orange, or lemonwood.

If these writers and bowyers are looking down on us today from the blue vaults of heaven, their eyes must be wide with surprise. For today arrows are fairly screaming through the air, propelled by the brilliant cast of superb wooden bows made of elm, ash, hickory, and oak.

Of course, we must give Duff his due. What he said was correct – if the bowyer makes all the mistakes Duff and his contemporaries made.

What were these mistakes?

Consider how the old-timers made bows. The American woods they used were yew and Osage orange. And often as not, they let these woods season sitting outdoors or in a shed. One extreme example was Mark Mauser, a friend of champion archer Robert Elmer. Mauser made a bow from a felled Osage tree that lay on the ground 18 years.

Next, these men made English bows. Called the "Mother of Archers" by Maurice Thompson, England was virtually the only influence white American bowyers followed until the 1930's. And the English bow was narrow and deep, with a rounded belly forming a D cross-section.

When making these bows, our old friends typically cut the bow to rough dimensions and immediately strung it. Then they began bending the bow to test its curve.

To be sure, the old boys got results with these methods. But they are an invitation to disaster for the fellow making a bow out of the "white woods," elm, hickory, etc., which in most subspecies are largely formed of white sapwood.

Osage and yew are highly resistant to decay. They can lie outdoors or stay in damp conditions for long periods of time. Ash, elm, oak, and hickory are a different story. They begin to decompose very quickly if left lying outside. I once split an elm log cut six months before and left in the woods. It was riddled with powdery rot through and through. By cutting only live white wood trees and storing the wood indoors, problems with decay can be avoided.

Osage and yew can stand higher levels of strain than nearly all of the white woods. This means Osage and yew can live with the narrow limbed design of the English longbow very nicely.

But narrow limbs are typically too much for the white woods. Odds are that the white woods will follow the string considerably if the limbs are narrow and the moisture content too high. String follow robs cast. Still, such bows are dangerous weapons and many archers would be pleased with them. And, as will be

*White wood stave, billets, and two flatbows.*

mentioned later, there are exceptions to the rule. But, on average, a narrow white wood bow will draw criticism when compared to the average narrow yew or Osage bow.

The answer, in part, is to make the second-string wood bow wider than a similar yew or Osage bow. If you want a good rule of thumb to follow, make the white wood flatbow's limbs two inches wide from handle to at least mid-limb (with thickness adjusted for the correct tiller). This width is more than enough to ensure the wood can stand the strain of shooting if the bow is about 66 inches long. All other things being equal, this design can produce a bow pulling in excess of 70 pounds while keeping string follow to a minimum. Lighter bows – for example, those at 55 pounds or under – can be made only 1-3/4 inches wide. If performance from a white wood is your first priority, these guidelines can produce excellent results.

With a white wood bow, plan to bend the bow only gently in the early stages of construction. If the bowyer strings the white wood bow – without first gently testing its curve – and then draws the bow, look out. It may break outright. Odds are high it will follow the string excessively. And weak spots in the limbs will become hinged, which means these small areas will show an extreme amount of string follow.

For white woods, first and foremost obtain a good tiller by only bending the bow slightly. This is easiest to accomplish with a tillering board and a long tillering string. Once the tiller is even, then the bow can be bent further with best results.

It is surprising to read that Duff and old-timers would consider making an ash or elm bow out of green wood, and then be disappointed it was overstrained when it dried. Dry wood is stronger than green wood, so it's hard to imagine anything else could happen with such an approach.

When I first began making bows out of white and second-string woods, I had my doubts. One fear was that such a bow would be acceptable in the beginning, but somehow it would break down or fall apart after a lot of use.

It never happened.

When properly designed and tillered, a white wood bow is extremely durable. It is worth mentioning that if an Osage or yew bow is poorly made, it, too, will break very quickly.

If it needs to be spelled out: A bow made of a second-string wood can shoot very hard and last a very long time, if the bowyer does his job right.

The next question is, can a second-string wooden bow be as fast as an Osage or yew bow?

They can very easily be faster.

I have made a number of English bows and flatbows of yew and Osage. The performance of some of them is markedly inferior to my best bows of second-string woods. When comparing my best second-string wood bows to my best Osage and yew bows, there is no evidence of any significant difference while shooting them. If the bows are of similar draw weight, the trajectory and hitting power of the arrows is essentially the same.

This involves a very important point. The wood itself will never guarantee great results in a bow. Great results depend on good design and good workmanship more than any other single factor.

By coincidence, I have in my possession an ash bow made the way the old boys would have made it. What a mess it is. Before most of us were born, some fellow tried to make this bow from ash, based on what he read in archery books of his day. Here's what happened: When our bowmaker began bending his bow, it was too heavy for him. So he worked down the sections of the limbs on either side of the handle, leaving the middle of the bow excessively stiff. In these areas, the limbs are no more than an inch wide, with a deep and rounded belly. The limbs began to follow the string badly. Small cracks appeared in the bow's back from the terrible strain. Worried, the bowmaker wrapped the scary spots with tape. Alas, one limb snapped off near the tip.

So much for the wrong way. What about a right way?

There are a number of possibilities. The approach I prefer with white woods is as follows. First, I cut the tree in the summer. If I need wood in the winter, I'll cut it then. But I prefer to cut the wood in the summer. I split the wood the day I cut it and immediately pull the bark off of ash, oak, elm, hickory, walnut, or birch. In the summer, the sap is up and the inner bark very wet. And when the bark is pulled off, the inner bark of these woods comes off with it. In the winter, the inner bark will stick to the wood and removing it involves more work.

 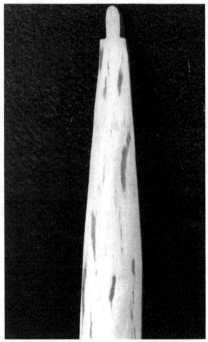

*The white wood at left was cut in the summer, when pulling off the bark also removed the inner bark. The wood at right was cut in the winter, when the inner bark sticks tight to the wood.*

*With winter-cut white wood, traces of inner bark are often left on the back of a finished bow.*

If you have to remove inner bark, carefully trim it as thin as you can with a knife or draw knife. Often, making a small cut in the inner bark will allow you to pull off a long piece. Once the inner bark is thinned, put the wood in the shower and let hot water dribble over it for about 30 minutes. The inner bark will then be soft enough to come up with a scraper. Steaming can also remove inner bark easily.

The beginner often confuses inner bark with real wood, because inner bark sometimes has layers that resemble grain. If you are not sure, test the outside with a knife tip. Inner bark is usually softer and more fibrous than the wood itself.

Next, I varnish the ends to reduce checking, then place the woods indoors. Sometimes hungry insects are attracted to the wood by the sap. If so, I hose the wood down with insect repellent. Then I let the wood sit about two weeks. In this time the moisture content will fall from in excess of 30% to about 15 to 20%. If I plan to cut splices to join billets, I do it after the two weeks have passed.

Once the wood hits 20%, it can now be dried fairly quickly. I do this with heat. At this stage, most pieces of these woods can stand up to 150 degrees of heat without any significant checking. To be on the safe side, 90 to 100 degrees is a safer bet.

A hot-box of the type used in making glass-laminated bows can be used. My device is simple and cheap. It consists of two six-inch diameter pieces of stovepipe, fastened together and stood on end. About a foot from the bottom of the lower piece, holes are drilled in the side. A screen is formed by lacing utility wire through the holes. The wood sits on the screen, and a lamp with a 75 or 100-watt bulb sits under it. Average temperature in the dryer: 100 degrees or so. Cost: about $12.

This cheap dryer has disadvantages. The wood closest to the bulb is warmer than the rest of the piece. A bit too damp and the end will check. And long staves must be flipped since only half will fit in the dryer. But if used on its own terms, the pipe dryer works very well.

An enclosed car sitting parked under the summer sun can also be used to dry wood. I have dried many pieces in such a manner. But 48 hours in the pipe dryer is worth 10 days in a parked car, because the car cools at night. The pipe dryer does not. My experience is that wood will fall from 14 to 9% if left in the pipe dryer 48 hours. Around 9% is a good target for moisture of white wood bows. At 12%, string follow can be considerable. At 9%, it can be very slight.

I check moisture with an electronic meter, but a meter is not necessary. This is a good test: once you feel the wood is dry, the new bow can be put on a tillering board (using a long tillering string) and bent to a level that equals brace height. If the bow shows string follow after sitting this way a few minutes, it's too wet. If it returns faithfully to its original position, moisture content is very close to 9%.

It should be stated for emphasis: There were no errors in the preceding paragraphs. This is exactly what can be done with the woods mentioned. Nothing is gained by letting whole logs of these woods sit around for months with the bark intact.

Bowmakers may be in the habit of letting yew and Osage season long periods with the bark on, and with some good reasons. Osage can check badly in the outer layers if the bark is removed too quickly. Ash, elm, oak, birch, hickory, and walnut will not. When you cut one of these trees, you'll be much better off splitting that log immediately and taking the bark off immediately afterward. The wood will dry out much faster.

Some bowmakers may have the idea there is some magic benefit to using wood cut years and years earlier. In some cases, there can certainly be a sentimental value to such an approach. But with white woods, there is absolutely no practical reason to let wood sit around for years. White woods can be stored for long periods without being hurt. But you can turn white wood into a bow very quickly, if you do it right.

My average white wood bow goes from green tree to finished bow in about 60 days. My record is something like 20 days. Some of my friends turn green white wood trees into finished bows just as fast as I do, and the above method is how we do it.

What matters is getting the wood to 9% moisture without damaging the wood. From a practical standpoint, that's all that matters.

Be warned that under some circumstances it may be possible to lower the moisture content of wood to as low as 4 or 5%. It is almost guaranteed that a bow limb this dry will break. Guard against putting the wood anyplace that gets hotter than 150 degrees. And avoid keeping wood at 150 degrees for several months or any similar extended period of time.

Here's another point worth mentioning. Almost everyone removes the sapwood from Osage orange, working their bows down to an interior growth ring. Many make yew bows with a thin layer of sapwood, or no sapwood at all. Both of these techniques involve removing the outer rings from the bow wood.

With healthy hickory, ash, elm, walnut, oak, and birch, you don't have to remove the outer wood. You can make the bow's back out of the wood immediately under the inner bark. If you pull the bark off in the summer, taking the inner bark off with it, the wood you are looking at on the outside of your stave is the back of the bow. And you don't have to do a single thing to it. The only exception is when the wood has suffered some deterioration, usually because of decay or disease.

A friend and I have a theory on how Osage became so popular for bows. Sometime around the turn of the century, a white man approached an old Indian warrior and asked what wood made a good bow. The Indian looked at him, remembering it was these people who destroyed the buffalo, burned the lodges, killed the ponies, trampled the land, killed the young warriors, and degraded the women.

This man should suffer, the Indian thought, raising himself to his full height.

"Osage orange," he said with a smile.

The point is you can make a great bow out of Osage orange. You can also make a great bow out of white wood, and it can be a heck of a lot easier and faster than using Osage. Part of the reason is that second-string woods are quite accessible, and it is fairly easy to find long straight wood.

To a man, my friends who have started getting great results with white woods have all grown reluctant to make more bows out of Osage. When we grab a piece of wood to make a bow, 95% of the time it's white, not orange. Second-string woods are habit-forming.

We should also remember that in the annals of archery history, many lusty and bloody chapters have been written by bows of white and second-string woods. They were used in prehistoric Europe and medieval England. North American Indians from coast to coast shot them.

Let's say a bowmaker is accustomed to making sinewed Osage bows. He can easily adopt white wood for a virtual copy of his Osage design. If he makes the white wood bow limbs slightly wider, say 30%, the sinewed bow should show no more string follow than a similar sinewed Osage bow. If his Osage limbs are 1-1/2-inch wide, for example, he should make the white wood limbs about 2 inches wide.

Our bowyer has to make sure the white wood is not damaged by decay, and the moisture content is low enough. Look for these indicators when searching for decay in a white wood: tiny holes or air pockets in the spring growth (the spongy wood separating the rings), and any powdery appearance when the wood is split.

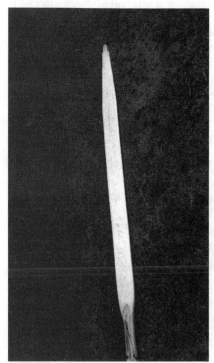

*The author's favorite design for a second-string wood, limbs two inches wide for most of their length, with the bow 66 inches long.*

*Elm bows based on the Meare Heathe artifact found in England and estimated to be 4700 years old.*

If the wood shows either, it may not work. Then again, it may. If the bowmaker has any doubts, there is a simple test which has proven very effective for me. Simply split off a small piece of the outside and make a tiny bow – about 6 to 12 inches long. If the wood will make a tiny bow that stands a good bend, then the big bow will do the same. If the small bow breaks, one option is to test the interior wood. Working the wood down to a single interior ring may work. Again, a small test bow can tell the answer. I'd recommend anyone trying a wood he has never used before to do a test with a tiny bow. This small bow need not be more sophisticated than a roughly cut slat of wood.

The bow I prefer to make of white wood is unbacked, 66 inches long and drawing as far as 29 inches, with limbs two inches wide extending from a narrow handle to well past mid-limb. The limb width narrows to the nocks. I have occasionally made limbs 2-1/4 inches wide. But two inches works well with every wood I have tried, at any draw weight. Making limbs wider than two inches along most of their length could hurt performance because of excess limb weight.

For no other reason than taste, I like to pattern these bows after the Meare Heath bow, a long yew flatbow made in Great Britain at about 2,700 B.C. (The Meare Heath artifact was probably 74 inches long, and had limbs about 2.6 inches wide.) While others have a fondness for Indian or medieval styles, I am fascinated with archery of prehistoric Europe. Among the oldest bows in existence are the Holmegaard bows, pulled out of a bog in Denmark. They are about 8,000 years old. The Holmegaards and their descendants – which were in use for several millennia – were made out of a white wood: elm.

At one time I shunned the thought of carrying a 66-inch bow in the field. Ultimately I realized that I'm 69 inches tall, and can manage to maneuver through the brush and trees with relative ease. I reasoned that if a 69-inch hunter can get around handily, a 66-inch bow should be able to go along with him. Carrying a 66-inch bow has only strengthened that view.

*Making a second-string wood bow long enough and wide enough (bottom) can easily avoid the level of string follow shown by more routine bows (top two).*

Another advantage of this long, wide design is that if the bowyer proceeds carefully, he can consistently produce unbacked bows of this type that follow the string less than an inch. This is easiest to accomplish when the stave has some reflex, or the billets are spliced together with some set-back in the handle.

Sinew backing is a favorite of many when making bows 62 inches or less with draw lengths up to 27 and 28 inches. I have used it to good effect on many such bows. Sinew does a superb job of protecting a bow's back. Its other great advantage is that it can greatly reduce string follow in a shorter bow. Without a sinew backing, shorter bows tend to show considerably more string follow, on average.

But I appreciate economy. I appreciate a design which allows me to produce a great straight-limbed bow in a minimum of time with a maximum of convenience. There are many approaches one can use in wooden bows. We should all follow our own drummers. Our own satisfaction should be our first concern. Yet bowyers should be aware that economy in wooden bows is certainly accessible if they want it. Approaches like white woods and long, wide unbacked flatbows are a good way to achieve economy. And a wooden bow with very little string follow is going to have excellent cast.

I have also made long, wide flatbows backed with sinew or rawhide. If one feels the urge, he can do the same. But be warned, get used to unbacked bows like this and they can be addicting. They are also highly durable. Because the stretching tension on the back is spread over so large an area, this type design is extremely durable when unbacked. My experience is if the back is in fine shape on a bow like this after several hundred shots, it will remain in fine shape indefinitely.

It is certainly not to be recommended, but I have made bows like this cutting through a ring on the back (when the rings are fairly thin) and leaving in gashes from the draw knife. And the backs of these bows are in great shape! I can cite no better evidence of how this design so nicely digests a bare wood back. (But for the record, good tillering, following one ring and making the back glassy smooth are the best insurance for unbacked bows.)

While I love this type bow dearly, it must again be emphasized there are other approaches a bowyer can use.

My friend Tim Baker has used white and second-string woods extensively. His ideas and approaches are based on many worthwhile tests, and are presented in detail in an earlier chapter. It is also worth mentioning Baker has had good results with kiln-dried ash, oak, and hickory. Many old books warn against using kiln-dried wood. If the wood is fairly soft, this is probably good advice. But hickory, oak, and ash are tough items. Baker's experience shows they are a worthwhile alternative when kiln-dried, with a moisture content around 9%. If you want to try such a kiln-dried wood, it would be smart to conduct a bend test with a miniature bow or small slat of the wood. When you buy any wood, you can never be 100% certain of the treatment it has received.

It is no accident that when American bowyers shifted from English to rectangular cross section in limbs, their opinions of second-string woods improved. By far and away, the best bowmaking book of the pre-fiberglass era is *The Flatbow*, written in the late 1930's by Ben Hunt and John Metz. They mention elm, locust, hickory, and walnut as bow woods. They also tell of a walnut flight bow that shot 341 yards. Sadly, this book is almost devoid of details on obtaining good results from these woods. But during its era, *The Flatbow* was almost revolutionary.

Dr. Dwight Bundy, a West Virginia bowyer, is a friend of mine who uses white and second-string woods. Being a fan of Indian lore and artifacts, he naturally has an interest in Indian bows. In addition to the wide, long flatbows mentioned above, he has also made bows using Eastern Indian designs. Most of these are 66-68 inches long. They are narrow and rectangular in cross section. The cross section of the handle matches the limbs, and the bow bends along its entire length.

Among these bows is a 66-inch unbacked elm bow that pulls 65 pounds. The width is a hair over an inch along most of the limbs. And this bow has no string follow. Zero. This is what can be accomplished when the stave has some reflex in it, and the bow tillered with tender loving care, never being strained more than its final draw weight. Not an easy thing to do with a narrow white wood bow, but Bundy did it.

*Dr. Dwight Bundy displays Indian-style bows of ash, hickory, elm, and black locust.*

Many writings cite a preference of Indians to make bows from trees killed by fire. Bundy's bow came from such a tree. And as a final touch of medicine, Bundy used this bow and an Indian-style arrow to tag his first primitive-archery whitetail.

Another friend of mine is Dean Torges of Ostrander, Ohio. Torges has a collection of bows he made using Osage and white woods. Among them is a remarkable specimen. It is an unbacked elm bow 64 inches long, pulling 67 pounds, with wide flat limbs. At this writing, it has been shot about 700 times, and it is still set back in the handle three inches! This bow is another example of what can be accomplished by tillering a white wood with the utmost care. Torges' bow is made of spliced billets. Each billet had a uniform reflexed curve in it. When brand new, it was set back in the handle 3-1/2 inches. First unstrung after shooting, the reflex falls to 2-1/2 inches. After several hours unstrung, it is back to three inches.

*Dean Torges holds a strung hackberry bow and an unstrung elm bow reflexed three inches after about 700 shots.*

The experience of Bundy and Torges are lessons for all of us. The quality of workmanship is a tremendous factor in the final bow. Torges also has a couple of extremely nice unbacked flatbows made of hackberry. He is the first person to my knowledge to use this wood in a bow. He was prompted to try it because he knew that working hackberry is similar to working ash. Torges has proven a tree not thought of as bow wood can produce superb results. Another lesson for all of us.

Let's talk briefly about some of the most common bow woods other than yew and Osage:

ELM – Elm comes in basically two types. One type is mostly white sapwood. This includes American, Siberian, and rock elm. The other type is slippery or red elm, which has a thinner white sapwood and a much thicker dark heartwood.

All these trees can make fine bows. I prefer to use a mostly white sapwood elm, because I think the wood is more robust and more resistant to decay. But it's a fairly minor point, because I have also made great bows from slippery elm. The only time I would remove the sapwood from slippery elm is when the sapwood shows rot and the heartwood doesn't.

Slippery elm can be split much like any other wood. It's work, because all elms have interlocking grain to some degree. The white elm trees typically have more pronounced interlocking grain and are murder to split. I cheat. I use a circular saw to make cuts on either side of the log, and hammer wedges into the cuts. Not exactly following the grain, but I have never had an elm bow failure with this method.

ASH – Ash is often considered in two classes. One has strong wood and one has weaker wood. The weaker ashes are black ash and blue ash. Almost all other ashes are in the stronger-wood class. The most well-known of these is white ash. Ash splits easily and works fairly easily, too.

OAK – White oak is usually considered the most reliable bow wood. But Tim Baker has made some nice bows of red oak.

BIRCH – Types of birch trees abound. According to wood textbooks, the wood is much the same in all of them. I'd make a bow out of any kind of birch. I have made several bows using paper birch. The best of the lot is 66 inches long, unbacked, with limbs two inches wide. The cast is good and I shoot it often.

HICKORY – Hickory comes in many types, all mighty tough. Pignut or smoothbark hickory is nearly unbreakable. As hickory likes to hang onto moisture, the moisture content of hickory falls slower than any other wood I have worked with. If the moisture content of a hickory bow is 12%, string follow will usually be excessive. For this reason hickory has often been called a sluggish wood. Get the moisture content down to 9%, and there will be nothing sluggish about a well-tillered hickory bow.

BLACK LOCUST – Black locust is not really a white wood because, except for usually thin sapwood, it isn't white. The other white woods mentioned above have one thing in common. The bark can be pulled off a green, freshly split log, and it's practically money in the bank no checking will occur on the back. Not so with black locust. Take the bark off a green piece and it can check on the back, not as often as Osage, but often enough. Best results are probably achieved by seasoning black locust like Osage.

Some bowyers have had good luck leaving a layer of sapwood on the back of black locust. Others have had their bows break almost immediately by trying it. It may depend to a large degree on the health of the tree. My experience is that the condition of black locust can vary considerably. In my own area, black locust borers make a mess out of almost every black locust tree by drilling them full of holes from one end to the other.

Many complain of black locust fretting, or getting compression fractures. Best insurance against this is making the belly as flat and smooth as possible, and tapering and tillering the bow carefully. Getting the moisture content down to 9% could also help, since damper wood is a bit softer.

WALNUT – I have used black walnut, and made the limbs from all white sapwood. Others have had good luck using other types of walnut. I have encountered walnut in which the outer rings will break easily when bent, but after working these pieces down to an interior ring have found wood which bends very well. Perhaps for this reason old-timers often backed walnut with hickory.

CEDAR AND JUNIPER – Many in the West have made superb bows of juniper, and its reliability is well-known. The sapwood is usually left on. My knowledge of eastern red cedar comes from Tim Baker, who has made a number of bows from it. He reports the tensile strength of unbacked red cedar seems low, breaking more easily on the back than other woods. Old-timers very often put hickory backings on red cedar, and no doubt this is the reason. Sinew-backing also works well with this wood.

MULBERRY – Two of archery's patron saints, Maurice and Will Thompson, made bows of mulberry as boys before the Civil War. Some old archery books give mulberry high praise, listing it as a good candidate for English bows. Like black locust, mulberry has a large dark heartwood. It is yellow-brown, covered by white sapwood. I have removed mulberry sapwood out of caution, but I do not think it is 100% necessary. If mulberry sapwood appears clear and sound, there is every reason to think it can be left on the bow's back. Old-timers often left it on, but trimmed it to a thin layer. A relative of mulberry is sassafras, which the Thompsons considered as good as mulberry.

MAPLE – Tim Baker has made a number of hard-hitting wide flatbows from sugar maple, sometimes called hardrock maple.

OTHER HARDWOODS – In addition to hackberry mentioned earlier, virtually any fruit or nut tree will make a bow if the tree can produce a long clear stave.

TROPICAL WOOD – No discussion of other bow woods would be complete without discussing tropical wood. The British began to use tropical wood for bows by the mid-19th century. Tropical woods such as lemonwood, lancewood, and snakewood have always had a first-string reputation in the minds of the old timers. The Thompsons bought bows of all three woods which had been made in England.

The most legendary tropical wood is lemonwood. Its real name is degame. It grows in Cuba, and by some accounts, in Central America. Like the best of tropical woods, it contains no visible rings. The grain can often be seen, but not always clearly.

Many old archery books describe sawing lemonwood staves while essentially ignoring the grain. This way, bowyers could cut the highest possible number of staves out of a lemonwood log. In the early 1940's, a good Osage or yew bow typically cost about $37. By comparison, a good lemonwood bow backed with silk (which was similar to a sinew backing in function) cost only $15. Until the 1950's, thousands of lemonwood bows were made. I have made several bows of lemonwood. The best is made in the 1930's flatbow style, 68 inches long, pulling 63 pounds, and unbacked. In one limb, the grain runs sharply off the back and belly of the bow.

Because lemonwood is so dense, it is extremely unlikely it would pull up a splinter in an unbacked bow. My experience is if pulled too far, the unbacked lemonwood bow will blow apart without warning. Lemonwood bows are rugged and highly durable unless the grain is severely tested. When it is, the party's over.

I once had a chat with an elderly gentleman who confessed that years earlier he snapped one limb of his neighbor's lemonwood bow trying to see how far it would pull. Sixty years after the event, my old friend still got a laugh out of that story.

Many old books warn against drawing the wooden bow with no arrow on the string. The writers were probably thinking of lemonwood when they wrote this. Old lemonwood target and hunting bows were usually backed. I own one with a fiber backing. These backings were probably designed to minimize damage if the bow ever blew apart.

It is worth mentioning that many old lemonwood bows were stained a darker color. Walnut was a favorite stain. The white woods are even whiter and brighter than lemonwood. I use an oil wipe stain on every white wood bow I make. Dean Torges does the same thing using aniline dye. Saxton Pope once wrote about an Indian bow apparently stained in some manner. There is plenty of good reason and historical precedent for staining white woods. If you're a hunter, you need camouflage, and staining white wood is a smart idea.

There are many, many types of tropical wood. The quality can vary and not all are as easy to obtain results from as lemonwood. Tim Baker has gotten good results from two types: purpleheart and goncalo alves.

It is possible to encounter problems when using white and second-string bow woods. If one is careful, he can avoid these problems. One potential problem is most of these woods – if unprotected – can absorb moisture under prolonged humid conditions. If the moisture content is 9%, it can rise to 12 or 14% in a couple of weeks of damp weather.

Osage and yew are less likely to do this. Consider staves of hickory and yew I had sitting next to each other for weeks on end. The hickory had a moisture content of 14%. The yew was 9%.

The best answer I can give to this problem is to keep the wood warm until the bow is finished. It will not pick up moisture if constantly heated to 80 or 90 degrees. Both Torges and I keep wood warm when we are not actually working on it. Torges uses a hot box and I use the inferior but still serviceable stovepipe dryer. Either costs only pennies a day to operate. A water resistant finish will prevent problems after a bow is completed. Certainly, finishes can only slow down water, not stop it totally. But rehydration is a slow process. It has never caused a problem for me in a finished bow, no matter how much rain splashes onto the limbs. Keeping paste wax on wooden bows is an easy and effective way to provide more protection against water.

Warping, another potential problem, can be caused by one of two factors. One is what woodworkers call reaction wood, which forms when stress is placed upon a tree because of how it grows. Cut the wood and it bends all over the place. In white wood trees with a trunk diameter under 10 or 12 inches, reaction wood is not very common at all.

Another problem involves cutting the wood into a narrow, long stave when still too green. A long, thin piece of green wood can warp easily. A thick, chunky green piece will warp very little. If you want to cut a thin, long stave, make sure the wood is as dry as possible before cutting the stave out of the half-log or quarter log.

Here's one example of what can be done: I once cut an elm and an ash during the summer. I split the pieces and immediately pulled off the bark. I had four half-split pieces. Each was wide, thick, and bulky. I put them in the back of my hatch-backed car. They were soaking wet when I did it. Each day the summer sun would raise the temperature in the car to 150 degrees. Four days in a row I got off work and found the car windows steamed up on the inside. I had to use a paper towel to wipe them off. Climbing into that car was like climbing into a sauna.

Water flooded from the wood like the cascade over Niagara Falls. About 10 days later, the moisture content of these pieces was 9%. There was no checking on the outside of the elm. One piece of ash had tiny checks where the grain curled on the back. I had planned on cutting the stave around that spot anyway. There was no checking on the straight-grained outside wood where the ash stave would be cut. The wood had been cut extra long. Checking on the ends was minimal. I sent the ash to Tim Baker and he made two bows. I spliced the elm together and made a bow from it.

It has been written often that thick-grained yew is weaker than fine-grained yew. Some say that fine-grained second-string woods are weaker than thick-ringed second-string woods. This may be true. But only a few hairs of thickness on the belly of wide limbs mark the difference between a 50-pound bow and a 70-pound bow. I have made several very serviceable bows pulling 65 to 70 pounds out of fine-grained elm. Let the wood itself tell you how thick the limbs must be to get the draw weight you want. And if the thicker limbs are heavier than thick-ringed wood, the ratio will be very small. And the difference in performance will so small as to be insignificant.

With almost all second-string woods (and Osage, too) the weakness is in the spongy spring growth that separates the rings. If the denser, solid summer wood in the rings is well defined and thicker than the spring growth, my experience is there is a good bow in the wood.

The worst thing I can say about thin rings is they require caution when making an unbacked bow. Thin rings are easier to cut through accidentally than thicker rings.

There are many variables in the white woods and second-string woods. As experience increases, so does our knowledge. No better example exists than the old-timer mentioned earlier who tried to make an English bow out of ash. This bow was given to me by a fellow who bought a collection of wooden bows made by our bowyer of the bygone era. And our old friend had learned his lessons well. My informant told me the best bow of the lot was made of walnut. And it had wide, flat limbs.

# WESTERN INDIAN BOWS

*Steve Allely*

In the fall of 1976, I was mule deer hunting in the high desert country of eastern Oregon. Despite not seeing any game, just walking in the fresh high altitude air, tinged with the scent of sage, was reward enough. While working my way up a small ridge where there were usually deer, I began finding pieces and fragments of obsidian points scattered about. Some were older atlatl points, while others were obviously made for use with the bow and arrow. The ridge wasn't a village site, since most of the camps were situated around some nearby springs as evidenced by the presence of obsidian flakes and fire cracked rock. The points up on the ridge had been, in all likelihood, broken and lost during hunting since it was an excellent place to find deer browsing in the dim hours of dawn and twilight.

Being a flintknapper, I felt an affinity for these earlier hunters and craftsmen. They may have been "primitive" by modern standards, but there was nothing crude whatsoever about the beautifully flaked points I found lying about.

Keeping one eye on the ground for more points and the other out for deer, I followed the ridge to a pleasant opening in the middle of several mountain mahogany thickets. This was a prime place to sit and wait, I thought, since several trails came together there, and the visibility was good in all directions. It was ideal.

And that's when I spotted it.

Nestled away in a clump of sage not ten yards away was an ancient stone hunting blind. The lichen-covered rocks had fallen down here and there, but the masonry work was still evident. Quite obviously someone else had considered this a good site in times past, and had perhaps brought down a mule deer or even a bighorn sheep on this very spot.

I began wondering in earnest about what kinds of bows and arrows the Indians once used in this place. Ironically, though the most disposable part of an archer's tackle, the points were the only remaining article of all their bowhunting gear.

It dawned on me then that I didn't really know much about what these points were once hafted to, much less what they were shot from, even though, as a knapper, I had made hundreds of points like the ones I'd been finding that morning. And to say nothing of quivers, manufacturing skills, materials used, hunting techniques and the like. Just replicating stone points was becoming old hat. What did the *rest* of the gear look like? I had to know. It was at that instant that the traditional archery "bug" bit me.

So from that point, I've been on a quest to find out more about the bows and arrows of the West Coast region, and have been fortunate enough to come up with some answers. Some were rare finds, such as the friend Ivan Sherk, who, as a boy, had been taught by an old Modoc Indian about hunting and making traditional bows and arrows. He, in turn, passed his knowledge on to me, so I've had the good fortune of obtaining information second-hand from an original source, as well as from study in dozens of museums and private collections. Some pieces of the puzzle are still missing, but after years of study a clearer picture of the weapons used by Western Indians has emerged.

By definition, when we speak of West Coast bows, we're talking about flat bows (both sinew-backed and unbacked) that were made and used by the Native Americans in the Far West. They ranged in use from the Chumash Indians in southern California northward to the Tlingit Indians on the Northwest Coast. A good portion of the northern and western Great Basin should be included, as well. There, flat bow fragments have been found in caves and were in use among the Paiutes and other peoples on both sides of the Cascade Range and on into the western parts of the Columbia Plateau. While these bows came in all shapes and sizes and varied from region to region, most were quite short by modern archery standards, especially the sinew-backed bows, some of which were as short as 30 inches (that's 76.2 cm. for you metric folk), while others, especially the unbacked bows, could be 50 inches or more.

Most of the sinew-backed bows averaged between 36 and 44 inches, which generally wouldn't be a functional length without the backing. In addition, they were often highly reflexed, resembling a shallow letter "C" when unstrung and viewed from the side. Sometimes the shrinking of the sinew-backing was solely responsible for the reflex, but some Indians in the California area reflexed their bows in a reverse position by heating or steaming them prior to applying the sinew-backing. Some bows were made while still green, which would make this process easier. To hold the bow in position while applying the sinew, they were sometimes actually strung backwards, then left that way until the sinew dried.

Generally the bows were made and well-tillered before sinewing. I've made my replica bows this way and even shot them, although never at full draw, especially on short bows. When the tillering is satisfactory, they are then recurved at the tips and reflexed. After the sinew is applied and completely dry, any final tillering and tuning of the bow is done.

Regular hide or animal glue was made for backing bows, but fish glue was a frequent substitute. Some people, such as the Sierra Miwok, added roasted Chlorogallum roots to their fish glue for a binder. Salmon skins and sturgeon jaws were most often boiled to make glue. In a primitive setting, glue was sometimes made in soapstone or shallow clay bowls. Water-tight cooking baskets could also be used by dropping in hot cooking rocks to generate boiling temperatures without hurting the basket. After the glue was made, it was often formed into small balls and dried for later use. A bow to be sinewed was lightly scratched longitudinally with a serrated stone flake or roughed up with an abrasive stone, and cleansed of oil or grease with a scrubbing of water and ashes. When needed, the dried glue was dipped into warm water and sort of "crayoned" onto the back of the prepared bow. Then the sinew, which had been previously split or shredded by pounding, was soaked or chewed to soften it. This wet sinew was laid down piece by piece onto the glue coating. After the entire back was covered, the sinew was carefully rubbed into the glue layer and then the whole bow wrapped in bark strips or twine to flatten down the sinew and keep it from lifting up during the drying process. This wrapping was especially needed if the bow had curved tips. After the sinew dried, a second layer of glue was applied over the sinew backing. Saxton Pope wrote of Ishi using this technique. In the days before electric crockpots this was the easiest method to use, and I've successfully sinewed bows in this manner.

Other Indians did dip their sinew strands in warm, liquid glue in the more common way. Some, such as the Miwok mentioned earlier, kept glue in their mouths so that when the sinew was chewed it was also being coated with glue.

Whichever glue method was used, a common trait on West Coast bows was the tight wrapping of the sinew-backing after the glue cooled and gelled and was no longer sticky to the touch. I believe there were some advantages to this. When the sinew layer was wrapped, the excess glue squeezed up out of the sinew strands, helping to insure a much stronger bond, and perhaps helping the sinew to work a bit more efficiently. The twine wrapping would retard the drying of the sinew somewhat, but this could be circumvented by removing a few wraps of the twine every day or so as it dries out. Often, on old bows, the twine and bark wrap marks can still be seen. The Maidu Indians of California sinewed their bows in this way to make sure the sinew-backing didn't crack or separate during the drying process.

Self bows with no backing were also made and used up and down the West Coast. One reason for the self bow's coexistence alongside the sinew-backed bows could be that the unbacked ones were used on wet days when it would have been hard to keep a backed bow dry. This may well explain why the sinew-backed bows become less common in the wetter northern climates, especially in Washington and British Columbia.

The width of the bows varied depending upon regional styles. Some were as narrow as 1-1/2", while some of the so-called "paddle bows" of the northern California Indians were as wide as three inches, or more. Between 2 and 2-1/2" seems to be a common average width. Oftentimes, the width depended upon how the bow was to be utilized. Saxton Pope, who recorded much about Ishi and Yahi archery, mentions that among the Yana Indians a light hunting bow would be three fingers wide, while a powerful hunting or war bow would be four fingers in width. I suspect that similar rules of measurement were in effect for most all tribal groups up and down the West Coast.

In cross section, most bows exhibited a flat, lenticular shape while in others the belly was quite flat with rounded backs. With others, this order was reversed, with the belly rounded and the back very flat. I have a well-preserved ancient bow which was found in a peat marsh in lower Klamath Lake in northern California. The bow is exactly three feet long, appears to be made of juniper and has a slightly rounded belly and a flat back. Crisscross diagonal scratchings are present on the back of this bow where it was once backed with sinew (which is no longer present). With the backing in place, it was probably lenticular in

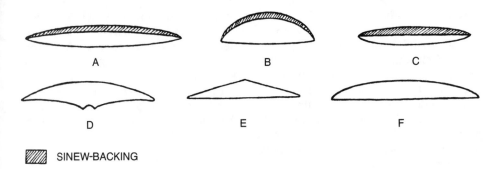

▨ SINEW-BACKING

*Bow cross sections: A) Hupa-Karok, B) Wintu, C) Ancient Modoc, D) Nootka, E) Nootka, and F) Kwakuitl.*

cross section with the wood forming one half and the sinew forming the other half. This little bow measures an inch and a half at its widest point and is preserved in a highly reflexed position.

Some other interesting cross sections occurred in bows from Washington and British Columbia, where rounded backs and grooves and flutes that run length-ways down the bow bellies can be found. Several Nootka bows I've seen were made this way. Others, like some of the Kwakiutl bows, had finely incised sets of lines carved or even burned into the bellies. Some of the Northwest Coast bows had ridges running down the middle of the back and belly, forming a flat diamond in cross section. Others had a ridge only along the back and formed a flat triangular shape. Some bows, especially from the Oregon area, had a trian-gular cross section near the tips of the bow, as well as in the handle, as if it were some sort of regional style.

A fragment of a prehistoric bow found in the Upper Klamath Lake marsh in southern Oregon was made in this fashion as well. It has a narrow, thick trian-gular shape at the tip which then gradually flattens out into the usual lenticular shape about six inches below the shoulder nocks. It has deep scratch marks preserved in the back for the adhesion of sinew and even has scorch marks still visible where the maker apparently attempted to recurve the tips with heat. It's unfortunate that we don't know what the rest of the bow once looked like.

I'll mention here that while this is an old design, I would be cautious about incorporating it into a bow you may be thinking of making. A ridge running down the back of a bow takes up a lot of the tension stress (and concentrates it) instead of distributing the force more evenly over the back, making it much more apt to break. Other problems can occur as well. I once made a 36 inch sinew-backed yew bow based on this design. It shot quite well, but since it was triangu-lar in the handle as well as in the tips, it eventually chrysalled and collapsed at the grip. This was partially due to the fact that I used inferior, low elevation yew, but while a triangular shape places extra tension along its ridge on the back, it also places extra compression along the belly due to the thicker cross section. This is especially true with a heavy sinew-backing, although I'm sure that shooting a 36-inch bow with a 20-inch draw stressed the design to its maximum limits. Had the bow been longer, chances are it would still be shootable today.

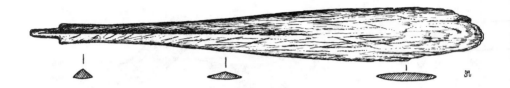

*Prehistoric bow fragment from Upper Klamath Lake, Oregon. Overall length 14 inches. Mid-limb at widest point, 1-15/16 inches.*

Recurved tips occurred on many Indian bows from the West Coast. Some were highly recurved, employing what is known as a "working recurve," while others showed no sign of recurves at all. Large working recurves, especially on longer self bows (without sinew), seem to show up more from the Oregon country northward. One long self bow I've seen from the lower Columbia River area had such recurves along with longitudinal grooves cut into the belly for the bow string at the bend, apparently to help keep it centered. Many bows from the Puget Sound area also had large recurves, particularly those made by the Kwakuitl.

Many of the shorter sinew-backed bows were bent only at the nock or shoulders to help prevent the bow string from slipping off while at full draw. This has happened to me a few times, and, after the shock wears off, it makes one a believer in bending the tips back to prevent it. One nifty trick, used by many Indians in the California region to bend the tips without breaking them off, was

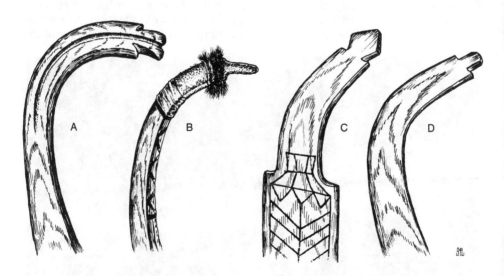

*Recurved tips: A) Self bow of oak, Lower Columbia River, B) Wintu sinew-backed bow of yew, with rawhide covered tips and fur wrap string silencer, C) Kwakuitl yew bow showing incised and burnt decoration lines on belly, and D) recurved bow of vine maple(?) presumed to be from western Oregon.*

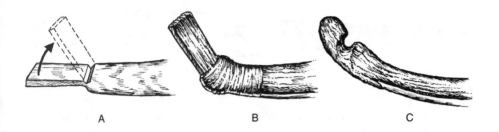

A                              B                              C

*A) Hupa bow tip showing kerf, B) same bow tip after sinewing, and C) Sierra Miwok bow showing built-up nock made from sinew.*

to cut a shallow "V" shaped kerf, or groove, on the back of the bow between the nock grooves. The area was heated or steamed, then the tips bent and tied into position. Any weakness incurred in the tip by cutting the groove would be more than made up by the laminating effect of the sinew-backing, which was applied over it. I owe this nugget of information to a mouse which chewed the sinew off of an old California bow, thereby revealing how the maker had bent the bow tips. Others, such as the Miwok Indians of California, solved the problem of slipping bow strings by building up multiple layers of sinew to form a sort of hooked-type ear at the tips.

Sometimes, in addition to this method, the whole end of the bow tip was encased in a glued-down wrap of rawhide for a distance of two to three inches. This was an almost universal trait on sinew-backed bows from the northeastern California region among the tribes from the Mt. Lassen and Shasta areas. It shows up some on northwestern California bows as well. One reason for this wrap was to prevent the sinew string from chafing the sinew on the end of the

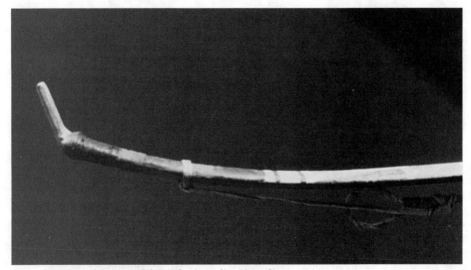

*Bent tab-style nock on one of the author's replica Hupa bows.*

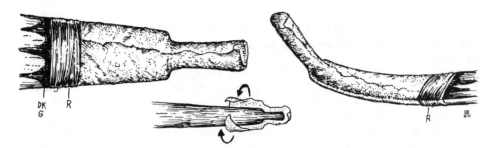

*Rawhide wrap on Pit River or Achumawi bow tip from northeastern California.*

bow. The rawhide provided a slight padding to the bowstring, which also helped keep it from fraying, and protected and strengthened the bow tip.

To prepare the tips of the bows for recurving, the bowyer often heated or steamed them. One clever Modoc technique for steaming bow tips was to apply a piece of wet moss to the end of the bow and then place a hot rock out of the fire directly on top of the moss. The hot rock acted as a steam iron to force the heat and moisture down into the wood. When the rock was cool enough to pick up, the bow was usually ready for bending by tying it into a form of some sort and leaving it until cool and dry.

One final addition found frequently on many bows tips was a strip of mink or otter fur wrapped around the tip of the bow just below the nock. This helped silence the slap of the bow string when an arrow was released, and still remains an effective counter-measure to the problem of game "jumping the string."

Types of wood used for bows on the West Coast varied depending upon what was available. Pacific yew was generally the favorite among many peoples, while juniper, ash, cedar, vine maple, oak, chokecherry, and others were also utilized.

Most old bows that I've examined, both backed and unbacked, have been made from Pacific yew. Most have no sapwood present on them, except perhaps along the margins of a sinew-backed bow. On every self bow made from yew I've seen, however, the sapwood was completely removed, and the grain of the heartwood cut through rather indiscriminately. It could be that in wetter regions in the Northwest, such a bow wasn't as brittle as in a drier and colder interior climate. I assume that the Native Americans of the region knew that the real "spring" in a yew bow lay in its heartwood.

Even when yew was available, though, it wasn't always a first choice to bow-makers. Ishi, one of the last survivors of a small band of Yana Indians, used juniper for his bows. Although a softwood, juniper is surprisingly springy and efficient, especially when sinew-backed. It seems to have been used more in semi-arid regions, particularly on the eastern slopes of the Cascade Range. It was employed widely by the Paiutes in the Great Basin area and by the Klamath and Modoc Indians, as well as by the natives to the north on the Columbia Plateau. Some raise their eyebrows when informed that juniper makes good bow wood, but I suggest they try breaking a limb of it in half sometime. It is fairly easy to season without splitting and, due to its softness, works well with primitive tools.

Cedar was also utilized by a number of tribes. The beautiful little bows mentioned earlier, made by the Miwok in California, were of cedar (usually from a limb according to old accounts). Lewis and Clark, while at Fort Clatsop at the mouth of the Columbia river in 1805-1806, recorded that cedar was used for bows by the Clatsop Indians; "Their bows are extremely neat and very elastic, they are about two feet six inches long and two inches wide in the center, thence tapering gradually to the extremities, where they are 3/4 of an inch wide, they are very flat and thin formed of the heart of arbor vita or white cedar, the back of the bow being thickly covered with sinews of elk laid on with a glue which they make from the sturgeon; the string is made of the sinews of elk also."

Some dispute that true white cedar grows in this area, but I think we can safely assume that it was a cedar of some sort. Further up along the Northwest Coast, yellow cedar was used for bows by the Indians who relied greatly on the cedar trees for much of their material culture.

Vine maple makes a surprisingly effective bow wood, provided a straight enough piece of it can be found. The lower Umpqua Indians in western Oregon, and others, were supposed to have made use of it for bows. Quite a few of the bows from this area, I suspect, are made from it since they have a light blond-colored maple look about them. I have an old self bow, reputedly from the Siletz reservation in western Oregon, which appears to be vine maple, though it's hard to be certain since it's painted on both sides with red ochre – but it definitely isn't ash or yew. I've not stress-tested any vine maple as of yet, but I think it quite capable of taking a great deal of overdraw, since some of these bows were less than three feet long and weren't even sinew-backed!

Ash and oak were used for bows, too. The stout self bow from the lower Columbia River with the recurved tips mentioned earlier is made of oak, as is one very similar to it which the Oregon Historical Society has in its collection. Others bows from these woods are in existence, both backed and unbacked.

One interesting account made by Alexander Henery, who took part in the fur trade along the Columbia River in 1814, gives some details of archery equipment and mentions a bow that could have been made from ash, or even oak. His party had lost some of their goods to the local Indians and had taken a hostage in order to try and get them back. His journal reads; "I now had the curiosity to examine the quiver of arrows belonging to the prisoner. It was made of a cub of a black bear, the bow was flat and very strong, and uncommonly elastic bent backwards as already mentioned. There was 70 arrows loose in it, and a parcel carefully tied up with cedar bark containing 10 more arrows, these last we examined minutely and found they were poisoned, in this opinion, Caesino (a local friendly chief) confirmed it, small strips of the skin of the rattlesnake was sticking to the barb of about two inches long, this skin is stuck on by means of some glutinous substance which Caesino told us was poison also. Their arrows are neatly made, and are of cedar and tipped with hardwood and bone about 5 inches, and sharply barbed with iron, and painted a very neat green, red, brown, and yellow, some of them are fired in socket so as to leave the barb in the flesh when received there. Their bows are made of a very coarse grained wood exceedingly well polished and smooth and overlaid with sinews."

A few other bows were made from oak, such as a Pomo self bow I've examined, and the Kalapuya Indians of the Willamette Valley region reportedly used it, along with yew wood. I'm of the opinion that when it comes to making bows, especially sinew-backed, one doesn't always need the ultimate in bow wood to make a weapon that shoots and functions satisfactorily. Ivan, the friend of mine who knew the old Modoc Indian as a boy, told me that the top of a Douglas fir limb with tight growth rings makes a decent bow when sinew-backed. Undoubtedly this will surprise many people who tend to think of 2x4's when Douglas fir is mentioned, but I think the little short, heavily backed bows could almost be thought of more as a sinew bow that happens to be built on a wooden frame. As long as the wood in the frame can take the compression and not collapse, the bow functions.

Both limbs and trunk sections were used for bows. Generally, the top of a limb was used because the growth rings were much closer together. Some tribes had traditions about from which side of the tree trunk to take the stave. Some Indians along the Oregon coast stated that the stave should come off of the windy side of the tree, while others said that it should be taken from the uphill side. Interestingly enough, these are excellent ways to avoid compression wood, especially in yew, which tends to be brittle. Compression wood is the side of the tree which takes the lean, or weight of the tree, and some of the Indians, at least, were aware of this and knew how to avoid it.

Staves were often split from large limbs and trunks in a living tree. In an excellent paper on this subject, Phil Wilke records a number of juniper bow stave trees in Nevada which still bear the stave removal scars. To remove a stave from the tree trunk or large limb, two 'V' shaped notches were cut at the upper and lower end of the intended stave. This was done with a simple cobble chopper or in later years with iron axes or hatchets. The stave was often left in the tree with the bark on to prevent checking while it seasoned. Then later, by means of a prying tool and perhaps some antler wedges, the stave could simply be split out of the tree between the two notches. Green wood can be split from a tree with this method, as well.

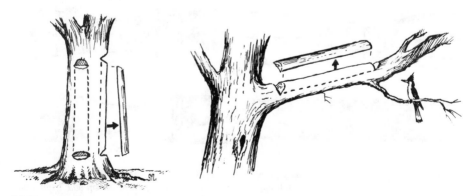

*"Split method" of bow stave removal from tree trunks and limbs.*

Some Indians preferred seasoned wood such as that cut from standing trees killed by fires. Others, like the Hupa, made their bows from green yew, carving it in a short amount of time to the desired shape. These green bows were then stored in humid places such as the sweat lodge until completely dry. One Shasta Indian I heard of made self bows from digger pine trees. His technique for seasoning his staves was to bury them in the mud of a stream bed and leave them for several months. Various seasoning techniques were clearly in vogue from place to place.

Bows were carved in a number of ways when the stave was ready. Often, according to many accounts, they were painstakingly fashioned with stone, shell, or even bone tools. Some of these tools functioned as knife edges while others worked like a planer or scraper. Rough stones such as sandstone and abrasive volcanic lavas were used as rasps. In the old days, stone adzes were sometimes used as well. Green wood is easier to work with stone tools, which may explain why it was often used. Pumice, fine sandstone, and horsetail rush were utilized for final sanding.

Some bows had hand grips on them while others didn't. Most sinew-backed bows had a wrapped buckskin grip. A few had a combination of buckskin and cordage while others were trimmed with fur at each end of the grip. On some of the short, backed bows the grip was offset so that when the arrow rested on top of the hand it was close to the center of the bow. Some bows from the Northwest Coast had grips of wild cherry bark wrapped over a padding of hair or, in later years, cloth of some sort. From the late 1800's, cloth grips show up on bows, as well.

A few bows from the northern California area had straps on the front of the grip which kept the bow from jumping out the hand when an arrow was released. This would seem to indicate the Indians were aware of the advantages of not gripping the bow too tightly, which reduces accuracy.

Many bows from the West Coast were painted, some elaborately, while others weren't painted at all. Painted bows from this region are usually associated with the beautiful designs executed by the Karok, Yurok, Hupa, Tolowa, Modoc, and

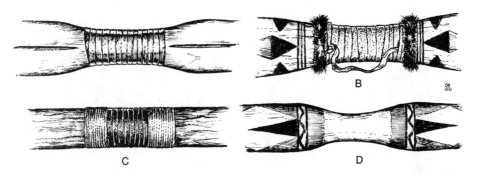

*Various bow grips. A) wild cherry bark on Nootka bow, B) buckskin wrap with fur trim and hand strap from northern California, C) combination of leather and cordage on Clatsop bow from mouth of Columbia River, and D) plain wooden handle on Modoc bow.*

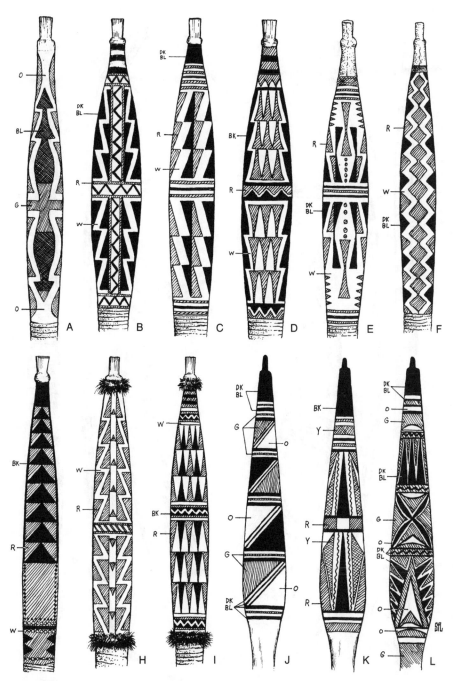

*Painted designs on bows from northern California and southern Oregon. A) Tolowa, B) Hupa, C) Hupa, D) Karok, E) Hupa, F) Hupa, G) Hupa or Tolowa, H) Karok, I) Hupa, J, K, and L) Modoc.*

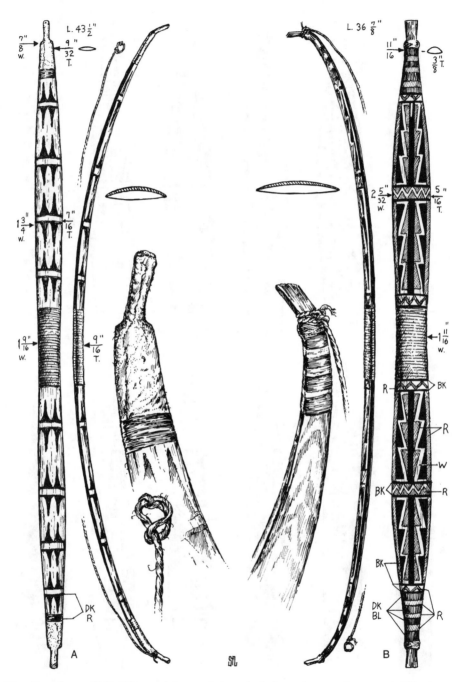

*West Coast bows. A) Pit River or Achumawi sinew-backed yew from northeastern California, with rawhide covered tips and two-ply string, B) Hupa sinew-backed yew from northwestern California with two-ply string.*

other nearby tribes in the northern California area. Many of these bows had striking triangular designs painted in various colors with black, red and blue the most common, along with occasional use of green, orange, and yellow. Often these were painted on a white background, which provided even more visual contrast.

Other bows made by neighboring tribes were a bit less elaborate. Further south into California, they tended to become somewhat less fancy with a few exceptions; the same is true further north into the Oregon and Washington area. The bows from these regions were fairly monochromatic with less use of multiple colors, painted with simple designs or a solid color, with red being a common choice. Some bows from the Northwest Coast were an exception, with beautiful designs reminiscent of the highly developed art of the region.

Many Indians in the Oregon area, especially west of the Cascade Range such as the Tillamook and the Chinook, occasionally painted the backs of their bows black and sometimes the bellies red. The reason may well be that a light colored bow in the dark heavy undergrowth typical of the region showed up like a beacon unless darkened. Some old arrows I've examined from this area, and others as well, had the foreshafts or several inches of the front ends painted a dark shade, perhaps for the same reason. Even if deer and elk are color-blind, they certainly notice a light colored bow, so painting weapons a darker shade makes good camouflage sense.

This is something to consider if you're contemplating making a replica bow for hunting. I no longer use bows painted with white backgrounds when I hunt in darker wooded areas, because the deer spot them too easily. The point is, try keeping the overall color scheme of the back of a bow compatible with where you're planning to use it. A brightly painted bow may look pretty and be authentic, but a nervous deer you'd like to put your hunting tag on may not be as convinced.

Paint pigments used on bows and arrows came from a number of sources. The white backgrounds were often made from white clay or sometimes pulverized rotten shell from old shell middens mixed with glue for a binder. Black could be made from ground charcoal, or, as Ishi mentioned, fish eyes. Red was often made by taking dull red or even yellow ochre and heating it in a fire to further intensify the color. Earth ochres such as red, orange, yellow, and green were ground, mixed with water, and then the water poured off into another container so that the fine sediment settled to the bottom. This was later removed and mixed with glue for a binder. The water-separated pigment could be dried, reground into a flour-fine powder, and then mixed with pitch or plant gums for a binder. Larkspur blossoms mixed with mountain grape berries and salmon glue made a dark blue used by many of the California Indians. Up on the Northwest Coast, copper oxide was used for a blue-green pigment and salmon eggs for a binder. In later years of course, after the coming of the whites, commercial colors such as vermillion were utilized. Unfortunately, much of the know-how about obtaining many of the old colors from native plants and other sources has been lost with time.

Bowstrings are something I'll mention only briefly. Most were of sinew and were two-ply, though I've seen some three-ply strings as well. Some of the Indians up on the Northwest Coast made finely plaited or braided sinew strings.

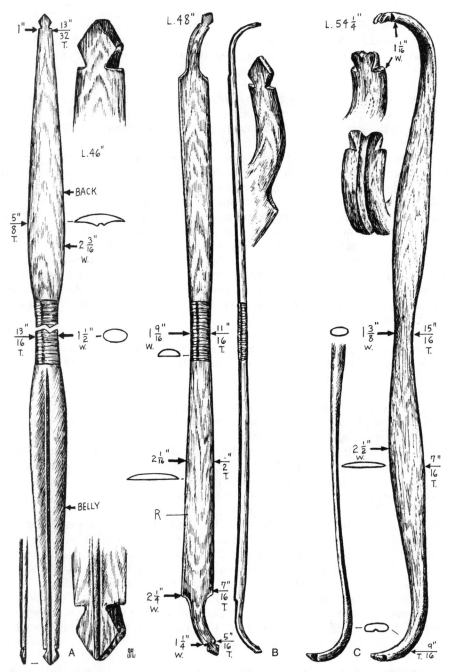

A) *Nootka self bow of yew with cherry bark grip from Northwest Coast, B) Kwakuitl self bow of yew with cherry bark grip from Northwest Coast, and C) self bow of oak from lower Columbia River, possibly Chinook.*

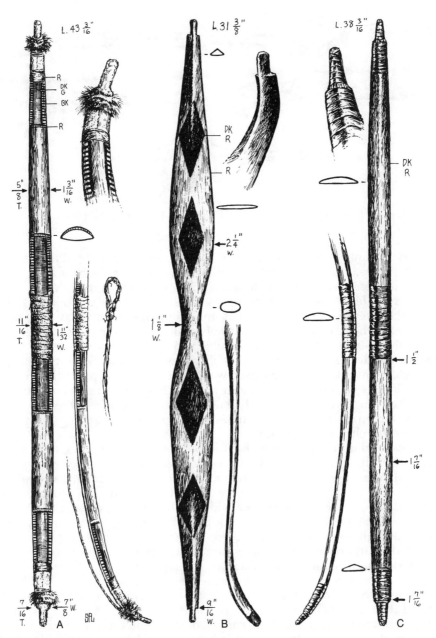

*A) Wintu-style sinew-backed bow from northern California with two-ply sinew string, and tips covered with rawhide and string silencer fur wraps, B) short self bow, possibly of vine maple, thought to be from western Oregon (exact tribe unknown), with triangular tips and belly painted similar to back, except in light and dark yellowish green, C) sinew-backed yew bow from Lower Columbia River with wild cherry bark grip and tip wraps (exact tribe unknown, but possibly Chinook).*

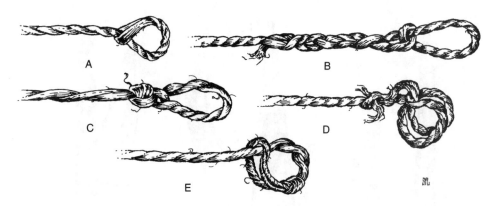

*Sinew bow string loops: A) Tolowa, B) Pomo, C) Wintu, D) Hupa, and E) Pit River or Achumawi.*

I've read accounts of bear, raccoon, and seal intestines being dried and twisted into bowstrings. Plant fiber, such as milkweed, nettle, or dogbane were used, but I think these were a substitute when sinew (or other animal by-products), weren't available. Most fiber bowstrings weren't nearly as durable as sinew, though they were less affected by moisture or humidity which may have made them a better choice on a wet day. Some of the Indians on the coast made strings out of whale sinew when it could be obtained. I've seen whale sinew, and it comes in wonderful lengths that makes elk sinew look short. Some strings were made with woven loops at their ends while others were simply tied with various half hitches each time they were strung. The loops were fairly common and vary in how they were made, but I've noticed few of the slip-noose style commonly found on Plains bows. Sometimes, to help water-proof strings, they were coated with pitch or even greased.

No bow would be complete without arrows. As with the bows, there was a wide variety up and down the West Coast. Basically, there were two types of arrows, **simple,** in which the shaft was a single piece of wood, and **compound,** made up of two or more parts, usually a foreshaft set into the end of a main shaft. Both types of arrows were used widely in the West. Lewis and Clark mentioned these in their journals at Ft. Clatsop; "...the arrow is formed of two parts usually though sometimes entire, those formed of two parts are unequally divided, the part on which the feathers are placed occupies 4/5 of its length and is formed of light white pine rather larger than a swans quill, in the lower extremity of this is a circular mortice secured by sinews wrapped around it; this mortice receives the one end of the 2nd part which is of smaller size than the first and about five inches long, in the end of this the barb is fixed and confined with sinews, the barb is either iron, copper, or stone – in this form forming at its point a greater angle than those of any other Indians I have observed. The shorter part of the arrow is of harder wood, as are also the whole of the arrow where it is of one piece only...." The journal goes on to state that these arrows would float well and could easily be recovered if a shot at waterfowl missed.

However, there were a number of additional reasons for making compound shafts. Although it may have been a bit of extra work to drill out the hole in the

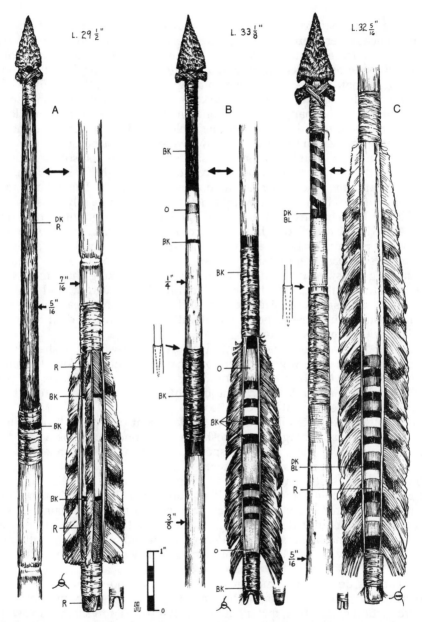

*West Coast arrows: A) Chumash arrow from cave find in Santa Barbara County, southern California. Point of gray Monterrey chert set in asphaltum and lashed with sinew. Phragmites cane main shaft. Hawk feather fletching. B) Shasta arrow from northern California. Compound shaft. Obsidian point set into nock with pitch and lashed with sinew. Sinew lashings are all painted black, possibly with pitch. Feathers thought to be Blue Grouse tail feathers. C) Pit River or Achumawi compound arrow. Obsidian point. Foreshaft and portions of main shaft have tiny cross grooves present from using horsetail rush for sanding. Redtail hawk tail feather fletching.*

end of the main shaft to accept the foreshaft, in case of damage to the point it became much easier to make and replace foreshafts than an entire arrow, especially if made from scratch with old tools. Just about any hardwood twig or shoot will made foreshafts, whereas it was much more difficult to find longer pieces for the main shafts. Often, when hitting a hard object, the end of the shaft shattered or split, making it necessary to cut several inches off in order to repair and renotch it. If this happened to a solid-shafted arrow several times, length was lost and eventually the arrow became useless by virtue of being too short.

Another prime reason foreshafted arrows were used was because some of the arrow shaft material employed for main shafts was simply too soft or hollow to support the direct impact of a shot and were too lightweight for serious hunting arrows. Phragmites cane arrows are a good example of this. The Indians added stout foreshafts to them and the weight factor made them deadly missiles capable of being launched from strong bows. This was true, too, of arrows made from red cedar or other straight grained conifers, as referred to by Alexander Henery and perhaps by Lewis and Clark, as well. Quite a number of arrows on the Northwest Coast were made of cedar. A number of other arrow materials have fairly good sized piths that run up the center, making them more like a piece of natural tubing. Elderberry shoots, nine bark, currant, and first year ocean spray shoots all have sizeable piths. While it's a good idea to place hardwood foreshafts in these type of woods, it's also easier to drill them out, especially with stone or bone tools.

When shooting at bigger game with this sort of arrow, the foreshaft usually comes out. You nearly always recover your main shaft, and tracking the animal may be easier due to a better blood trail because the arrow no longer plugs the entry wound. I've never read anything like this in an ethnography report, but, speaking from experience, it works quite well.

And finally, foreshafts allowed quick replacement of a point broken in the field, an obvious advantage. The foreshaft could conceivably be a carryover from the days of the atlatl, since the spears, or darts as they're called, had the same sort of foreshaft mechanism in common use.

Single shafted, or self arrows, showed up in much of the Far West and were longer than those found in the Great Plains area, usually 27 to 33 inches long. One reason for long arrow lengths may have been a need for accuracy, as the West Coast people hunted on foot and had to make the first shot count. Shaft grooves were found on some Western arrows, although not as frequently as on the Plains. Usually, there were three of them, and they tended to be shallow and quite straight.

One curious detail that sometimes shows up on solid-shafted arrows from northern California and southern Oregon was a wrap of sinew present on the forward section of the shaft, making it look as if it were a foreshafted arrow. I've seen this on Klamath, Modoc, Shasta, Hupa, and Karok arrows. The Maidu were said to have made their arrows this way, as well. This was always sort of a puzzler until I measured the distance from the rear nock to the sinew wraps on some old arrows. It usually was from 22 to 25 inches, which is about the draw limit for many short bows. It seems logical that the sinew wrapping could well be drawpoint markers that work by feel. If a foreshafted arrow was made so that

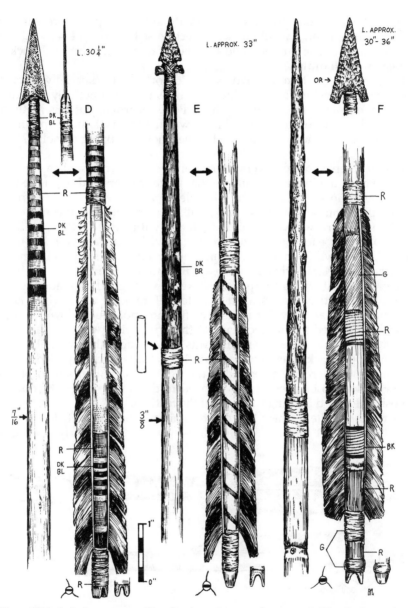

L. 30¼"

L. APPROX. 33"

L. APPROX. 30"- 36"

DK BL

D

E

OR →

F

R

DK BL

DK BR

R

R

G

3/8"

R

7/16"

R

BK

R DK BL

1"

R

0"

G R

*D) Hupa solid-shafted arrow, possibly of syringa, from northwestern California. Iron point. Horsetail rush smoothing marks on shaft. Hawk wing feather fletching. E) Klamath or Modoc solid-shafted arrow with forward sinew wrap. Obsidian point. Hawk wing feather fletching. Possibly from northeastern California or southern Oregon. F) Phragmites cane arrow from the Great Basin in southeastern Oregon. This drawing is a reconstruction based on fragments of arrows from several caves, including Roaring Springs and Catlow Caves. Canadian goose wing fletch. Foreshaft of greasewood. Stone point is "Rose Spring" style, although side notch points were more common among the Northern Paiute in northern Nevada and southeastern Oregon.*

the draw limit would come to the spot where the sinew wrap was present on the main shaft mortice joint, it would make perfect sense to apply the same idea to a solid-shafted arrow. The hunter could feel the wrap of sinew hit the knuckle of his bow hand at full draw.

I've tried this on my hunting arrows and it works well, especially when I'm concentrating on placing the shot. Many Indians shot instinctively and didn't always use the exact same draw length, as Pope recorded, but this method at least indicated the maximum limit of a draw. This theory is pure speculation, but it seems to be a logical explanation for the sinew wrapping on solid-shafted arrows.

Fletching feathers generally were shorter on Western arrows when compared to those found on the Plains. It could be that if the feathers laid upon the bow's grip, they made noise when drawn. The silence factor wasn't as important if thundering up to buffalo on horse back, but it was an important consideration for foot hunters. Arrows were usually fletched with three feathers held with sinew wrapping at each end, and sometimes with glue, as well. Up on the Northwest Coast, two feathers were commonly used, both split quills and two whole feathers laid flat in what's known as **tangential** fletching.

Feathers were split with a sharp stone flake, or were gently pounded to separate the quill. Often they were soaked in water before being used, which helped them to stretch out and lay flat on the shaft when not glued down. Feathers were usually attached at the nock end of the arrow first with a wrap of wet sinew. Frequently, the web of the feather was lashed under the sinew along with the quill. After the back sinew-wrap dried, the feather could be pulled forward without slipping, where it was bound at the front with another strand of moist sinew. If glue was to be used, it was applied to the underside of the quill just before positioning and binding the front of the feathers.

Most arrows had the feathers laid on straight, but some were fletched with a definite helix or twist to them. The feathers were trimmed fairly close to the

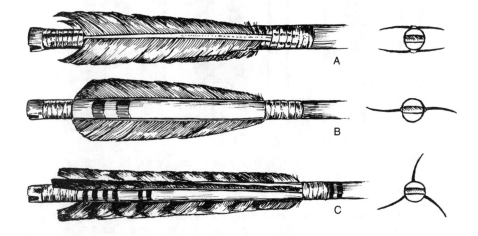

*Types of fletching. A) Tangential, B) two split feathers, and C) three split feathers.*

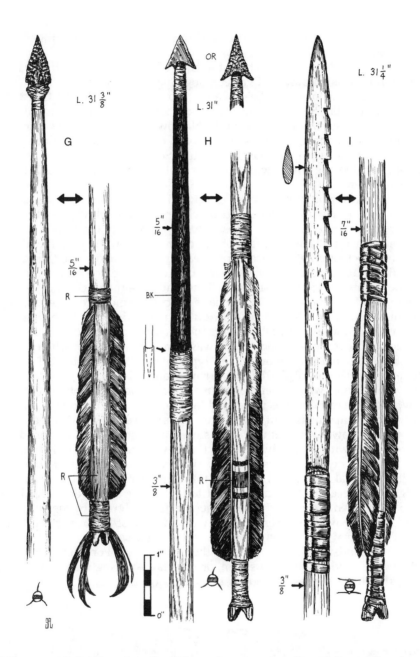

L. 31 3/8"

G

L. 31"

H

L. 31 1/4"

I

*G) Self arrow with obsidian point collected in northern or western Oregon. Exact tribe unknown. H) Chinook compound arrow from Columbia River area. Main shaft of red cedar. Unidentified fletching feathers. Small iron point, similar in size and shape to stone points described by Lewis and Clark. I) Nootka compound arrow, red cedar main shaft, bone foreshaft and point. Goose feather tangential fletch with wild cherry bark wrapping.*

185

shaft with a sharp stone flake, though sometimes they were singed to the desired shape.

Generally, sinew was used to bind the ends of the feathers but if it was lacking plant fiber was employed. I've seen dogbane on some old Phragmites cane arrow fragments from Great Basin caves. Up on the Northwest Coast, from about the Columbia River northward, wild cherry bark was commonly used. This may be because the dampness of the Northwest tended to make sinew lashings a bit less practical, whereas cherry bark can be stretched slightly when wrapped and is fairly impervious to moisture. Some Indians who did use sinew wrappings coated the sinew with pitch for waterproofing, or painted it with a pitch-based paint.

Types of arrow wood on the West Coast varied widely from region to region and, like with bow woods, depended much upon availability. Most tribes had their particular preferences but substitutes were readily employed when the first choice wasn't at hand. A few of the main arrow woods were: wild rose, syringa (or mock orange), serviceberry, ocean spray (or arrowwood), hazel, currant, Indian plum (or oso berry), ninebark, chokecherry, elderberry, red osier (or dogwood), snowberry, maple shoots, willow, and Phragmites cane.

Conifer wood was used for main shafts on compound arrows, especially in northern areas, since it could be split out in perfectly straight pieces. Some woods used for these split-timber shafts included red cedar, Port Orford cedar, fir, spruce, and even yew wood, which was sometimes used for self arrows and foreshafts. As mentioned before, many types of hardwood will work for foreshafts along with any of the harder arrow woods listed above. In the Great Basin, where wood was sometimes scarce, greasewood, mountain mahogany, willow, and even cattail stems were used for foreshafts on Phragmites arrows.

This isn't a complete list, but covers the main arrow shaft woods used.

Shoots for arrows were cut and then stored in bundles until seasoned. They were straighted with heat or by bending them every day as they dried until seasoned, which, in my opinion, is the easiest way to do it. Arrows were reduced in size with stone flakes snapped in half to form a planer scraper (in the same way the edge of a piece of glass can be used today). After they were carved down close to the desired form, they were further sanded and trued by means of a pair of sandstone arrow smoothers, which worked almost like a sort of "sander lathe." The shaft was spun on the thigh and rotated between the two grooved halves of the sandstone blocks held together in the hand. For a final smooth finish, they were sanded with Equisetum, or horsetail scouring rush. Often, on old arrows, the tiny grooves caused by the ridges on the rush can still be seen,

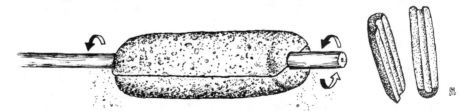

*How sandstone shaft smoothers were used.*

resembling threading on a machine bolt. Up on the Northwest Coast, sharkskin was sometimes used for sandpaper.

Phragmities cane arrows were usually cut when green and stored until dry. They were then straightened with heat by gently bending them over a hot grooved stone, frequently steatite, heated in a fire. A foreshaft was normally added and sometimes a wooden "nock plug" in the rear for the bow string. After fletching, they were pretty much ready for use "as is."

Many of the better-made arrow shafts were **barreled,** or were thickest in diameter in the center or a bit forward from center. The merits of this will be addressed in more detail in a chapter in Volume II of *The Traditional Bowyer's Bible,* but suffice it to say that they were much more balanced and flew well even when tipped with the so-called small "bird" points (which are, in reality, points for larger game). I've seen some Hupa arrows from northwestern California that were so beautifully made and barreled they appear to be made from dowels – until the knots in the shaft revealed they were made from a shoot.

The flared nock common on most Plains arrows wasn't found much, if at all, in the California area. But from the Columbia River northward it showed up regularly, especially on cedar arrows. Whether this was due to the use of a pinch grip arrow release, or is an adaptation to withstand breakage of soft woods from the force of the bowstring upon release is not certain.

There were many kinds of points in use on West Coast arrows, some of them quite elaborate. Stone points were in use up until historic times. Obsidian, or volcanic glass, was probably the most common material used, followed by jasper, agate, chert, opalite, petrified wood, and others. Bottle glass was used in later times along with iron and some copper, although the metal points tended to be much smaller than those found on the Plains. Generally, points were hafted with pitch, then lashed with sinew which was sometimes painted or covered with pitch. Ground slate points were used on the Northwest Coast along with ground shell. I've even seen a few carved from soapstone, or something similar to it.

Points made from ground antler and bone were also used. Many arrows from the Northwest Coast had a long barbed bone point up to seven or so inches which doubled as a foreshaft. Most all of these were set into red cedar main shafts. Other types of bone points in other areas looked more like a typical arrowhead. The northern California Indians sometimes made a multi-barbed bone foreshaft tipped with a stone point. One elaborate prehistoric type from the Columbia Plateau region had a carved bone point set into a carved and

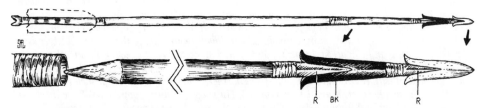

*Prehistoric arrow from Dechutes River in northern Oregon. Cedar main shaft with hardwood foreshaft. Carved and painted wooden point tipped with second carved point of bone.*

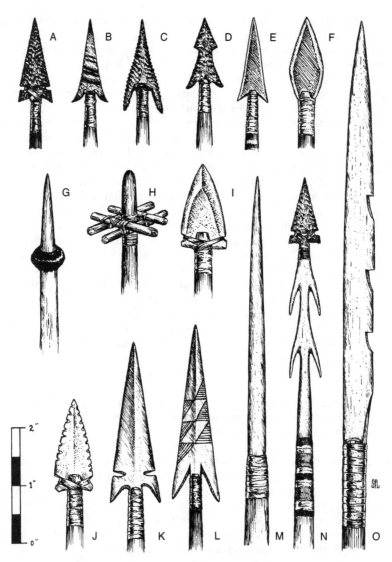

Points on West Coast arrows. A) Shasta obsidian side-notch. This type of point was used widely in the Western U.S. B) Banded agate stemmed point typical of Columbia River area, C) Gunther barbed, or Rogue River point of jasper from southern Oregon and northwestern California. D) Unique "double-pointed" stone arrowhead occasionally found along the Columbia River and its tributaries. E and F) Late style metal points found along the West Coast. G) Klamath water-skipping duck arrow showing the pitch ring which acted as a hydroplane. H) Laced stick bird arrow made by Ishi. I) Ground slate point from northern California. J) Ground shell point from northern California coast. K and L) Two types of Hupa bone or antler points. M) Bone tip shaped like a wooden foreshaft, from northern California. N) Hupa barbed bone foreshaft tipped with stone point. Possibly for war use. O) Barbed bone point set into red cedar shaft and lashed with cherry bark. Nootka, Northwest Coast.

painted wooden point. This was then hafted into the end of a hardwood fore-shaft socketed into a main shaft of cedar. A fairly labor-intensive missile.

The wooden blunt tip was quite common, and was used throughout the region for small game arrows. Often these had a reinforcing wrap of sinew just behind the tip to prevent splitting. I can say from experience that it's a waste of arrow points hunting rabbits in a rocky area with stone tipped arrows. For birds, a type of blunt was often used that can only be described as looking like a tic-tac-toe design of short twigs laced to the front of the arrow with sinew. Another ingenious type of arrow that the Klamath and Modoc Indians made was for shooting waterfowl sitting on water. A Phragmites arrow with an insert-ed foreshaft of hard wood had a small ball of sinew coated with pitch molded around the shaft about one inch back from the sharpened wooden tip. When shot at a duck on the water, the pitch ring acted as a hydroplane and made the arrow skip across the water for a short distance. If the point of aim was just below a bird on the water a hit was almost guaranteed. I've made and shot some of these arrows and they work well. Some old arrows had these "skipping tips" carved from the solid piece of wood used for the foreshaft. On some, the sinew lashings on the whole arrow were coated with pitch to make them waterproof.

Many arrows were painted, as was referred to in the excerpt from the Henery journals. Like bows, they varied widely from place to place, but it is sometimes possible to pick out what region they're from based on how they were painted. Generally, like on Plains arrows, the ownership crest was present under the fletchings but sometimes it extended farther. Patterns differ, ranging from the common cross bands of color to barber pole-like spirals. Sinew lashings were often painted, possibly to help repel moisture. And, as mentioned earlier, the foreshafts or front of the arrow was frequently painted, which may have been to darken it and help in camouflage. Most arrows were painted with only one or two colors but sometimes more were used. Red and black were the most common with blue, green, yellow, and others following behind.

Quivers, of course, were needed to keep arrows protected and there were many types. Some were made from prized animal hides. In northern California, quivers were made from otter, martin, mink, bobcat, raccoon, deer heads and necks, and sometimes bear. Quivers from this region were usually case-skinned, turned inside out, and decorated with abalone shell disks, various types of beads, feathers, and woodpecker scalps, especially on prized otter quivers. Some were lavishly ornate and others plain and utilitarian. Often they weren't soft-tanned but left a bit stiff so they would better retain their form.

Usually, the quiver was a single container which held both bow and arrows, with no separate bowcase. The smaller mink and martin quivers held only a half dozen arrows or so. It's quite probable that they were mainly for short hunting excursions. Case-skinned pelts with the fur side out, as well as hides of tanned buckskin, were used in other areas. They usually had a carrying strap added. Moss or dried grass was stuffed into the bottom to serve as padding for the deli-cate stone or bone tipped arrows.

Up to the northwest, where things were often done quite differently, many quivers were side-opening. Lewis and Clark commented on the quivers they observed; "...the quiver is usually the skin of a young bear or that of a wolf

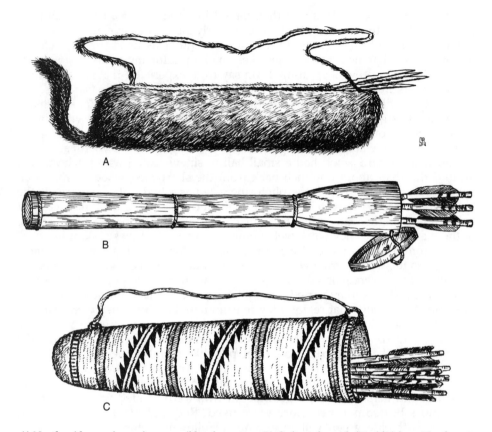

*A) Nootka side-opening quiver, possibly of sea otter, B) Cedar tube with fitted lid from Northwest Coast tribes. C) Modoc basketry quiver of split tule.*

invariably open at the side instead of the end as the quiver of other Indians generally are, this construction appears to answer better for the canoe than if they were open at the end only." One old painting I've seen of a Nootka hunter shows him carrying a side opening quiver, with the arrow tips protruding from what might be a sea otter pelt. Side-opening quivers would have some protective advantages if used in wet climates, such as the Pacific Northwest. The arrows could be completely protected inside this type of quiver as could the short 30 inch sinew-backed bows that Lewis and Clark referred to, which may be one reason the bows were made so short.

Wooden tube and box type quivers were also used along the Northwest Coast. Made from cedar, some had lids that fitted down on them like a circular hat box lid. Some may have been more of a type of storage box to store and protect arrows until needed for the hunt.

In the Great Basin, and in the fringe areas near marshes, quivers were sometimes made from tule. Some were simple and made from unsplit twined tules and others were beautiful examples of the basketmaker's art, complete with

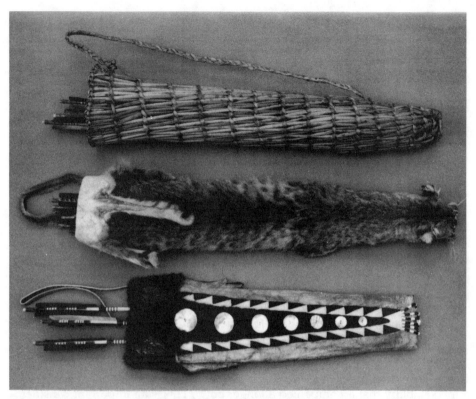

*Author's replica quivers. Top) Klamath-style quiver made from unsplit tules. Middle) Case-skinned bobcat with fur side out. Bottom) Hupa-Karok-style otter quiver with fur side in, decorated with black flannel, white deer hair, and abalone shell discs and beads.*

interwoven designs. The Klamath and Modoc were especially noted for this type of quiver.

Columbia Plateau quivers showed some influence from typical Plains-style quivers. Bowcases began to appear on some quivers and they often had carrying straps, or bandoliers, highly decorated with beadwork. Interestingly enough, I've seen old photos of Indians holding such quivers with what can only be described as a flat bow sticking out of them.

Shooting these flat bows from the West Coast is something I've not yet mentioned. Overall, flat bows are a design that work well since they spread out the compression and tension and shoot quite fast if properly made, especially if backed with sinew. The Native Americans had a wide variety of shooting techniques that ranged from shooting the bow horizontally all the way to vertically, along with a wide array of arrow releases, as well. Admittedly, the short bows can be tricky to shoot if you aren't used to them, since any errors made during shooting are magnified. If you're interested in replicating one of these bows and shooting it well, my advice is to make it longer than most of the originals, though some of the old bows from the region pushed 55 inches (I would take

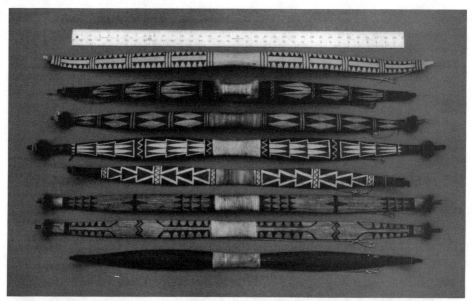

*Some of the author's replica bows. Top to bottom: Klamath-style self bow of juniper; Modoc-style sinew-backed juniper; Klamath-style sinew-backed yew; Karok-style sinew-backed yew; Hupa-style sinew-backed yew; Pit River or Achumawi-style sinew-backed yew; Maidu-style sinew-backed yew; and western Oregon sinew-backed yew.*

this to mean that there were individuals who liked longer draw lengths and the added stability that accompanied a longer bow). This is an important consideration if you intend to hunt with such a weapon. A rule of thumb is to double your draw length to arrive at the length of bow. A sinew-backed bow can be made shorter still.

People sometimes have interesting reactions when they see these bows for the first time. Once, during archery deer season I was walking back after an unsuccessful morning hunt and spotted two other bow hunters. I walked over, intending to strike up a friendly conversation as to who had seen what that morning. They seemed to regard me rather suspiciously, however, after spotting my bow. Of course, they were decked out in the latest in bowhunting fashions, right down to the maple leaves painted on their faces. Their bows were modern compounds, or "four-wheel drive bows" as I teasingly call them. After viewing me rather askance, one of them finally had to ask if my bow "was African or something?" I explained that it was a copy of a Karok design, as were the stone tipped arrows. He then asked if the bow even pulled 30 pounds, which is 10 pounds under the legal limit. I'm not sure he believed me when I said it drew 47 pounds.

Quite a few people ask about the weight of these bows and they're usually surprised when told that something so small and light can pull over 60 pounds. Most of the Indian bows that I've seen average between 35 and 60 pounds, depending on their intended use. The serious bows for large game fell somewhere in the 40 to 50 pound range. After using replicas of these bows, along

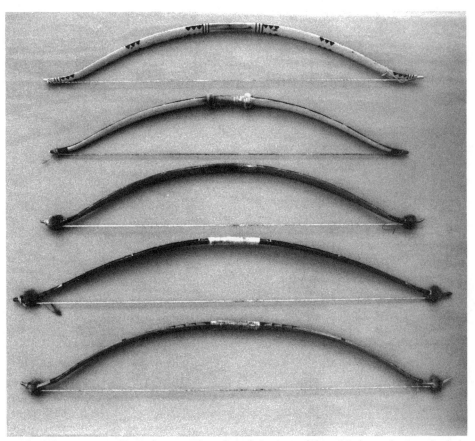

*Author's bows, strung. Top to bottom: Klamath-style juniper self bow; Modoc-style sinew-backed juniper; Klamath-style sinew-backed yew; Karok-style sinew-backed yew; and Pit River or Achumawi-style sinew-backed yew. Strings are two-ply elk and deer sinew.*

with the up-close style of hunting employed by the Indians, I've discovered that 50 pounds is plenty of killing power. Being able to shoot a bow accurately and placing a shot are the most important considerations, so my recommendation to any serious replicators and hunters is make a bow which can be shot comfortably, which will improve accuracy.

I recently decided to alleviate a minor case of cabin fever by stringing my juniper Klamath bow and going for a jaunt down a desert canyon to bother a few rabbits. The rabbits proved elusive, due possibly to a golden eagle which had been working the canyon. The Native Americans had once used the area, too. There were a couple of small rock shelters nearby with smoke blackened roofs and a scattering of obsidian flakes near the entrances that bore witness to earlier visitors.

I was soaking up the solitude of the place when a thought suddenly stopped me in my tracks. When was the last time someone hunted in this canyon with a juniper bow and cane arrows with greasewood foreshafts? Probably a long, long time ago.

A sense of symmetry, of rightness, slowly dawned at the thought of keeping some ancient traditions alive and returning these weapons to their place of origin.

# GLUE

*Tim Baker*

A glue IQ question: How can two boards be glued together with water alone? Answer: wet the boards, then freeze the water.

This is not especially valuable information for those of us living below the Arctic circle, but it does illustrate the qualities glue must have: 1) Glue must have good wetting ability; 2) Glue must adhere well to the surfaces being glued and; 3) After being applied glue must cease being a liquid, becoming internally solid and strong.

Intuitively we assume that glue adheres by penetrating liquid roots into surface pores, where, after setting, the roots become mechanically locked in place. This is about half right. Glues operate at the molecular level, and, in the world of the molecule, electrostatic attractions rule. Surfaces must like each other before mating. Glue does adhere better to porous surfaces, and mechanical gripping does play a part, but much of the advantage of porous and corrugated surfaces derives from the fact that greater surface area permits more molecules to embrace.

Half the glues on the market claim to be "stronger than wood itself." And for the most part they are telling the truth. Many glues are stronger than many woods, IF applied properly.

*Glue joints most often fail because surfaces have not been prepared properly, or because the glue has not been mixed or applied properly.*

If one Romeo glue molecule reaches for his Juliet, but instead touches an invisible-to-us film of oil or dust, the marriage is off. To get the most from glue, naturally oily woods, such as Osage, should be degreased shortly before gluing. *Other wood surfaces should be machined shortly before gluing.*

If this last admonition seems unreasonable here is a simple and eye-opening way to demonstrate its soundness: take a piece of smooth hardwood which has been exposed to the air for a few weeks. Leave one portion untouched; plane or spokeshave another portion, exposing smooth, interior wood. Place one drop of water on each portion. The drop placed on new wood will spread out and soak in; the drop placed on old wood will tend to bead up like raindrops on a waxed car. Glue finds such surfaces similarly appealing and repellant.

Contrary to intuition and general practice, surfaces to be glued should not be roughed up with rasps, sandpaper, hacksaw blades, or the like. That's like trying to get traction on loose gravel. Even unmarred, perfectly sound wood

*Two water droplets placed on surfaced and unsurfaced areas of a maple board (photo taken after ten seconds). "New" wood, left, soaks up water like a sponge. Even ten minutes later the "old" wood droplet was still clearly elevated.*

surfaces rip loose before the glue fails; scoring the wood only weakens the gluing surface further. Scoring bow backs before sinewing does not seem to weaken the wood/sinew bond, possibly because the sinew itself is the weak link in the wood/glue/sinew chain. When a sinew backing is peeled from a limb neither the glue or the wood fails; sinew fibers themselves split apart longitudinally.

Surface area can be increased by creating clean, sound, matching grooves. The most highly strained glue bonds in archery history were found at the horn/wood boundary in Turkish flight bows. About 1/16" male/female sawtooth grooves were inscribed on both gluing surfaces. Surface area was increased, and because of a snug mating, the resulting glue line remained fine.

Like bow wood, good glue must have high breaking-strength and flexibility. Some jobs require less strength, more flexibility – mounting stone points, for example. Some jobs require more strength, less flexibility – splicing billets, for example. Some jobs require a very high level of both – sinew-backing a working recurve, for example. Fortunately, abundant natural and synthetic glues exist for all such needs.

## REASONS FOR GLUE FAILURE

Oily or crumbly wood surfaces. Inadequate sizing. Large gaps – glue is not a filler. Repositioning surfaces after glue has begun to set – or jell, in the case of animal glues. Clamp pressure too high or low. Curing temperatures too high or low. Removing clamps too soon. Stressing joint too soon.

If a glue is too thick, its wetting properties diminish and the bond is weak. But up to that point, thicker mixes are stronger for two reasons: One, such mixes contain more glue relative to solvent, and two, thinner mixes shrink more as volatiles depart. This creates internal stress, using much of the glue's strength just holding itself together. Shrinking stresses also develop at the glue line, contributing to failure at this point.

Glue lines which are too thick suffer the same internal stresses and have the same dangers. Gaps can be seen as very large localized gluelines. Glue lines should be no more than a few thousandths of an inch thick for most glues.

In general, glues which set by drying, such as white and yellow glues, need thinner glue lines. Glues which set chemically, without solvents, such as epoxy, will tolerate thicker glue lines and gaps. Epoxy is especially tolerant of gaps because it is totally made up of solids.

In general, lighter clamping pressures should be used on thin glues, heavier pressure on thicker glues. Let glue-line thickness be your guide. Small gluing surfaces need less pressure. Perfectly snug fitting surfaces need less pressure. The more perfectly-mated the surface, the stronger the bond.

## NATURAL GLUES AND ADHESIVES

Collagen is a protein which forms connective tissues in animals. It does a good job of holding animals together. Remove that collagen and it can be used to hold other things together as well.

If you doubt the strength of such a primitively derived product put a thin layer of hide glue on a pane of glass and see what happens. As the glue dries and shrinks chips of surface glass are pulled free. Hide glue has 10,000-plus lbs of tensile strength.

One of animal glue's most valuable qualities is that it can be made to set up at will: kept warm it remains liquid, allowed to cool it sets to a hard jell. This is especially valuable, for example, when gluing horn bellies to wood cores, as in Asiatic composites. A considerable amount of time is required to bind or clamp horn and core together, during which time the glue jells and loses its wetting qualities. Once bound in place mild heat can be applied, liquifying the glue long enough to re-wet all surfaces.

Use animal glues at 140 degrees for wood or vegetable fiber backings. Heating the materials to be glued to 100 degrees or above will help prevent premature jelling. Use at about 120 degrees for sinew, or other materials of animal origin.

It's important to size surfaces before gluing. Sizing is simply a first coat of glue. Like a coat of primer, it soaks in and seals the surface. Without it, a thirsty surface may soak up too much glue, leaving the glue line starved and weak. Use slightly thinner sizing for dense wood, thicker for porous wood.

Use about 100 lb per square inch clamping pressure after gluing. On average, keep the surfaces clamped for 12 hours. Wait six days before fully straining the joint. Less time will be needed in dry air, more time in more humid air.

Make permanent liquid hide glue by adding acetic acid, or vinegar. Or use fish glue which remains liquid at room temperature.

Flexible hide glue can be made by adding glycerine in weight equal up to the dry weight of the glue. This is an old book-binding formula.

"Mouth glue" can be made by adding one part sugar to four parts glue. This mixture melts in the mouth and is handy for gluing in the field.

Knox™ gelatin is extremely good glue. Knox™ reports that some of their gelatin is made from bone, some from hog skin, and there is no way to tell which is which without testing. But both are very strong.

Hide glue has justifiably been criticized for softening in humid or rainy weather. But having to use plastic glue on an otherwise purely aboriginal wood bow surely takes the bloom from the rose. Any bowmaker with an IQ exceeding his draw length will probably be able to figure a way to seal his bow from moisture, at least for a day or so at a time.

Water resistant hide glue can be made by adding tannic acid, Formalin, or formaldehyde. These can be added either to surfaces to be glued, to the glue surface itself, or can be mixed with the glue. Tannic acid can be extracted from tree barks, especially oak. Old literature reports that hide glue can be waterproofed by adding 40% linseed oil, but my test results showed marginal effects at best. Tung oil works better, possibly because it dries to a harder film more quickly. Even with tung, however, the resulting glue is only mildly water resistant.

Professional gluemaker Bob Main believes that formaldehydes which naturally occur in woodsmoke tend to waterproof sinew-backed bows. He feels that sinewed bows cured in the rafters of a smoke-filled lodge would not let down as quickly in damp air.

## HOW TO MAKE ANIMAL GLUES
The very highest strength animal glues are easy to make on your stove at home.

Animal glue is made from the fibrous chains of proteins in animal connective tissue. Heating such tissue in water dislodges these chains, suspending them in a water solution – animal glue. If temperatures are too high for too long the chains become too short, and the glue too weak. Temperatures should be kept below 180 degrees.

The less glue is "cooked," at any temperature, the stronger it will be. To reduce cooking time tissue can be plumped up by soaking for a couple of days. It can be plumped even further by adding a small amount of lye, exposing the protein chains to easier assault by water. One side benefit of plumping with lye is that oil and grease become soap, easily flushed from the stock. The lye must be washed clear before cooking begins. Generally a mild acid, such as vinegar, is used to neutralize any residual lye. Stock prepared in this way needs far less cooking, yielding stronger glue. But not all that much stronger.

Glue made quickly, from unplumped stock, is only slightly weaker, but much easier to make.

SINEW GLUE – Make from leg or backstrap sinews, or from sinew scraps. Put sinew stock in a large pot and cover with water. Simmer at 170 degrees for about 24 hours or more, stirring occasionally. Toward the end remove the lid and let the mix evaporate down to a very light syrup – just barely thicker than water. During the last hour of simmering occasionally scoop off fat, foam and impurities. Bring the mix to a light rolling boil for the last ten minutes or so. This will not degrade the glue, but will roll all impurities up to the surface where they can be scooped off.

*A rolling boil brings fat, foam, and other impurities to the surface. Adjust the boil until a discreet island of trapped debris localizes in one area. Chaff can then be removed completely and easily.*

*Left to right - glue from fish bladder, sinew, Knox™ gelatin and Knox™ combined with tung oil. Strength seems related to clarity. The fish bladder glue is amber in color, but clean and transparent. Sinew and hide glues are more milky and opaque. Gelatin is highly filtered for clarity. First-pouring sinew and hide glues, for example, are more transparent. If plumped up with lye, and cooked for just an hour or two, glue will be glass-clear and of the highest strength.*

While removing this chaff, keep the temperature high enough to prevent a skin from forming on the surface. The very strongest part of the glue skins up first. No need throwing the best glue out with the waste.

The longer glue cooks, the darker and weaker it becomes. The **first pouring,** after ten hours or so of simmering, is the strongest glue. The Turks used first-pouring glue for their highly strained horn-sinew flight bows. You may want to set this first pouring aside for the most demanding jobs. Stronger glues soak up moisture more slowly. Bows which are sinew-backed using first-pouring glue will hold their poundage better in moist weather.

Continue simmering the remains for 24 hours or more, or until the stock mass no longer reduces. The resulting glue is slightly less strong, but still excellent. Even the weakest hide glue is more than strong enough for almost all gluing needs.

If you're in a hurry don't bother simmering. Bring the sinew to a full boil right away and hold it there for two or three hours. Strain off impurities as above. Let the mix boil down to a light syrup, and you're finished. This quick-glue will be virtually as strong as slow glue. Continue simmering the remaining stock as usual.

This quick method does not yield as much glue per pound of sinew from the first pouring, so you may want to start with more sinew than usual.

Pour the light syrup through a fine-weave cloth to filter (discretionary). Then pour into wide trays or plates and let jell. Pour about 1/2" deep or less.

You now have a large petri dish. Bacteria may convert your glue to smelly gruel before it has time to dry. To speed drying cut the jell into 1/2" to 1/4" cubes, sprinkle onto a clean surface to dry. Wind, or a fan, speeds the process. Keep cool and out of the sun to prevent melting. When hard and dry, store out of the reach of insects and mice. If kept dry, its shelf life is unlimited.

If you misjudged the glue's pre-poured viscosity – if the glue is too watery – it may not jell rigidly enough to hold its shape for cutting. A half-hour in the refrigerator will fix that.

To use, soak the much-shrunken dried granules in sufficient cold water to cover. Wait a few hours, until they are plump and jelly-like throughout. Heat to 160 degrees and stir until uniform, then let cool to a working temperature of 110 to 140 degrees, depending on the materials to be glued. If necessary, thin to a medium-light syrup. The glue pot should be kept below 140 degrees. At 175 degrees animal glue will loose over 2% of its strength per hour. Successive remelting also weakens animal glue.

HIDE GLUE. The same process as for sinew. Makes slightly stronger glue. Hide scrapings, a by-product of buckskin tanning, work well. Hide scraps should be pulverized, since the paper-thin hide scrapings release their glue faster than sinew. Quick-cooked first-pouring hide-scrapings glue takes only one hour. Otherwise, let the mixture simmer at 170 degrees for ten hours, or until the scrapings are no longer diminishing in bulk. Hide tanning, and how to produce proper hide scrapings is a chapter in itself. This information is included in two excellent articles on the theory and practice of hide glue making found in the Fall '91 edition of the *Bulletin of Primitive Technology.*

BONE GLUE. Requires involved acid processing to separate minerals from collagen. Sinew and hide glues are stronger than bone glue, and much easier to make.

*Two commercial "hide" glues. As a general rule, lighter colored glues (left) are stronger. Darker glues are likely bone glues. Stronger glues also smell "cleaner", while weaker ones have a sweet, oily smell, especially when hot and wet.*

FISH SKIN GLUE. A moderately strong glue, but weaker and more brittle compared to the weakest hide or sinew glue. Old literature reports fish glue as weaker but more flexible than animal glue. Maybe fish were different back then. Fish glue that I've bought or made is about as flexible as peeling paint. Other home-brew fish glue makers (the world's second smallest minority group) report the same. But it's fun to try different glues, and it is convenient having always-ready liquid glue on hand.

Remove flesh, fat and scales. Wash the skins. Cut into strips or squares, then proceed as for sinew and hide glue. Fish skin glue does not jell at room temperature, but remains liquid. Pour into trays and let dry down to a medium syrup. To store as a liquid add boric acid as a disinfectant.

Fish glue can be dried as a solid: Once the "leather" stage of drying is reached peel the glue free from its tray. When hard and dry break into small flakes for storage. Like hide glue, dried fish glue has unlimited shelf life.

FISH AIR BLADDER GLUE. Same process as for sinew, hide and fish glue. Fish bladder glue jells like animal glue. It is also as strong and flexible. The old literature reports this glue was preferred by composite bow makers. The unidentified bladders I've used yield glue that is slightly stronger than hide glue, and slightly more yellow-amber in cast. Other fish-bladder glue makers (the world's smallest minority group) report the same.

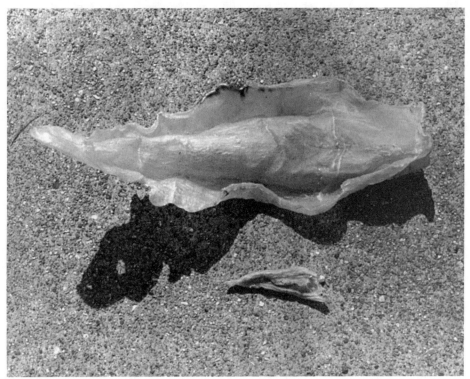

*A Chinese fish market may stock fish air bladders. Simply asking for fish air bladders won't always work, show them this picture. Size ranges are extreme. Medium-sized bladder, four to seven inches long, cost about $10 per pound. If there is a nearby source, you may fine it more convenient using fish bladders than sinew or hide scrapings.*

Certain species of sturgeon were preferred in the old days, and this fish might yield stronger glue, but I doubt if there would be a significant difference.

Jeff Schmidt recently completed an Asiatic composite bow which shot a flight arrow 500 paces. He used sinew glue made on his kitchen stove. Jeff does not feel his glue-line thickness or clamping pressures have been idealized, yet his glue did the job. Earlier in this century, composite bows were made with casein glue, vastly inferior to hide glue, yet these bows held together for awhile. The point being that stove-top hide glue is awesomely strong, stronger than you will likely ever require, and that there is no need to search the corners of the earth for exotic fish bladders.

SILK GLUE. Hide glue is made of protein. Sinew glue is made of protein. Fish glue is made of protein. And what is silk made of? Protein!

As I dropped the silk into boiling water the very air was charged with wonder and invention. I tried to imagine the strange and exotic qualities silk glue would have. Very tough, very elastic, pure white, beautiful. This was going to be great.

Six hours later I looked in the pot and found two things: boiling water, and a pristine mass of perfectly unaffected silk.

Two other non-sources of glue are hooves and horn. Despite common belief, dictionary definitions, encyclopedia entries, and other literature, glue cannot be made from hooves.

CURDLED MILK GLUE. Casein glue can be made from curdled skim milk or low-fat cottage cheese. Milk becomes somewhat water resistant after curdling. When dry, it loses considerable strength after some time in water, but does not dissolve. The curds do not make a smooth textured glue, but by adding lime, about 5% by volume, the curds break down to a smooth consistency. Lime also makes curd glue fairly waterproof.

Furniture in Egyptian tombs was assembled using sour milk-lime glue. One can only guess why, when stronger animal glues were available. Possibly because of milk glue's longer assembly times. Fish glue can be worked almost as long, but fish glue is not waterproof. And unlike fish glue, milk glue is odorless.

Casein glue can be used on wood having up to 15% moisture content. It will also bond to oily woods.

My strongest casein glue to date was made with low-fat cottage cheese. Wash and strain the cottage cheese until the curds are clean. Drain for fifteen minutes – removing as much free water as possible yields thicker, stronger glue. Add 5% lime by volume, stir well and let set one hour, stirring occasionally. Strain and use. Apply liberally, no sizing needed. Apply just enough pressure to hold work in place.

Preparing hide glue with casein glue instead of water yielded negligible moisture protection.

COMMERCIAL CASEIN GLUE. Contains dried curd casein, lime, sodium salts and a fungicide. The sodium salts render the casein water soluble – so it can be mixed. The lime waterproofs it again. Commercial casein glue is hard to find but still available. Insects, mice, mold and bacteria will eat casein.

If you wish to make your own dry, storable casein glue, dry and grind curds to powder. To use, stir this casein powder into a solution of water, lime, and lye.

BLOOD GLUE. Blood thickened with wood dust or lime dries to a moderately strong, water-resistant glue. Until the mid-40's, pig and cattle blood were used to manufacture plywood.

## PLANT RESINS

Injured conifers, especially pines and spruces, "bleed" pitch or rosin, and though not particularly strong, if prepared correctly the pitch is flexible and waterproof. Pitch is used for hafting points and blades, and can also waterproof sinew, rawhide, and gut bindings.

Fresh rosin is too sticky and must be heated or boiled to thicken (Caution! Pitch is flammable and should only be heated outdoors with great care.) Heat the rosin just enough so that when cooled to room temperature it is firm but not brittle. Old, hard rosin can be softened by melting and adding new rosin or beeswax. To increase its strength, add about one-tenth (10%) powdered charcoal to melted rosin. Charcoal can also be pressed into the surface after application to eliminate stickiness. Flintknapper Scott Silsby adds 1/4" fibers of dogbane to increase strength and flexibility. Flax, milkweed, nettle, and other plant fibers would likely work also.

## SYNTHETIC GLUES

EPOXY. Versatile. Excellent for splicing billets. Fully waterproof. Does not shrink while setting. Fills gaps fairly well. Runs moderately. No glue line. Expensive, smelly. Sets in minutes or hours depending on type. Medium to low clamp pressure. The various viscosities and setting times available make this a very versatile glue; dual syringe dispensers make it very convenient. Long or short assembly time, depending on type. Long shelf life.

CYANOACROLATES – "Superglue". Limited use. Sets instantly. Expensive, smelly, poisonous. No glue line. Runs badly. Poor for filling gaps. Good for filling checks, fletching, holding threads down, and spot repair work. It's wise to keep solvent handy, for separating body parts without surgery.

RESORCINOL™. Excellent for splicing billets. Fills moderate gaps. Does not run. 100% waterproof. Dark glue line. Fairly inexpensive. Wood moisture content must be below 12%. High clamping pressure of about 200 p.s.i. needed. Above 70 degree mixing and curing temperature needed. Acidic woods, such as oak, will need 100 degree-plus temperatures. Tolerates high temperatures. Long assembly time. Cleans up with water. One year shelf life.

WHITE CARPENTER'S GLUE. Fairly versatile. Can be used for handle splices, backings, miscellaneous. Inexpensive. No glue line. Odorless, dries quickly. Runs badly. Short assembly time. Not good at high temperatures or high humidity. Must be applied at room temperature or above. Cleans up with water. Long shelf life.

YELLOW CARPENTER'S GLUE. Very versatile. Holds up under higher temperatures than white glue, is somewhat more moisture resistant. Does not run as badly as white glue. Better for handle splices than white glue. Slightly amber glue line. Inexpensive. Odorless, dries quickly. Short assembly time. Cleans up with water. Moderate shelf life.

UREA PLASTIC RESINS, Weldwood™. Stronger on less dense woods. Mixed from powder. Highly waterproof. Inexpensive. Brittle. Shrinks as it dries. Bridges gaps poorly. Poisonous dust. Moderate clamp pressure. Wood should be between 8 and 12% moisture content. Best applied at about room temperature. Does not tolerate high temperatures. Long assembly time. Cleans up with water. Long shelf life.

POLYESTER RESIN – "fiberglass resin." This glue does not adhere well to wood, shrinks while curing, is brittle, and cracks easily.

## A DO-AT-HOME GLUE STRENGTH TEST

This test is fairly crude, but within an accuracy range of 10% or so, it will let you compare relative strengths of different types of glue, and of different "cookings" of animal glue. This test will help you optimize glue making, selecting, mixing, applying, and curing.

Where animal glues are concerned, laboratory jell-strength tests are accurate at judging internal cohesive strength, but not so good at measuring how well a given glue will adhere to a given surface. By using actual samples of material to be glued, this test is more dependable in this regard.

Rock or sugar maple was used in these tests because it is non-ring-porous, strong, and widely available. Samples are cut into one-inch squares, 1/2" thick. A one-inch end wrench can be used as callipers. It's important to work the to-be-

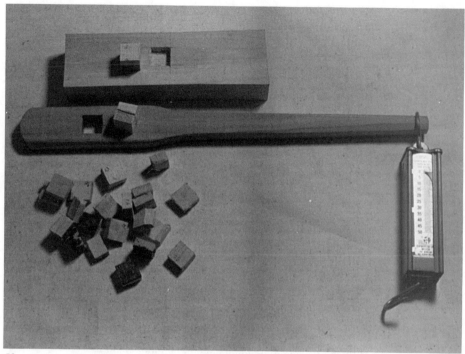

*Glue testing apparatus, showing spring scale and samples.*

glued surface with a plane or such shortly before gluing. Glue applied to unsurfaced, "polluted" wood fails about 30% sooner than on fresh wood. Cut long one-inch wide strips and plane the entire strip before reducing to squares – it's almost impossible to surface individual squares without creating a slightly crowned surface.

Prepare and apply glue as per directions. Glue two squares together at recommended temperature and pressure. Let dry, or set, for recommended times.

Scrape or file surplus glue from the sample's edge to reveal a clean, distinct glue line. Excess glue will throw readings off. Chisel a 1" square hole into a hickory baseboard, another 1" hole into a hickory wrench, as illustrated – ten minutes work with a sharpened screwdriver.

The sample is set into a square socket so it can be gripped on all four sides. When held on only two sides in a vise the wood fails before even medium-strength glue fails.

Set one side of the two-square sample in its base socket, and place the hickory wrench on the other square. Maintain about a 1/8" gap between base and wrench, with the glue line in between. Position a spring scale 1/2" from the wrench end, keeping the scale at 90 degrees to the handle. Pull until either glue or wood fails, noting poundage at the moment of failure.

As determined by the above test, here are relative strengths of various natural and synthetic glues and adhesives. Surfaces were prepared well, glue directions were followed carefully, and surfaces were sized where appropriate. At least three tests were made with each glue.

Candle wax.........................................................1 lb
Double stick tape ............................................. 1 lb
Contact cement ................................................ 3 lb
Cottage cheese alone, clamped.........................4 lb
Powdered skim milk and lime paste............... 5 lb
Pine pitch........................................................6 lb
Ice................................................................... 9 lb
Duco™ "airplane cement"...............................10 lb
Curds and lime...............................................16 lb
Commercial Casein ........................................ 18 lb
Urea resin ......................................................18 lb
Cottage cheese/lime ......................................20 lb
Epoxy putty....................................................23 lb
Resorcinol™ ...................................................25 lb
White glue – on unsurfaced wood..................25 lb
Epoxy, "Five-minute"™................................ 28 lb
Cyanoacrolate, "Slow-Gap"™.........................30 lb
Fish glue.........................................................33 lb
Rabbit skin canvas sizing ...............................34 lb
White glue – on surfaced wood ......................35 lb
Commercial liquid hide glue...........................35 lb
Sinew glue .....................................................36 lb
Bone glue, sold as hide glue ...........................36 lb
Yellow glue.....................................................38 lb
Hide glue .......................................................38 lb
Cyanoacrolate: "Zap-Gap"™ ..........................40 lb
Fish bladder glue............................................40 lb
Knox™ Gelatin ............................................... 42 lb
Epoxy "Two-Ton"™...................................... 44 lb

Above about 35 lb the maple samples themselves begin to fail. Relative strengths of the strongest glues are therefore less dependable, resulting from interpretation of the failure rather than simple measurement.

Earlier in the century spliced billets were commonly joined with casein glue. Few failures were reported, so we can assume a relative breaking strength of about 20 lb (based on the above test) is adequate for handle splices.

# SPLICES

*John Strunk*

There are several types or styles of splices used to join bow billets. I have seen many different splices, and although they all seem to work, some have more wood-to-wood contact and are therefore stronger. Logically, the more surface area making contact, the greater the strength obtained. At one time a spliced bow was not as desirable as a single-pieced stave because hide glues were used to hold the joint together, and even though hide glue is strong, it isn't water-proof!

There have been many stories of archers in the 1920's using hide glue to splice their bows. On damp days, the bows simply came apart at the splice joint. Shooters could be seen heading for their cars with the two pieces of their bows under their arms! Of course, they had spare bows in their cars so they could continue shooting. The folded bow would simply be re-glued when they got home.

Another story tells of archers wearing gloves so the perspiration from their hands wouldn't cause the hide glue to absorb moisture. Again, hide glue is strong, but waterproof it isn't!

One great advantage to using splices is that it is easier to split out 40" billets from a log free of knots and other defects than find a clean, straight 72" piece. Another way to look at it is a 100 pound log is easier to pack out of the woods than a 200 pound log. By splicing wood together, you can also replace a broken limb and thus salvage a damaged bow. My first shootable longbow was made by splicing together the two good limbs from my first two failures.

Another advantage of splicing billets is that it allows you to have matching wood on both limbs of your bow. This is especially true if you are making a "snake" bow, or a bow with many crooks in it. It also allows you to put some "setback" into the limbs. With Osage or one of the white woods, the back of the billets should be worked to a single yearly growth ring before splicing.

## MAKING A SPLICE JOINT

There are several ways to splice a pair of billets together. Here is a method I have used that would be appropriate for a beginning bowmaker, though it should be noted that only the "Z" splice will work with this technique, since it is the only splice where both ends are identical. Trim the ends of the billets to remove any small drying cracks and cut them to approximately 38" long. With the billets this length, you will end up with a 72" bow stave after gluing them. If

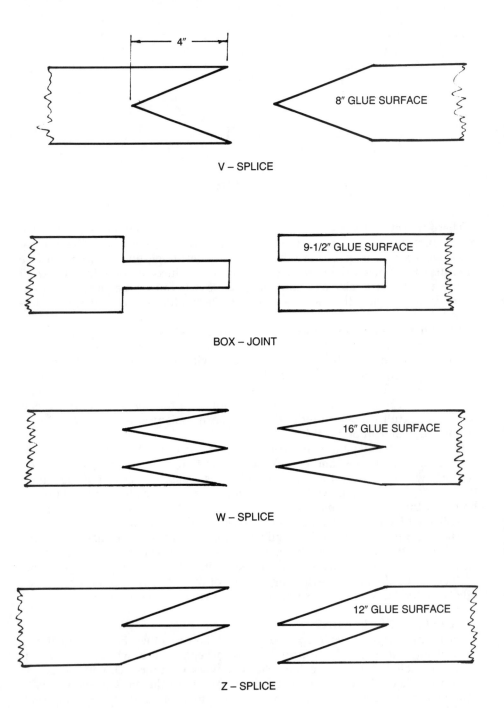

*Various styles of splices, showing relative gluing surfaces.*

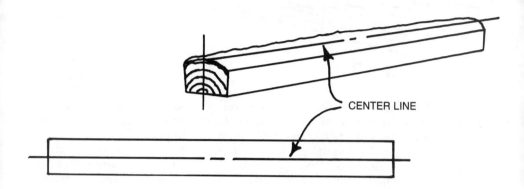

*Centerline drawn on billet.*

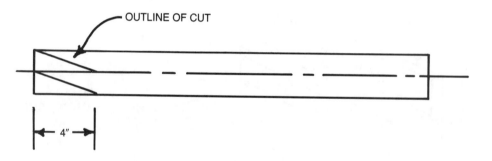

*Splice drawn on top billet.*

you find that the stave is too long, it can always be shortened later. Now draw a centerline down the back of each billet and extend it over the ends to the belly side. Follow the diagram and do this to each billet. Now look them over and pick the ends to be the handle section. Any end that has a natural bend which curves upwards towards the sapwood would be my choice for the bow's tip. Measure a distance of four inches from the ends chosen to be the handle of your bow. Draw an outline as shown. I draw this pattern on the handle section of only one billet.

Now place this billet on the top of the other and fasten it in place with C-clamps or tape. Be sure to keep the clamps or tape approximately 12" from the ends to be spliced. This allows room for sawing the joint. NOTE: The billets must be stacked belly to back as shown. You are now ready to saw the outline of

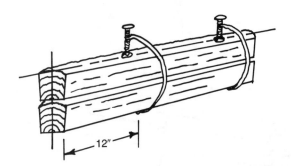

*Billets clamped together in preparation to cut splice.*

the splice. I do this with a bandsaw; however, a good, sharp handsaw works fine. The billets can also be cut one at a time. Once you finish cutting, you may adjust the fit by sanding or filing the pieces until they fit perfectly.

In my case, where I am splicing a lot of billets, I have devised a jig that works on my bandsaw. Using this plan, a jig can be made to fit any bandsaw that has a miter slot in the table. If you plan to do only a few bows, however, I wouldn't take time to make a jig.

Once the splicing cuts have been made, a few cuts with a woodworking plane will make the parts fit snugly together. Planing is only necessary on the outside slope of each piece.

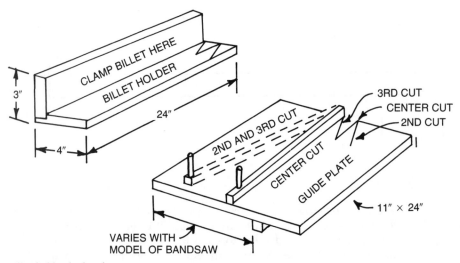

*Billet-holder for bandsaw.*

If any splice other than a "Z" is used, the different patterns are drawn out on each billet, and the cuts made with bandsaw or handsaw.

Note that your two center lines will line up with each other when the joint is tested. If the joint has gaps due to sloppy cuts, make thin shims and fit them into the cracks. This works well and produces wood-to-wood contact. Don't try to fill gaps with glue because it will be brittle and may cause problems later. Another trick is to soak the ends of the wood in water for five to ten minutes and then force them together. The moisture will cause the wood to expand and improve the fit. One caution: if you soak the wood, it will be necessary to allow the wood to dry thoroughly for a few days before gluing.

## GLUING THE SPLICE JOINT

Probably the best glues for splicing are Urac185™, Weldwood Resorcinol™, or a heat-setting epoxy. Resorcinol™ has been around for most of this century, and is used primarily to repair wooden boats. It has a distinctive, dark-purple color which can be recognized in many old bows.

Always follow any glue's directions precisely, or a glue failure could result, and you'll be walking back to your car with your bow under your arm. I prefer a strong glue such as a 12-hour, heat-setting epoxy for bonding the pieces. Another tip is to soak each end of the joint in acetone to remove oils from the wood that may affect the glued joint's strength.

*Finished "Z" splice with bow cut out.*

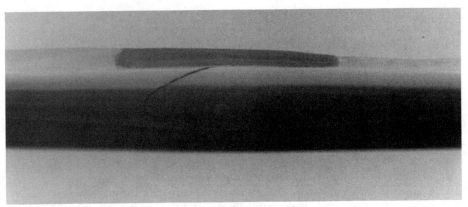

*Splice showing wooden pin glued into hole drilled from the side.*

When the pieces fit properly, apply the glue and slide them together snugly. Drill a 1/4" hole through the joint from side to side. Fit a 1/4" dowel into this hole to prevent the pieces from slipping apart as the sides are clamped. Now, tighten the clamps firmly to hold the joint. Some thin cardboard strips should be placed between the wood and your clamps to prevent sticking them together. Now, direct a light on the joint for heat, or place it in a heated box and cure the glue overnight at approximately 120 degrees.

The joint is now complete, and you are ready to proceed with the bow as if it were made from one solid piece.

# SINEW-BACKING

*Jim Hamm*

If you have recently tried making a phone call and gotten an "All circuits are busy" recording, I have a confession to make. This is probably due to the long-winded conversations held by your faithful authors; from Texas to California to Alaska to Ohio to Oregon, and many points in between. These marathon, circuit-jamming calls usually center around the relative qualities of various bow woods and the nuances of myriad bow designs. Theories and counter-theories fly fast and furiously, though contrary to what my wife maintains we have yet to actually discuss how many bows can dance on the head of a pin.

Anyway, the one topic that invariably begins the longest arguments concerns the merits of sinew-backing a bow. Jay Massey, a man of vast practical experience under actual hunting conditions, always backs his weapons with sinew. Paul Comstock, an accomplished hunter in his own right, almost never does. The rest of us lean one way or the other, depending upon our latest Toxophilic success (or failure).

The reason for the wide disparity of viewpoint is there are so many pros and cons associated with sinew-backing.

On the positive side, it is hard to argue with the fact that sinew, when used within certain parameters, is incredible material. By shrinking as it dries and imparting that tension to the bow, sinew reduces or eliminates string follow. As discussed earlier in the chapter on Performance, string follow is the arch enemy of arrow speed. Some maintain that string follow makes a bow sweeter shooting, but if you're interested primarily in speed from a bow, then sinew-backing may be the answer.

For a highly stressed bow such as a static recurve or horn bow, the elastic sinew is essential to prevent breakage. The top 10% of the back does about 50% of the work with the sinew taking the strain from the wood, allowing the bow to be pulled farther without danger of failure. Sinew-backing will, in fact, render a bow almost unbreakable; often even miraculously saving one that has pulled up a fatal splinter on the back. The fibers of sinew in their matrix of hide glue hold down the back of a bow and keep a splinter from developing into a break.

The advantages of sinew are clear, allowing the bowyer to make shorter, highly stressed bows which are practically invulnerable (though it should be noted that a poorly tillered bow may break in spite of the sinew).

Unfortunately, the disadvantages of sinew are just as clear.

On bows longer than 64" (for a 28" draw length), sinew-backing becomes a classic case of diminishing returns. The longer a bow is made, the less it will be stressed, making the stretching property of sinew less apparent. In fact, since sinew and glue are heavier than wood, a backing becomes a detriment after a certain length because of increased mass.

And since a properly designed and tillered longer bow seldom breaks anyway, sinew is not needed to keep it intact.

Aside from these factors, sinew backing is a great deal of work, usually doubling the amount of time to make a bow. And, for some bowyers, sinew and hide glue are often difficult or impossible to obtain.

But the biggest drawback to sinew is that the hide glue which holds it in place is water soluble. If the bow is immersed in water, or subjected to long periods of damp, foggy weather, the performance suffers as the sinew absorbs moisture and stretches, and the bow can even break. This can be a serious consideration, though it's only fair to state that if Jay Massey uses sinew-backing in Alaska, under the most demanding weather conditions imaginable, then it's not exactly delicate.

In any case, whether or not you have any intention of making a classic sinew-backed short bow, the technique is extremely useful to know, if not to make a short recurve then to save a favorite longer bow which develops a life-threatening splinter on the back.

## PREPARING SINEW

Sinew, or tendon, can be found in any animal, though to obtain workable lengths sinew from animals at least as large as deer or antelope should be used. Horse and cattle sinew will work, though I prefer to get it from wild animals such as elk, moose, or buffalo because the stretch, and ultimate performance, seems to be better. A bow backed with buffalo or elk tendon has better "medicine" without a doubt, though this facet might be more difficult to prove.

Sinew comes from two primary areas on an animal. The first is **leg**, or Achilles' tendons, which run up the back of the leg from ankle to knee. The sinew in the back legs is a bit longer than the front legs. Deer normally yield an 8 to 10 inch piece while a larger animal's will be 10 to 14 inches. Most slaughter houses which process deer and elk routinely cut off all four legs at the knees and discard them. A benevolent plant owner may give you access to these legs, and a barrel-full can yield several hundred from a couple of hours work. Simply run a sharp knife between the tendon and the bone, slicing through the hide, then cut the ends of the sinew loose at ankle and knee. Reasonable care should be exercised to utilize all the length available, especially at the ankle, where the tendon will divide in half, or "Y." With practice, the entire operation takes under thirty seconds.

Once removed, the limp, moist sinews should be placed, not touching, on a flat surface and allowed to dry thoroughly. It is a good idea to flip the tendons over after a day or two, to insure that they are dried completely. A word of experience: animals, especially dogs and raccoons, love fresh sinew; they can wipe out your hard-won supply in short order. So it pays to dry the tendons where varmints can't get to them. Steve Allely says he sometimes splits the fresh tendons with a dull knife tip into smaller strands, which allows them to dry more quickly (this could also save time during the pounding and reduction

*Hind leg of a whitetail deer.*

*Hide cut away showing tendon, or sinew, on back of leg.*

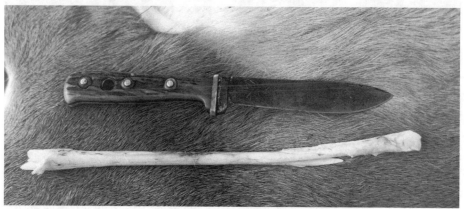

*Fresh leg sinew.*

phase). When totally dry, the translucent, amber colored sinew can be stored indefinitely or pounded into threads. More about this in a moment.

Sinew can also be found on top of an animal's long back muscle, known as the backstrap. When the hide is removed, the two long, silvery sheets on either side of the backbone are **back sinew.** It differs from leg tendon in that it is thin and wide, rather than a thick, round mass about the size of your thumb. Cut one end loose up in the neck area, then carefully cut and pull the sinew away from the underlying meat, until it disappears down into the pelvic region. For a deer, these strips are normally 12 to 15 inches long, while in a bigger animal, such as an elk, they may be up to 18 inches or more. Once the sinew is free, all particles of meat must be removed. An easy way to do this is to spread the tendon out on a smooth board, then hold a knife at right angles and scrape the meat away. Be sure to do both sides, as any remaining meat will turn rancid.

Storage of back sinew depends upon the intended usage. It works well as bow backing material, but also makes excellent strings and is useful for fletching and attaching points. In these applications, it is preferable to freeze the tendon rather than dry it. When thawed and ready for use, it will be like fresh sinew, slightly sticky with a great deal of stretch. In this condition, you can tie on feathers more neatly and make a stronger, smoother string. Dried and reconstituted back sinew has these qualities to some degree, but not as much as fresh or frozen sinew. If intended for backing, however, treat it exactly like the leg tendon, thoroughly dried and then stored.

*Location of back sinew, in this case a whitetail deer.*

*Cleaning a fresh back sinew by scraping free any meat or fat.*

To prepare dried leg sinew for backing purposes, separate it into individual threads. Pound the tendon with a hammer to loosen the outer covering, or sheath, which is discarded. This outer covering is sinew, also, but it is very difficult to separate into threads, so if there is an adequate supply of tendons it is best not to waste time on them. The inner core that is left will be about the diameter of your little finger (for elk), and is pounded with the hammer until it begins to separate and come apart. I use a two pound hammer and a section of railroad track, but a hammerstone and a smooth, hard wooden surface will work just as well, though with a bit more effort. Or a wooden mallet can be used on a stone surface. Whatever is used, care must be taken not to strike the sinew with the sharp edge of a hammer or rock and cut the strands.

Now, pull the tendon apart. Sometimes it can be pulled into two halves, but more often smaller pieces have to be pulled free from the main bundle. Because sinew is tough material, with the fibers interlocking, two large pairs of pliers are helpful in this initial reduction. The main bundle should be separated into six or eight pieces at this stage.

How many tendons does it take to back a bow? It depends on the bow length and design, as well as the desired thickness of the backing, but for an average bow it takes three or four elk legs or about eight deer legs. It is better to have too much than not quite enough, so I always do a couple extra. I like to take all of the sinew through the process at one time.

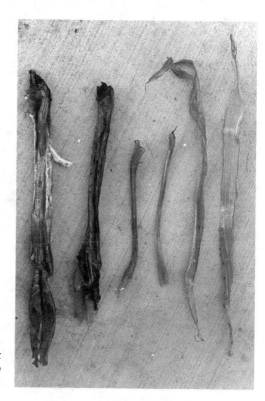

*Dried tendons. L-R, two elk legs, two whitetail deer legs, two whitetail deer backs.*

*Reduction process for leg tendons. L-R, dried sinew, outer shell loosened, separation of inner sinew begun, single sinew separated into about eight pieces, and final thread size.*

These six or eight pieces can now be pulled apart by hand. Reduce the size of the fibers to about that of small twine. Buffalo sinew is much softer and easier to separate, while elk and most deer is a bit wiry and somewhat stiffer. The finer the threads, the neater the finished job will be, though if a snakeskin will cover the sinew or aesthetics are not important then larger strands may be used and a great deal of time saved. The function does not seem to be affected by the size of the threads, only the finished appearance.

*A bundle of sinew, showing size of threads.*

*Sorted sinew bundles of different lengths.*

The threads are sorted into bundles according to length; I usually have three or four separate lengths of fiber being worked at once. When you accumulate ten to fifteen threads in a bundle, place it between the pages of a magazine, then turn the page. This keeps the different length bundles separated and prevents them from tangling. Do not concentrate entirely on longer bundles, they make the sinewing job go faster but some shorter lengths will also be needed to finish the ends and sides.

Reducing the pounded tendons into threads is tedious and time consuming, and usually takes from four to eight hours for enough to back a bow. Halfway through, you may well begin wondering what possessed you to make a wooden bow, and especially one with a sinew-back. There isn't really anything wrong with a compound, you'll be thinking, or for that matter your trusty old 30-06. But don't despair, the more care taken at this stage the smoother the finished backing will be. And when you launch that initial arrow from a bow made with your own hands, you'll fully understand, perhaps for the first time, why you went to so much trouble.

Processing back sinew into threads is much the same, though with a couple of pronounced differences. First of all, the back tendon can be worked between the hands and pulled apart into threads with no pounding and less effort. But be aware that it will take many more backs than legs, about fifteen to twenty for an average bow.

Also, the reduction can be speeded up with the use of a **comb,** made by driving short nails into a board. Rub the entire back sinew briskly between the

*"Comb" made by driving sharp nails through a thin slat.*

*Pulling back tendon across the points of the nails.*

hands, to begin the fiber separation, then grasp the piece at one end where the sinew is usually cut straight across as opposed to a long taper on the other end. The entire piece is repeatedly pulled across the sharpened points of the comb, shredding the sinew into fine threads, though they are still attached to the short section held between the fingers. Leave the tendon this way, so the threads do not become tangled, until ready to back a bow. Dip the entire tendon in glue, cut off the solid end, then lay the sinew on the bow.

The reduction process for a single back sinew is much faster than with a single leg sinew. But the total time may still be close to the same because it takes so many backs tendons which are time consuming to remove from an animal. Also,

*Shredded tendon ready to place on bow.*

finding enough back tendons is difficult, as modern butchering methods usually cut across it and large numbers are rarely available at processing plants.

Once the sinew is prepared, whether leg or back, it can be stored indefinitely until ready to place on the bow.

## PREPARING THE BOW

The back of the bow, ideally with one annual growth ring faithfully followed, must be prepared so as to give the sinew and glue a surface to which it can adhere. Carefully roughen the back with a new hacksaw blade. Hold the blade at right angles to the back and scrape lengthwise without making a cutting motion. Be certain to roughen the entire back, though the grooves should not be deep.

Some do not roughen the back at all, but simply apply the sinew onto the smooth pristine surface. Based on the findings in the glue chapter this may be an equally acceptable method, and insures that the growth ring used for the back is left intact. Usually, whenever I've had to remove the dried sinew from a bow, the wood and sinew come apart, rather than the glue failing, so the glue is not the weak link in the chain anyway.

Whether the back is slightly roughened or left smooth, it must be **degreased.** Some woods, such as Osage orange and cedar, contain an oily resin which prevents decay. But any wood can be contaminated with oil from the hands or airborne dust and grease, so follow this step no matter what type of wood is used. Poor surface preparation is one of the leading causes of glue failure.

In the old days lye, in the form of hardwood ashes and water, was used to cut the grease and clean the back of a bow. Today we can use lye in the form of crystals, usually packaged as a drain cleaner. Mix it with water (4 parts water to 1 part lye) and brush it on the bow. *Take great care* not to get the lye solution on the skin or in the eyes, as it burns like acid.

Another option is to scrub the back of the bow with naphtha soap. John Strunk has also used Acetone for cutting any grease, with good results. No matter what solution is used to wash the bow, rinse it afterwards with boiling water to completely clean it. Once the bow has been rinsed, back and belly, allow it to dry.

Sinew-backing, or for that matter, any type of backing, begins with the glue, in this instance hide glue. In a previous chapter the properties and home manufacture of hide glue were explained, and I will only add here that almost any grade will work to hold the sinew to the bow, although the better the grade, or strength, the better the adhesion and performance the sinew will give. Liquid hide glue should not be used, however, because it takes practically forever to dry.

The powdered glue (about 1/2 pound for one bow), with enough cold water to cover it, is set aside for thirty minutes to allow the glue to swell. Then, place the glue mix in a double boiler and heat it to between 140 and 150 degrees, adding additional hot water as needed, until the glue is in solution. It should be about the consistency of thin syrup. Once the glue is totally liquified lower the temperature to between 110 to 120 degrees, or until it is very warm, but not unbearably hot, to the touch.

*Work bench with bow ready for backing. Note double boiler for keeping glue hot and sinew bundles of different lengths spread out for convenience.*

When the degreased bow is dry from the hot water rinse, the back should be **sized** by brushing warm glue over its entire surface. Then allow the sizing to dry. This step is simple but important. If the back hasn't been sized, the pores of the wood may soak up most of the glue from a bundle of glue-saturated sinew, resulting in a poor bond between sinew and bow. This situation directly affects high blood pressure in bowyers due to the resulting broken bows. The sizing fills the pores and cavities in the roughened back, allowing all of the glue in a bundle of sinew to stay in place and hold it to the wood. So, control the stress level in your life by sizing the back of the bow.

After the sizing has dried, the much-labored over sinew is finally ready to begin its ordained task.

## APPLYING SINEW

I like to have things neatly arranged on the workbench before beginning this step: the bow in a steady position with small blocks placed under it if necessary, the double boiler for the glue – ideally with adjustable heat or a thermostat (your wife probably won't mind if you borrow her crock pot, as long as she never gets a whiff of what it was used for). Also, lay out several dozen bundles of sinew, of different lengths, along with an insulated cup with more hot water and a stirring stick. You will need a smoothing tool such as a metal rod, bone, or a wooden dowel. Keep it in a cup of water so the glue will not build up on it.

*Using fingers to flatten sinew bundle while stripping away excess glue.*

To begin, grasp one of the longest bundles of sinew in the center and dip it in the warm glue. Swish it around and completely saturate the sinew threads. Change hands, so the area under the fingers can absorb glue, too. When the bundle is totally limp, usually after 20 or 30 seconds, lightly squeegee out the excess glue with the free hand while straightening and flattening the bundle at the same time. Don't force out too much glue, especially on this first layer; there should be plenty left to give good adherence to the bow.

Lay the bundle of sinew lengthwise across the center of the bow. Do this by holding the bundle near the middle with both hands. Stretch the sinew by pressing it firmly to the wood while moving the hands out toward the ends of the bundle. With the fingers, press down any places where the sinew is not lying flat. Always work from the center of a bundle to the ends; this stretches the sinew and prevents the ends from becoming tangled. It is important not to let the ends curl, they should be laid out in nice straight lines in order to obtain the maximum benefit from the sinew. Now use the smoothing tool to further flatten and smooth the sinew, still working from the center to the tips. When finished, replace the tool in the cup of water to prevent glue buildup and pick up a fresh bundle.

*Smoothing sinew bundles with a bone tool.*

*Laying first row of sinew down
the center of the bow.*

Repeat the process of saturating the sinew in the glue, then lay this bundle end to end with the one already in place on the bow and smooth it down as before. These bundles of sinew will spread out into a strip about 3/4 of an inch wide as they are smoothed and flattened. Continue placing bundles end to end until there is a continuous strip down the center of the bow. The shorter bunches of sinew sometimes come in handy on the ends, to fill in a space of only a few inches. Lap any extra sinew around the ends and onto the belly of the bow.

Once the initial strip down the center of the bow is placed, the first course, or layer, is finished one half at a time, from the center strip to each edge. Remember how the very first bundle was placed across the exact center of the bow, with one half on one limb and one half on the other. This next strip will be staggered in relation to the first. These bundles are placed next to and touching the first strip, and are flattened as before, until they are blended and smoothed into the existing sinew. Continue placing bundles in this strip until it stretches from end to end, or until the bow narrows at the handle or the end and the sinew reaches the edge.

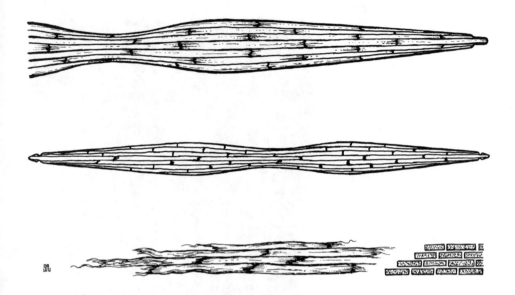

*Bundles should be staggered, like bricks in a wall.*

The placement of the bundles in relation to the bundles already on the bow is stressed because the splices should look like the bricks in a wall, with the seams staggered. Splices should never run all the way across the bow in one place. Proper application forms sinew into a solid matrix on the back, with no weak spots. This is, in truth, natural fiberglass.

Continue the first course of sinew until it covers the entire back of the bow and also extends over the edges and partially down the sides. This helps hold down splinters which can pull up on the edges of the bow.

Now that the first layer of sinew is in place, a few thoughts are in order. Some bowyers maintain that each course of sinew must dry completely, sometimes for several weeks, before additional courses are added. I have tried drying each course as well as putting on the total amount at one time, and can find no advantage to letting each course cure individually. Applying all of the desired sinew at once saves a great deal of time and is just as effective.

Some have insisted and occasionally written that great lengths must be taken to apply sinew in a high-humidity, high-temperature environment, some even going so far as to sinew bows in the bathroom with the hot shower running, making the room into a giant steam bath. These methods are, I believe, well-intentioned but in error. Ideally, once we have a sinew bundle stretched and smoothed into place, the glue will hold it in exactly that position, imparting ALL of the tension as the sinew dries and shrinks to the bow. Since the liquidity of glue is determined both by the water content and the temperature, it follows that contrary to keeping the glue warm and moist, which allows the stretched sinew to move, we want it to cool and gel as soon as the sinew is in place. I have had much better results backing bows on cool, dry days than on hot, muggy ones. A steam room would be even worse than a muggy day, negating some, if not a great deal, of sinew's effectiveness by allowing the sinew to shrink without imparting that power to the bow.

A variation on dipping the dry sinew in the glue is to pre-soak the bundles. This can be useful if the sinew is stiff and wiry, as is sometimes the case with elk legs or most back tendons. Lay several bundles at a time in a pan of water, and when they are limp, pick them up a bundle at a time, squeeze out as much water as possible, then dip it in the warm glue. Thoroughly saturate the bundle with glue, perhaps by dipping and stripping the glue a couple of times, then place it on the bow. This method is not any faster than using dry bundles but allows a smoother finish if the sinew is a bit stiff.

You may notice that after ten or fifteen bundles are placed on the bow your hands become incredibly sticky. Wash your hands in warm water to avoid sticking to everything, like the Tar Baby (and don't blame me if you choose to use your wife's new cup towels to dry your hands afterward).

Also, during the backing process, the glue in the pot will thicken due to evaporation. Add a splash of hot water occasionally and stir the glue thoroughly to maintain the proper consistency. I normally add a bit of water each time I stop to rinse my hands.

After the first course is in place, a second, if desired, is immediately added on top of it. Be sure to stagger the seams between bundles like on the first course. This layer can stop at the edge of the back, if you wish, instead of continuing down over the sides.

In order to have a smooth final finish, it is very beneficial for the sinew back to be mounded, or crowned, down the center. If the bow's back does not have a natural crown this can be accomplished by the way sinew is applied. After the second course is in place, a single strip, one bundle wide, can be placed down the center of the bow. Two more strips can be laid over this one down either side of center. Another full course can then be laid across the entire back.

How much sinew to put on a bow? Even a single course gives a great deal of protection against breakage, but for added effectiveness use three or four layers to increase speed in a short bow. More can be added, but keep in mind that the thicker the sinew, the more susceptible the bow will be to losing weight when the weather is warm, and gaining weight when it's cold. It will also tend to lose more weight in conditions of high humidity or rain. Once it is dry, the sinew's thickness, except on a horn bow, should not be over 25% of the bow's total thickness. When the sinew is first applied, and is still moist, it will look as though there is a tremendous backing. But once seasoned, the sinew will shrink down to a much thinner layer, following every contour of the bow's back. A good starting point might be to put on four complete courses.

After applying the total amount of sinew to the bow, dip your fingers in the glue pot and rub a generous coating over the back and sides.

When the sinewing operation is complete, the glue can be covered and stored in a refrigerator for several weeks. To reconstitute the glue, simply warm it in the double boiler, or even in a carefully monitored microwave, and add a bit of warm water to adjust the consistency. However, if stored too long in the refrigerator the glue will begin to mold, so for long term storage freeze it, then warm when needed. It can also be thoroughly dried, then covered with warm water 24 hours before needed.

## CURING AND FINISHING

When the actual sinew-backing process is complete, the sinew and glue immediately begin curing or drying out. You may leave the bow in place on the workbench for the first twenty-four hours to allow the glue to gel and begin to solidify. Do not expose the bow during this initial period to sunlight or high temperatures as this would tend to keep the glue in a liquid state and allow the sinew to move, or shrink, without imparting that shrinkage to the bow. Even placing the bow in front of an air conditioner is not a bad idea, as the cool, dry air gels the glue.

Some bowyers wrap the fresh, still moist sinew back with an elastic bandage or, in the case of West coast Indians, with strips of bark to give a smooth finish. But I have never found this step to be necessary, and in some cases it might even slow the curing by retarding evaporation of moisture from the sinew and glue. And a perfectly smooth finish can be obtained without resorting to wrapping.

After twenty-four hours the backing will be fairly hard on the surface and have a slight "give" when squeezed. You may move it outdoors during the daytime, where the sun can shine and wind can reach it. Both sun and wind aid in driving water from the sinew and glue. In the event of cold or rainy weather, a fan blowing on the bow in a warm room accomplishes the same goal.

A trick to allow the sinew to exert more tension as it dries is to stress the bow by placing the tips on supports and hanging a weight from the handle. This must be practiced in moderation, as too much weight will break the bow, but it permits the sinew back to shrink farther and apply the extra tension to the weapon.

Animals will eat the sinew backing and the glue which holds it on, so protect the bow accordingly. I once repaired a bow for a doctor who somehow lost his bow in the woods. When he found it a week later a coyote had stripped every particle of sinew backing and glue from one limb, while the other limb was untouched and pristine. After soaking free the remaining sinew in a horse trough, I rebacked the entire bow. And I only thought I had seen everything up until that point.

The fresh sinew-backing should be seasoned until it is dry. How long does it take? It depends. Factors effecting drying time are the thickness of the sinew, quality of the glue, relative amount of glue, humidity, temperature, and air flow just to name a few. In a fairly dry climate the backing should be cured in about ten days. For a thick backing or high humidity two weeks or more are needed. Some Asian composite bows were seasoned a year, but then, if a bow broke during battle, the bowyer who built it was reportedly beheaded, which makes for meticulous craftsmanship, to put it mildly. A drying time of two weeks is normally adequate, though it can be cured for much longer without detrimental effects. Be aware that the sinew will continue to cure for several months after a bow is finished, slightly raising the strength, and even several years later will increase in reflex during periods of low humidity.

For a bow with recurves, it is a good idea to wrap the tips once the sinew has hardened somewhat. Use sinew bundles dipped in glue, just like the backing, and wrap the entire curved area tightly to prevent the shrinking sinew-backing from eventually pulling away from the wood. The wrapping can also be done with thin rawhide or silk thread, though these will not be quite as effective.

Once the backing is completely dry, it is ready to finish. Begin by scraping the sinew with a knife blade held at right angles to the back. If a snakeskin will be applied over the sinew, then only the most pronounced ridges require scraping. But a painted or plain back should be smoothed with the blade just as rasp marks are scraped from wood. In fact, the dried sinew and glue behave much like wood during this process.

After scraping the ridges, use a sanding block and coarse sandpaper, about 120 grit, to further smooth the back. It will become apparent at this stage why a crowned back is easier to finish than one which is flat or has valleys in it. When sanding is completed the back will be smooth but dull, with tiny tufts of sinew protruding.

Before the finishing begins, warm a thin solution of hide glue in the glue pot. Now, simply dip two fingers in the glue and rub a coat over the entire back and sides. After a minute or two the glue will begin to set up, or lose its tackiness. At this point, dip a paper towel or cotton cloth in warm water, lightly wring it out, then firmly rub down the length of the bow once. Like magic, this finishes the backing, covers any sinew threads and leaves behind a smooth, glossy surface.

When dealing with sinew backing, there are additional ramifications of which you should be aware.

First, as a sinewed bow is initially tillered and pulled to full draw, you may hear the sickening sound of wood breaking. When your heart starts beating again, you'll notice the bow is not broken but that there are tiny cracks running across the backing through the glue. The sound you heard is that of the glue cracking, and while it's identical to that of a bow preparing to explode, the cracks in the glue cause no performance or durability problems – though extreme cases are a sure sign the bow was made by a beginner. The cracks are usually due to too much glue being used, which is another way of saying that not enough was squeezed out with the fingers when the sinew was saturated. Poorer quality glue is also more susceptible to this. The condition is relatively harmless, though a bow sinewed with far too much glue can make enough noise when drawn to spook game! While we're on the subject, it is vastly entertaining to stand behind a friend who is pulling his new bow to full draw for the first time and break an arrow shaft just behind his head. His knees rarely fail to buckle. I probably don't need to mention how hazardous this can be if your friend doesn't possess a profound sense of humor.

I never pull a bow which is to be sinewed until the backing is on it. Pulling a bow stresses the wood, giving it a greater or lesser degree of set, which tends to counteract the effects of the sinew. Some bowyers completely tiller a bow, bringing it to full draw and even shooting it, but this seems like an unnecessary strain on the wood as well as risking the chance of breakage. A sinew-backed bow is usually shorter than prudent for an unbacked bow at the same draw length. Since the sinew is what allows a shorter bow to be made, it stands to reason that pulling it before backing is just asking for trouble. Trouble as in a dead bow. It is acceptable, but not necessary, to mildly floor-tiller the bow before backing in order to bring the limbs into approximate equilibrium.

Since the foremost drawback to a sinew-backing is its susceptibility to moisture, some measures can be taken to make it more water-resistant. First of all, use the best quality glue you can find or make for sinew-backing. The better the glue, the more resistant to moisture it will be.

Perhaps the most practical moisture protection is to cover the sinew with a snakeskin. This process is described in the section on Other Backings, but I would like to mention here that since the skin is waterproof, use as little glue (and water) as possible to hold it on over a sinew-backing. Too much glue will trap water under the skin and soften the sinew, which allows it to contract and lose some of its tension, which will lower the weight of a tillered bow. On a related note, I once made the error of applying a snakeskin directly on top of a fresh, just-applied sinew backing, which seemed to make perfect sense at the time. But after two weeks, since the moisture could not escape, the sinew was still soft and it finally began to rot (as in stink). I had to soak it off and start from scratch. The point is, the less moisture between snakeskin and sinew, the better. The best method I have found is to use fresh or frozen snakeskins. Apply a thin coating of hide glue to the sinew-backing with the fingers and when nearly dry, after a few minutes, put the snakeskin into place. The inherent moisture in a fresh skin will bond with the glue and hold the hide securely.

A sinew-backing, even one protected by snakeskin, is still vulnerable to dampness, especially along the edges. This area should receive special attention when a bow is sealed. Another problem area is on the upper limb, where the loop from the bowstring slides when unstrung. The nocks, too, often have the protective sealer worn away by the string. Some of the modern Verathanes and Urathanes are fairly durable, though if you wish to use a more traditional finish on a bow the areas mentioned should get periodic attention, especially if the weather is bad. Jay Massey, a traditionalist even down to the finishes he uses, has told me of the constant battle over keeping a sinew back dry and functional in the unending fog and rain which often besets Alaska's hunting season.

It is beneficial to place a finished bow in the sun whenever possible. The warmth drives out moisture, which increases the sinew's tension and improves performance. Experienced hunters who use sinew-backed bows quite often place their unstrung weapons in the sun when they are not in use. The Turks, who made the famous flight-shooting horn bows, took the principle even further. They placed their bows in a specially heated box several hours before a shoot to extract every last ounce of energy, though the bows must have been allowed to cool to ambient temperature before being shot. A bow that has been artificially heated will be like limp linguine if strung and fired. At least, when I once retrieved a bow from an enclosed vehicle on a summer day here in Texas (the temperature in the vehicle must have been 160 degrees, or more), I was shocked upon immediately stringing and shooting it. The 65 pound bow pulled about 45 pounds, and the arrow had the trajectory of a brick.

If sinew-backing a yew wood bow, the sapwood should be removed before the sinew is applied. A heavy layer of sinew will, in some cases, actually rip the yew sapwood away from the heartwood.

A disconcerting phenomenon occasionally encountered with a sinew-backed bow is the development of **belly cracks** in the wood. Not every sinew-backed bow does this, but it's not uncommon, either, and the cracks are sometimes fairly extensive. I've always felt like the drying, and shrinkage, of the sinew exerts tension on the belly by pulling up on the sides, resulting in the belly cracks. Jay Massey observed that very old, dry wood is worse about developing the cracks

*Tension cracks in the belly of a yew bow (top) and an Osage bow.*

and feels it is due to the sudden influx of moisture into the dry wood. Once he mentioned it, it dawned on me that the older wood that I have sinew-backed seemed more prone to the problem, too. Tim Baker has chipped in with a most insightful observation. As any material is stretched, it narrows considerably; witness a rubber band. When a bow is drawn it stretches the sinew-backing, making it narrower, thus exerting lateral forces onto the wood, which produces the belly cracks. The jury is still out, but any of these theories, or a combination, could be responsible. It is worth noting that for some reason bows sinewed with back tendon rarely develop these cracks. What is certain, however, is that if tension cracks develop they cause no problems and should not be looked upon as a flaw. They do not weaken or jeopardize a bow in any way, and only show that the sinew is performing its job of providing tension on the back. If cracks occur in a finished bow which is intended for rugged all-weather use, the belly should be carefully resealed with a waterproof finish to protect the bow.

In some cases, backing a bow is necessary to increase the poundage. An average layer of sinew three courses thick will raise the weight from five to ten pounds. To increase the weight even more, shorten a bow in addition to sinew-backing it. A bow can be shortened until it is only twice the length of the arrow, and sometimes the weight can be raised twenty pounds or more.

A self bow which pulls up a splinter on the back can often be saved by applying a layer or two of sinew. I once made a bow as an experiment, to see how far a self bow could be pulled before breaking. It had at least a dozen knots on the back, and, as a result of ferocious overdrawing, eventually developed a splinter on both sides of most of them, almost twenty splinters in all, any one of which would have drastically shortened the life of a bow. I finally sinew-backed it, and was surprised to find that the splinters magically disappeared. The bow, which had been on the brink of expiring only a short time before, was completely cured.

Sinew-backing is not for every application, but sooner of later you will have need for its remarkable properties: for a short bow, a bow with a flawed or questionable back, or a bow which develops a splinter. Sinew is a tool which belongs in every bowyer's bag of tricks.

# OTHER BACKINGS

*Paul Comstock*

From the dimmest days of prehistoric Europe to modern times – across Europe, Africa, South America, Eastern North America and the South Sea Islands – men have made and used wooden bows which were not backed with sinew.

You can do the same.

In the 1980's, sinew was so highly touted that some may wonder if a wooden bow is capable of good speed and durability unless it has a sinew back.

The answer to that question is: It depends on the bow and its design.

If a bow is fairly short and drawn fairly long lengths, then you have a piece of wood that is being strained severely. Such a bow – with no sinew back – will typically experience high levels of compression on its belly. This compression can very easily result in a large amount of string follow which robs the bow of good tension early in the draw, reducing cast per pound. In addition, if the belly is severely strained, then the back also faces considerable strain. Any slight problem in such a bow with no backing could result in a splinter on the back or fracture of the bow.

If we take this type of bow and give it a good sinew back, several things change.

To begin with, the sinew backing shrinks as it dries, pulling the bow stave into more of a reflex than it had originally. Sinew is also capable of taking over a large part of tension work in the bow's back. The harder the sinew works, the less strain on the wood of the bow. Even the bow's belly can gain protection, because the sinew backing can reduce the size of the section of limb under compression. String follow is usually kept to a minimum.

On top of all this, the tough sinew backing keeps a tight rein on the wood in the bow's back by holding down splinters.

Our short wooden bow thereby gains performance and durability from a sinew backing. Without it, odds are high such a bow is simply under too much strain to be a good, durable weapon.

There is a way to avoid the need for a sinew backing, by making a bow that does not need sinew for performance or durability. The way to do it is reduce the strain in the wood of the bow.

This is easiest to accomplish by making the wooden bow long enough and wide enough so that the strain on the wood is minimal. With relatively little compression of the belly, string follow is kept to a minimum and cast per pound at a maximum. And the strain on the back is also greatly reduced, lessening the danger of splintered backs and fractures.

How long is long enough? In most cases, 66 inches is adequate for a flat-limbed bow with a narrow, rigid handle. A particularly skilled bowyer can make a fast-shooting, unsinewed flatbow 63 or 64 inches long which has very little string follow. This is easiest to accomplish by increasing the width of the limbs. If the limbs are on the narrow side, it is a good plan to make the bow 68 inches long. (The lengths in these examples can digest a 28-inch draw length.)

How wide is wide enough? If seeking a bow pulling 60 pounds or more, and using a wood like Osage, yew, or lemonwood, it is my preference to make the limbs at least 1-1/4 inches wide. The limbs would be that wide from handle to at least mid-limb, with the thickness taper adjusted for the correct tiller.

If using ash, elm, hickory, birch, or some similar wood, I would make the limbs two inches wide from handle to mid-limb for a bow pulling 60 pounds or more. For weights under 60 pounds, I would make limbs of these woods about 1-3/4 inches wide.

These are personal preferences which have yielded good results under a broad range of circumstances.

No one – alive or dead – has tested a greater variety of designs and types than Tim Baker of Oakland, Calif. Baker wrote this volume's chapter on Design and Performance. In it you will read more on how to design a wooden bow so the wood alone can stand the strain of shooting.

Or, you can back it with one of the following:

**THIN AIR**
There is a great deal to say for wooden bows that are backed with thin air. That is, that are backed with nothing at all.

If the object of making a wooden bow is a combination of accuracy, speed, durability, and economy (ease of construction), then the man-sized straight-limbed bow is – and has been for thousands of years – the undisputed champion among wooden bows. No other design can perform so many functions as well simultaneously, and with great consistency among a large group of samples – particularly if the man-sized bow is a flat bow. This style of bow is the ideal candidate for no backing. Such a wooden bow must be long enough for the draw length, and wide enough for the draw weight and wood species used. If the wood in such a bow is not overstrained, meaning the bow was designed correctly, there will be very little string follow.

A properly designed unbacked wooden bow is incredibly robust. And therein lies its main beauty and attraction. Carry it with impunity in driving rain, snow, mist, and fog. The backing will never come off. Because there is none.

Many hunters know the experience of getting caught in a rainfall so fierce that they have to wring out their undershorts when it is over. Under such circumstances, carrying a bow with a backing held on with water soluble hide or wood glue can be a nerve-wracking experience. With an unbacked bow, it isn't.

Every smart bow-maker will use some kind of waterproof finish, be it tung oil, spar varnish, frequent applications of grease, or whatever. All these finishes protect wood when applied heavily enough. Do they protect backings well enough? Maybe yes, maybe no.

I have seen backings of rawhide, sinew, and snakeskin develop loose spots. Rawhide and snakeskin are particularly vulnerable, since they are put on as a sheet. A sheet has edges. Things can creep under the edges. Like water. Bingo. Loose spot.

My deep affection for unbacked bows developed in part from one evening spent in a howling rainstorm so windy it would literally blow the arrow from the bowstring. By the time I had sloshed back to my car, the rawhide on one limb of my Osage bow – put on with wood glue and liberally varnished – was completely off from handle to limb tip.

By comparison, sinew is a matrix assembled from threads. In my experience, it is statistically less likely to pull loose along the edge in wet weather – assuming it has some waterproof finish. That damp sinew will cause the bow to lose poundage is another issue.

A bow can be left unbacked when there are no problems. Sometimes if there are problems, the bow can still be left unbacked.

The main question is this: Is the condition of the bow's back such that it may splinter? If the answer is yes, then back the bow. The main purpose of most backings and sinew is to keep the bow's back from splintering. And thereby from breaking.

An unbacked bow may be backed after it develops a splinter. In most cases, the splinter is completely arrested, and the bow goes on to have a long life.

Some back problems can be encountered no matter what type of wood is used. One of the most common is knots.

When a knot appears in the back of the bow, level with the rest of the back, the danger exists that the back will splinter around the knot.

In many types of wood, knots are often found in the middle of a lump which is naturally higher than the rest of the back surface. Such a high spot is subjected to less tension than the lower wood of the back, thus strain is reduced there. If a knot in such circumstances measures no wider than 10 or 15% of the rest of the limb, you can expect such a bow will be quite durable.

A fairly wide knot places additional strain on the wood between the knot and the limb's edges, but making the limb wider in such areas will compensate. When the knot lies level with the surface of the back, one option is to create artificially what the tree did not do naturally – make the knot sit in a mound of wood higher than the surrounding surface.

This is accomplished by taking rings of grain off the back, and leaving extra wood surrounding the knots. If the rings are particularly thick, it may not be necessary to cut through the rings. That is, the knot can still be left high and the same ring will be in surrounding wood. This could cause trouble in an over-strained bow.

Veteran makers of Osage orange bows, typically pretty knotty stuff, are the most active proponents of this technique. Even small knots – called pins – are often raised on the back of an unbacked Osage bow, since they too can splinter.

With the "white woods," oak, elm, ash, hickory, birch and similar trees made up mostly of white sapwood, knots are much less of a problem in an unbacked bow. Mainly because of the ease of finding knot-free wood, at least when compared to the task of trying to find knot-free Osage.

When making long, wide flatbows of white woods, I usually make no attempt to raise a pin. I have never had a pin splinter on such a bow. Over-strain the bow, however, and it could happen. If the limbs are wide and the bow was made from a small log, there will be a high crown in the middle of the back. To state it another way, the middle of the limb's back will be thicker than the edges. Under these circumstances, it is proportionately safer to lay out the bow so any knots or pins are not on the high crown of the back. Also, with such a high-crowned back, avoid a situation where the radial grain crosses the crown at sharp angles, as the wood can split in such spots. With a flat level back, any winding grain is much safer.

The next consideration in making an unbacked bow is this: Are the rings thick enough? The ideal for an unbacked bow is to make the back follow one ring from one end to the other. Or at least from each tip to the handle.

However, if the outer ring is paper thin, it may be too weak to make an unbacked bow. With such wood, the bow may break very quickly. Because a really thin outer ring can be compromised by almost anything, such as a faint scratch left by a scraper, or the slightest bit of excessive strain.

It is my experience (in woods other than yew and other conifers) that if the outer ring is at least 1/16th of an inch thick, I can make an unbacked bow from the wood. To understand better what we are saying here, let's talk briefly about rings of grain. Most trees are ring porous. This means there are two kinds rings. The spongy-looking rings are the spring growth. The hard, solid-looking rings are the summer growth. Rings of summer and spring growth alternate in ring porous wood.

When you make an unbacked bow, you want the outer ring to be of summer growth. When we speak here of an outer ring at least 1/16th of an inch thick, we are talking about a solid summer growth ring.

When using a summer-cut piece of white wood, following one ring on the back is particularly easy. If the wood is immediately split and the bark pulled off, the inner bark will also come off. All that's left underneath is the outer ring.

The most common practice with Osage is to remove the white sapwood. If the rings of heartwood are quite thin, it becomes a considerable job to work the wood down to one ring. Many Osage bow-makers don't even try. They cut across the thin rings on the back and back the bow. For unbacked bows, they often prefer Osage with thicker rings. It makes the job of working the back to one ring much easier.

If the outer rings are thin and the inner rings are thick, there is another option. Rip off the outer rings and work down to a thick one, which will be much easier to follow. This can be done with Osage and the whitewoods when ring structure permits.

Following one ring on the back remains the best insurance. But does an unbacked bow really have to follow one ring in 100% of all possible cases? No. The real danger of cutting through rings on the back is when the edge of the cut ring is not parallel with the limb. Look at illustration A. The edges of the exposed rings run across the limb. Any of the exposed edges in this illustration could splinter.

Look at illustration B. The edge of the exposed ring is parallel to the limb. This exposed edge is far less likely to splinter. Look at illustration C. This limb is more likely to splinter than the limb in B, because more rings have been cut through. The more rings you cut through, the more risky things get. Look at illustration D. This limb is less likely to splinter than A. Because only one ring is cut through.

The limb in illustration E follows one ring. But pieces of another ring can be seen on top of the outer ring. A bow made like this in no danger of splintering.

The risk of splintering in examples A to D can be increased by certain circumstances. For example, if the spring growth is quite thick – as thick as the summer growth – the risk of splintering would be higher when compared to an equal bow with much thinner spring growth. Also, cutting through thicker rings can be expected to increase the risk of splintering, when compared to cutting through thinner rings.

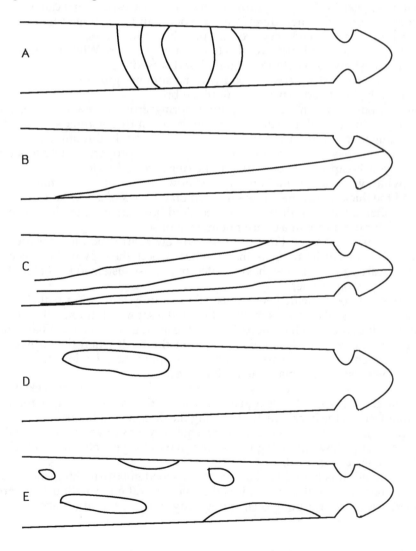

The bowyer can sometimes cut through rings and get away with it, but the ideal is still to follow one ring in the back.

Polishing the uncovered back to a glassy shine with fine sandpaper and steel wool can be beneficial as any gashes or tool marks could result in a splinter if the bow is overstrained. Also, burnishing the back with a piece of round glass, such as an empty olive bottle, helps smooth the wood and compress the back's fibers.

When making an unbacked bow out of white wood, the bowyer must determine if the wood has suffered any decay. An Osage tree which has been lying in the woods since it fell over three years ago can make a bow, because Osage heartwood is very resistant to decay. Ash, elm, hickory, etc. will rot, and they can rot fast.

When these woods rot, they often take on a punky, powdery appearance. Air gaps may appear in the spring growth. In extreme cases, air gaps can appear in the summer growth. Such deteriorated wood can (sometimes) make a bow when backed. If unbacked, they are very poor bow candidates.

The best way to avoid such wood is to cut only live trees. While it is rare, even live trees can show such deterioration if ill or diseased.

I once encountered a piece of wood with no summer growth in the outer layers. Naturally, I just had to try it. Naturally, it broke.

Some woods do not have weak, porous spring growth. Yew is one of them. Exposing spring growth by cutting through rings on ring porous wood increases the danger for splintering on a wooden bow's back. But since the spring growth in yew has some strength and integrity, it is proportionately less risky. Even so, yew is capable of splintering if the rings are badly violated.

For whatever reason, makers of yew bows have for many, many years reduced the thickness of the white sapwood on the back of a yew bow. Yew sapwood is often a half-inch thick on the tree. And bowyers have tended to cut the sapwood thinner, to about a quarter of an inch or so.

Many years ago, Saxton Pope did tests on yew heartwood and sapwood. He concluded while harder to break than the heartwood, the sapwood bends easier than the heartwood. This may have created or at least sustained the habit of cutting yew sapwood thinner.

The rings of good Pacific yew are usually painfully thin. It is a real challenge to follow one ring of a yew stave while taking the sapwood thinner. It is so difficult a task, it borders on the impossible for the average craftsman. What usually happens is many rings become exposed on the back when the sapwood is thinned, which greatly increases the danger of splintering. Under these circumstances, the most reliable plan is to back the bow.

If you want to make yew bows, and you'd like the bows to be unbacked, then don't thin the sapwood. Leave it just as it was on the tree. One ring is automatically followed on the back, greatly reducing the danger of splintering.

There is another mighty good reason. Thicker yew sapwood – up to half an inch or so – cuts down on string follow and makes the yew bow more efficient – all other things being equal.

This little tidbit is a long-kept secret of the wooden bow-making craft. As far as I have been able to determine, it is the sole innovation of Arthur Lambert Jr. Lambert was sort of a pompous, snooty guy who was a target archer in the

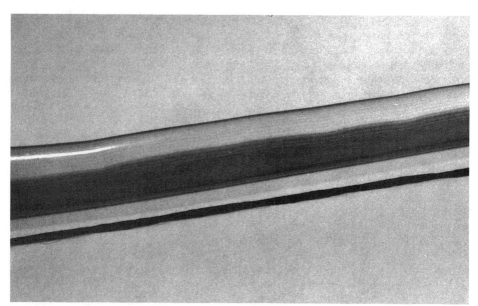

*This yew bow was made without removing any of the thick sapwood. This made it easier for the unbacked bow to follow one ring on the back, and helped reduce string follow.*

1920's. But he was no dummy. He wrote a book in 1929 called *Modern Archery*, and although an obscure volume, it stands as one of the best archery books of that era. Long before Hickman, Nagler, and others began working in archery physics, Lambert possessed some clear and correct ideas of how wooden bows tick.

In his book, Lambert advocates thicker sapwood on yew bows as "sound engineering." In an English yew bow, he wrote, it was perfectly acceptable for the sapwood to constitute up to a third of the bow's thickness. He told about taking such a bow to an archery tournament. At first, other archers criticized him for leaving the sapwood so thick. But when they saw how well the bow shot, they suddenly clammed up.

Because yew sapwood is weaker than the heartwood, it bends easier. To put it another way, it takes less energy (or pounds of pull) to bend yew sapwood. With the sapwood on the back, the neutral plane on a yew bow shifts closer to the belly than on an all-heartwood bow. Leave the sapwood about a half-inch thick, and the neutral plane is even closer to the belly.

The neutral plane separates the sections of the limb being stretched and compressed. Compression makes a wooden bow limb follow the string. In Lambert's thick-sapwood bow, a greater percentage of the work is done by the wood under tension. By reducing the compression, string follow is also reduced. Rare pieces of yew will have sapwood thicker than a half-inch. In order to imitate Lambert's success, make sure that enough of the belly of the yew bow is heartwood so that no sapwood is placed under compression. Yew sapwood cannot stand compression as the heartwood can. Those who have made solid yew sapwood bows have little good to say about them.

I have a 68-inch, 65-pound, unbacked English yew bow made following Lambert's advice. What a peach it is. It was made from a straight piece of wood with a slight deflex in one limb. Thoroughly broken in – and left strung up to 10 straight hours – this bow shows only slight string follow. I wish Lambert could have been with me when another wooden bowmaker examined this weapon and exclaimed, "No way this thing pulls 65 pounds with no more string follow than that!" At the limb tips on this bow, the sapwood is 3/8 inch thick and the heartwood 1/8 inch thick.

Despite the advantages of long unbacked bows, the question should be asked if they are the right choice for the first-time bowyer. More than a few bowyers made a good unbacked bow on their first try. But if a novice has any doubts about his skill, it would be smart for him to back his first bow or two. An unbacked bow can break if not properly tillered. A backed bow made exactly the same way, however, could survive. The difference could be between having a wooden bow or having firewood.

It is also a good plan not to subject an unbacked bow to a whopping bend until it begins to be well broken in. This can be accomplished by leaving the bow strung four to eight hours or so. Or by drawing the new bow a number of times at short draw lengths, increasing the draw gradually with more series of pulls. If the bow is any good to begin with (i.e., well-built and properly designed), neither of these methods will increase string follow excessively.

## RAWHIDE

Throughout the golden era of "civilized" wooden bows in America, from the late 19th century to the advent of fiberglass, rawhide was the most common backing used on wooden bows. Sinew did not gain any significant popularity among white bowyers until the 1930's and 1940's.

In his book *Hunting with the Bow and Arrow,* the legendary Saxton Pope says he and his companions had many bows break in their hands until they started backing them with rawhide. This speaks significantly of the difficulty a novice could experience without using some kind of backing.

Pope and plenty of other old-timers who wrote on the subject said the rawhide they used was very thin clarified calfskin. In the 1990's, clarified calfskin has gone the way of the flapper and the Model T. I have known people who have looked long and hard for clarified calfskin, and have never found a shred of the stuff.

A bow I once saw was backed with something resembling rawhide, but was as clear as glass. One observer said it was clarified calfskin. Couldn't prove it by me. I also have a tough time believing rawhide can be made completely transparent without some sort of chemical treatment.

The itch over clarified calfskin stems mainly from old writings about it. According to Robert Elmer, another archery legend, it was possible to put some glue on the back of the bow, press damp clarified calfskin onto the back, and it would dry out for a perfect backing job.

For those with experience in backing bows with regular rawhide, this is an amazing account. Because using regular rawhide has been known to involve sanding, wrapping, regluing, and use of inventive language. Just imagine if you had something easy to use! It appears the only response to that statement is: Dream on.

Just in case your life depends on getting clarified calfskin, I have one informant who has an idea where it may be obtained. He suggests suppliers of musical instrument equipment and materials may be a source, since (he says) clarified calfskin is used in the manufacture of banjos.

While clarified calfskin may be extinct, it is fairly easy to obtain rawhide. The type I have used is white cattle rawhide. Others have also used cattle rawhide which is brown and translucent. Thickness of these two types can vary from fairly thin to fairly thick.

Others have had good luck making their own rawhide from deer skin. My informants tell me it is very strong and thin.

Backing a bow with regular rawhide need not be any more of a hassle than backing a bow with sinew.

My early bows had rawhide backing put on with wood glue. The results ranged from lousy to so-so. I began to get far superior results when I started putting rawhide on with hide glue. It was far less messy than runny wood glue, and the rawhide stuck better. I scraped the rawhide thinner after the whole works was dry.

Others, however, do obtain satisfactory results with wood glue, but they thin the rawhide before gluing it on. This is typically accomplished by going over the rawhide with a belt sander, uniformly reducing its thickness. For example, the talented John Strunk uses Elmer's™ carpenter's glue to apply rawhide to his English-style longbows. But first – using a drum sander on a drill press – he sands the flesh side until the rawhide is about 1/16th of an inch thick. John glues down the flesh side since the hair side, which will be showing, has the smoothest appearance.

Strunk next softens the rawhide in water and puts glue on the back of the bow. He warns not to use too much glue, or it will end up running all over the place – a mistake you won't want to make twice. Most rawhide is so short that separate pieces must be cut for each limb. I have long been in the habit of overlapping the rawhide about 4 to 5 inches at the handle, since it was necessary to keep the rawhide in place with my early, crude gluing technique. But it is not 100% necessary.

Strunk uses a skive joint to butt the ends of rawhide strips at the handle by beveling the edges of the rawhide so the beveled edges are placed one atop the other, thus equaling the thickness of the rest of the rawhide. The overlapped section need not be more than 1/4 inch long, and if done correctly is difficult to see when finished.

Strunk wraps the bow and rawhide with Ace™ bandage. Starting at the handle, he wraps the bow so that each wrap covers half of the previous revolution. Once the wrapping begins, he pulls on the nock end of the rawhide strip to remove air bubbles.

After 24 hours, he removes the bandage wrap. The rawhide is typically somewhat damp at this stage, so he allows it to sit another 24 to 48 hours. It is possible to put the bow in a hot box at about 100 degrees to speed up drying.

I have tried placing bows with thick rawhide backs in a hot box and had the rawhide warp from the limb's surface. The significant difference is that Strunk first thins his rawhide to 1/16th inch. The rawhide that warped on me was considerably thicker.

Once the rawhide is dry, Strunk sometimes trims the edges with a spokeshave set for a fine cut. He says a scraper (such as Richard Baugh's Bowscraper) is better and I certainly agree. I have also done clean work of trimming rawhide off the side of a bow with a Stanley Surform™ tool and sandpaper on a block.

One advocate of deer rawhide is Ron Hardcastle, another maker of terrific wooden bows. Deer rawhide, he says, "has no equal." He uses hide glue to fasten the moistened strips to the bow limbs. Hardcastle often uses rawhide to back edge-ringed bows. Since the back of these staves are perfectly flat, he uses another board for a press. The rawhide is clamped between the stave and a press after the glue is applied and the rawhide positioned on the limbs.

I have also used this method with board staves. I have found it helpful to place felt, cloth, or paper between the press and the rawhide in case leaking glue adhered the backing to the press. It is also helpful to imitate Strunk by removing the press after 24 hours to let the rawhide dry further. A long oak plank is a very good press for this method. Hardcastle has found it helpful to put the rawhide on the raw board stave and trim the rawhide simultaneously with working down the sides of the bow. He has also wrapped rawhide backings with gauze until it dries.

My friend and neighbor Dean Torges has done enviable work in applying rawhide backs. He thins thick rawhide with a belt sander before applying it with white wood glue. He likes to wrap the damp rawhide with string, also my favorite method. Using string leaves a lot of the rawhide surface exposed to air, which expedites drying, although string can leave marks on the finished rawhide. But it the string is fairly thick and not spun too tightly, the marks will be faint. I typically scrape the rawhide thinner after the gluing job is finished. This removes any string marks and leaves a rough, non-glare surface of which I am fond. I have gotten best results by wrapping the string around the bow and rawhide at eight revolutions per inch.

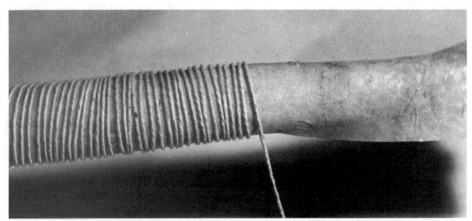

*Wrapping with string at eight revolutions per inch is one way to secure rawhide onto a bow until the glue dries.*

*A rawhide-backed yew longbow.*

The white rawhide will still be white on the finished bow. For camouflage, one can paint the back or put on varnish mixed with stain. If you use a varnish, it's a good idea to test it to see if it cracks. Smear some on paper and let it dry thoroughly. Then bend the paper to see if the finish cracks. If it does, it will also crack on the bow's back and be very unsightly.

It is imperative that the rawhide and the back of the bow be clean before you glue on the backing. If either the rawhide or the wood have been sitting around for weeks on end exposed to dust and grime, better sand the gluing surfaces to make sure there is no dirt whatsoever on them.

One day I was out shooting a very good 65-pound elm bow. Very good except for one thing. The rawhide was dirty when I glued it on. I kept noticing the backing was raised slightly in spots on the edges. I shrugged this off and kept shooting. Until the rawhide pulled off the lower limb taking part of the wood with it, creating a mass of shreds and splinters with a loud crunching bang.

## SNAKESKIN

Snakeskin is used mainly as a decoration. Most pieces of snakeskin are thin, weak, and tear easily, making it doubtful that they could hold down splinters well.

Some put snakeskin on what would be an otherwise unbacked bow, ostensibly for camouflage. Others put it over sinew backings to protect and waterproof the sinew.

Snakeskin comes in several different forms, one of which is green snakeskin, essentially snake rawhide. Another is a tanned hide with a leathery surface on the inside which is very tough and difficult to tear. I would not hesitate to use such a piece of snakeskin in place of rawhide. In addition, Jim Hamm says the skin of a bullsnake is thick and tough and may be valuable in holding down splinters.

Another type is tanned (according to my informants) with glycerin. Glycerin-tanned snakeskin has no leather on it. It resembles green snakeskin, but is soft

*Snakeskin-backed bows. Top to bottom; bullsnake, rattlesnake, and exotic skin from Malaysia.*

and somewhat oily. I would expect a glycerin-tanned skin could not be glued unless the glycerin was washed out, and I have no evidence that this is even possible.

Hamm takes matched, fresh snakeskins and freezes them, then thaws them before putting on the bow with hide or wood glue.

Dean Torges has put green snakeskins over bare wood backs using wood glue thinned with water. The snakeskin is first softened in water, then Torges prefers a second person's help in applying it. While one holds the end at the handle, the other presses down the skin and works out all the air bubbles. When the bubbles are gone, Torges says the skin can be moved around until it is in the correct position.

Torges finds it unnecessary to wrap the green snakeskin, and trims it when wet. If an air bubble is evident in the finished job, Torges puts a small slit in the bubble and uses a 20-gauge hypodermic needle to insert glue. The excess glue is squeezed out.

Green snakeskin comes complete with scales. Torges waits until the backing job is finished before removing the scales. One alternative is to put two-inch tape over the snakeskin and wait two hours. Pull the tape off and the scales will come with it. Another possibility involves using acetone or lacquer thinner on a coarse cloth and rub against the grain of the scales, lifting them off.

Hamm lets the skins dry a couple of hours after they are positioned, then trims the edges with a razorblade. Strunk also prefers green snakeskin, saying it is easier to trim the edges of the finished job.

Leather-tanned snakeskin could probably be glued on dry, but a better gluing job could be expected by wetting the snakeskin first.

## FISH SKIN

John Strunk is the modern era's pioneer in using fish skin as a wooden bow backing. Obviously, it takes a good-sized fish to produce skin large enough to back a bow. Sturgeon is Strunk's first choice, and he has produced many gorgeous Osage and yew bows backed with sturgeon skin.

Sturgeon skin is just as attractive as snakeskin, and there is also evidence it is tougher. Strunk believes it provides some protection to the bow's back.

He uses dried sturgeon skin – essentially sturgeon rawhide which has been stretched to dry then degreased with acetone. Once dry from the degreasing, the flesh side can be sanded.

Not every sturgeon skin is big enough to do an entire limb. No problem, Strunk says. He cuts the strips of skin as long as he can, then butt splices them on the limb as necessary using the skive joint described in the section on rawhide. Strunk stresses the overlap must be small or it will leave a bulge in the finished backing. He glues the sturgeon skin to the bow with the same procedure he uses for rawhide and snakeskin backing.

When the whole job is finished, he wraps any skive joint with size D nylon fish line. Red is his favorite color, judging from the bows I have examined. If one limb requires a wrapping to cover a skive joint, he places another wrap in the same spot on the opposite limb for a symmetrical appearance.

The idea of wrapping a wooden bow may seem a bit odd to someone whose experience is confined to fiberglass-laminated bows. But it is a very justifiable technique with a long tradition. The prehistoric Meare Heath bow (described in the chapter on Other Bow Woods) was wrapped with both leather and sinew according to archaeologists. Many wooden bows in the early 20th century were wrapped. Saxton Pope said a cedar bow backed with hickory should be wrapped every few inches, similar to fishing rods of that era. He recommended this step because of the water-soluble wood glue used on these bows.

Strunk uses the same kind of wrap used on fishing rods. He begins by taking a section of string and laying it lengthwise along the limb. The string is formed into a "U" shape. He then takes a second piece of string and wraps the limb with both ends of the U protruding from beneath the wrap. He finishes by sticking the end of the string he is wrapping with through the loop formed by the closed end of the U. By pulling on the open ends of the U, the loose end from the wrap

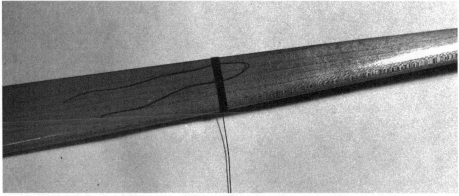

*This is a good way to secure a string wrap on a bow where the backing strips butt together. One piece of string is wrapped over a second piece forming a "U." The loose end is put through the closed end of the "U." By pulling on the open ends of the "U," the loose end is pulled under the wrap. All loose ends are snipped off, and a neat wrap is the result.*

is pulled underneath. All that remains are the two open ends of the U, which he snips off. It is an easy and attractive method of wrapping a limb.

Strunk sometimes uses the wraps where the horn nocks meet the wood. You may put on a pair of horn nocks and be displeased with the appearance of the fit. If so, wrapping the base of the nocks will improve their appearance.

Like many other bow-makers, Strunk's success with a new technique began with experimentation. If you have access to large fish, you may discover other species which make successful bow backings.

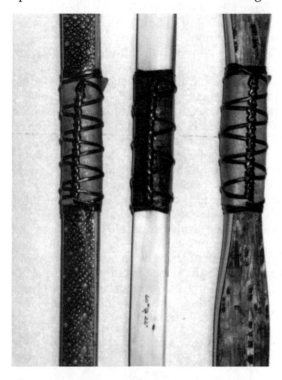

*Backed bows. L-R; sturgeon skin, rawhide, and cherry bark, all made by John Strunk.*

## TREE BARK

Once again, John Strunk leads the way with a new technique: backing bows with bark from the wild cherry tree. Extremely tough and hard to tear, it makes a most functional bow backing.

The fibers in wild cherry bark run only in one direction – around the girth of the tree. And that is how Strunk cuts strips for backing. Cutting strips running the length of the tree would cut through these fibers, destroying the bark's strength.

To obtain this bark, he looks for dead wild cherry trees, especially one which has been dead four to six months. The bark will come off fairly easily, but if it sticks, he "fleshes" beneath the bark with a knife as if he were skinning a deer. After removing the bark, he staples it flat to lengths of plywood so the bark will not curl while drying.

Because the strips of bark come from around the tree, and not along its length, the strips average only 14 to 16 inches in length. He uses the skive joint described earlier to butt-splice the bark on the bow limbs.

Because he dries the bark so it remains flat, Strunk can lay the bark pieces on the bow and trace the outline of the limbs. Then, he cuts the bark to the limb's dimensions with scissors. Do not try to overlap the bark onto the bow's sides, he says, because the bark will split.

Because the bark is only about 1/32nd of an inch thick, it can be glued on dry. He prefers to use an epoxy glue which allows him long working time. If using white wood glue, he applies glue to the sections of bark one at a time, as he glues them on.

Strunk started off wrapping the backing with Ace™ bandage and leaving it until dry. Now, however, he uses strips of inner tubes for the wrapping, which gives much better results by compressing the bark into any recesses.

Once the backing is finished, he rubs it with steel wool. This knocks off any loose scales and gives the bark a shiny surface. The result is an attractive backing which may show colors of white, maroon, turquoise, gray, or silver.

All indications are that wild cherry is an extremely tough bark. Strunk says it is difficult to split wild cherry without removing the bark first.

(While it is not the same technique used by Strunk, Dwight Bundy made a bow out of shagbark hickory with the bark left intact.)

Strunk can also back bows with strips of maple veneer, if the grain is straight enough.

## SILK

According to Robert Elmer, silk backing was introduced in 1939 by Clarence Hickman. Hickman was a professor of physics who, along with Forest Nagler and Paul Klopsteg, did a considerable amount of engineering investigation with bows and arrows in the 1930's and 1940's. Maurice Thompson and Saxton Pope were pure savages at heart. But Hickman etal. were cold, calculating scientists inspired to wring every possible foot per second out of archery tackle. The poetry, romance, and soul which had been such a large part of archery apparently held little fascination for the physicists. Their testament, a book called *Archery, The Technical Side,* is a collection of scientific articles crammed with charts, force-draw curves, and high-speed photographs gleaned by connecting wooden bows and arrows to every laboratory gizmo and widget in existence.

This work had at least one benefit. The physicists' findings accelerated the switch from the D-shaped English longbow cross-section to a rectangular longbow cross-section. The men dubbed the rectangle "more efficient." In plain English, the rectangular cross-section makes it consistently easier to produce a bow with less string follow – all other things being equal – when compared to the D-shaped cross-section. By reducing string follow, cast per pound is increased.

The physicists failed to acknowledge, however, that this miracle innovation had been in use for centuries by Native Americans. (We know today it was also used in prehistoric Europe.)

The physicists' work had larger and darker implications. Their compulsion to increase arrow speed – by often very small percentages – founded a school of thought that was ripe for the advent of synthetics. With the emphasis now on speed at all costs, gadgets, sights, releases and compound bows were a logical progression.

Hickman's silk backing was produced commercially in strips ready to apply to bows. The backing had a short career. A few years after he conceived it, World War II imposed strict rationing on silk and it was no longer available for bows. When peace returned, Hickman began producing backing material of the plastic Fortisan™ (see upcoming section on Extinct Backings). Why? Because Fortisan™ made a bow shoot a bit faster than silk.

Most old writings on Hickman's silk backing are maddeningly vague. They usually say it was "raw silk fibers in a matrix of glue, applied under tension." The reader of these works can only guess what the matrix glue was, or what kinds of glue would fasten it to a bow, or how it should be applied under tension.

Elmer's *Target Archery* states that silk backing was quite thin – 0.035 of an inch – and its tensile strength per inch of width was 1,250 pounds. Mighty tough!

Elmer said it could stretch 3% without taking a set, which is well beyond the stretch on the back of a well-designed wooden bow. The backing should be stretched 1% when applied to a bow. For most bows, he said, this meant stretching the backing 1/2 to 3/4 of an inch.

The net effect was very similar to a sinew backing.

The professional bow-makers of the 1930's used a jig to apply a silk backing. Alton Safford, who lives near Los Angeles, worked for several manufacturers of wooden bows before World War II. One of them was the Los Angeles shop of James Easton Sr., later founder of the Easton aluminum arrow company.

Safford told me that Easton's bowyers used a jig which suspended the manufactured silk backing strip horizontally between two rods. The rod at one end was actually a ratchet, which could be cranked to wind one end of the strip around the rod, stretching the strip.

With the strip now under tension, the next step was to size the back of the bow with casein glue. The bow was placed on top of the backing strip, belly up, then the whole works wrapped with inner tube until the glue dried.

If you want to back a bow with silk, you can imitate Tim Baker, who uses silk cables on bows. Cables are a technique widely used on Eskimo bows. (The Eskimos used sinew cables.) Baker was inspired to use silk cables by Richard Baugh, who developed the Bowscraper. Baugh made a bow with a nylon cable which worked well.

This requires a bow with a back which would not otherwise splinter, although the cable will provide some protection by taking quite a bit of tension work away from the back of the wood. It also requires using rather large pin or shoulder nocks which hold the thick loops of the cable in place. The loops of the bowstring can be placed over the same nocks, resting on the loops of the cable.

Silk thread is wrapped around one nock, run down the back of the bow, wrapped around the other nock, run down the back again, wrapped around the nock again, etc., until upwards of 50 or 60 strands are on the back. The silk can be pulled snug as it is wrapped around the nocks. Then some sort of short lever (such as bone, horn, or antler) is stuck between the two large bundles of strands. Use the lever to twist the bands, much like a child sits in a swing and spins to twist the swing chains.

The silk can be twisted and twisted until it is very tight. If the lever is long enough, it can be left in place to prevent the cable from untwisting. The cable may be tied to the limbs at several spots to help keep it in place.

I tried such a cable on a 45-pound wide-limbed flatbow, 64 inches long. The tightened cable boosted the weight to 50 pounds and removed every trace of string follow. And it shot very nicely. One hitch, however. This bow had a fairly high crown, which means the limb was thicker in the middle than the edges. Every third or fourth shot the cable slid to the side of the limbs and no amount of tying would stop it from happening. The best answer to this problem is to use a bow with a fairly level back.

Baker has also used linen successfully for a cable bow (see next section).

## PLANT FIBERS

When Tim Baker began experimenting with natural bowstring material, he wondered if plant fibers would have any value as backing for wooden bows.

In essence, he learned that any plant fiber which makes a string can indeed be a successful bow backing. Specifically, these fibers can be glued onto a bow's back to prevent splintering.

Potential fibers include linen, jute, yucca, sisal, and hemp. Baker has done most of his work with linen. He prefers to obtain linen from raw flax plants. (Although manufactured linen string is a possible option.) Linen fibers run the length of the flax plant, surrounded by harder material which makes up the rest of the flax stem. Baker spreads the flax out in his yard where the dew and rain can keep it damp (an ancient process called retting), and turns it occasionally for a few weeks until the stems are partially decomposed, then pulls the linen strands free.

*Tim Baker made this bow backed with parallel twisted strands of linen.*

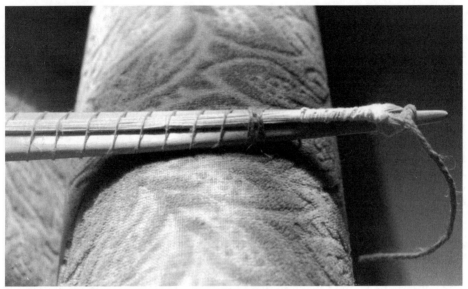

*This bow has a cable backing of linen ready to be twisted.*

His method of applying linen is very similar to applying sinew. If necessary, he cuts the linen fibers to the correct length for the bow limb. Then he dunks a bundle of strands in hide glue, wrings out the excess, and lays the bundles straight on the bow's back, with the ends of the bundles overlapping. Baker has also twisted linen into cords, and glued the cords side-by-side on the bow's back, creating a very distinctive appearance.

A finished linen backing has a dark color with a rough texture – a good camouflage combination for a hunting bow. Other plant fibers could be expected to produce the same appearance.

Baker says linen works well when applied to a reflexed stave. This pre-stresses the linen and allows it to perform some of the tension work on the back.

He has also used linen to create the cabled bows discussed in the earlier section on silk.

### WOOD

Backing a bow with another piece of wood is a technique with a long history, and is particularly useful when making bows from board staves.

The most common wood for bow backing has been hickory. Ron Hardcastle is an experienced modern proponent of hickory backings. Hardcastle says hickory backings may be applied in three ways: flat ring (with the edges of the hickory rings on either side of the backing strip), edge ring (with the edges of the rings showing on both inside and outside of the backing at close to a 90-degree angle), and bias ring (when the hickory rings meet the surface of the backing at less than 90 degrees; for example 45 degrees).

Hardcastle says all these configurations will work as long as the longitudinal grain does not twist off the backing strip, which can only be avoided by cutting hickory trees which have no spiral grain. If cutting the hickory trees yourself, you will instantly recognize spiral grain when splitting the log because the grain twists around the girth of the trunk like stripes on a candy cane. Such twisting grain usually can be spotted in the standing tree by a twisted appearance in the bark where the grain curves.

When someone else is cutting the hickory for you, Hardcastle believes the best insurance is to instruct them to discard wood with spiral grain.

If spiral grain hickory is cut into backing strips, Hardcastle warns the problem may be difficult to identify by sight alone. In such a piece, it may be possible to study the wood closely and see the open pores of the earlywood pointed in a different direction where the grain twists.

Hardcastle typically uses hickory strips 3/16th of an inch thick. To get useable strips, have them cut on a top-line table saw by a competent cabinet-maker. A planer can also be used to flatten the strips.

He will either use a strip long enough for the entire bow, or butt the strips at the handle. First, he scrubs the hickory backing with soap to remove any oil. If the bow is Osage, he also scrubs the Osage.

He prefers to glue on hickory backings with Weldwood Resorcinol™ – possibly the finest epoxy glue for wooden-bow work.

The backed bow can be either straight or reflexed with good results, says Hardcastle. He usually clamps the bow along its length as the glue dries, but has also obtained satisfactory results by piling bricks three-high on the prone stave and backing until the glue is dry.

He warns that some wood advertised as hickory is in fact, pecan. Pecan does not have the tensile strength of hickory, and should not be used in a thin board backing.

In addition to hickory, another wood used in the past for backing is elm. I have never been able to find any specific details on how these elm backings were applied, but it was recognized in the old days that elm has quite good tensile strength.

My experience with solid elm bows is fairly extensive, and there is no doubt in my mind that consistent results cannot be obtained if the elm grain is cut through in any way on the backing strips. The alternative is to take fairly good-

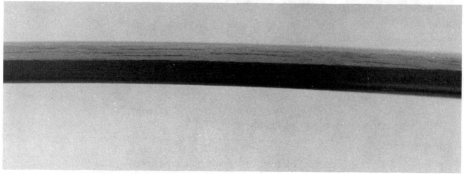

*Osage bow backed with a slat of hickory.*

sized elm logs and cut off thin strips of the outside, so that the backing follows one ring. This technique means that the great advantage of hickory backing – i.e., the ability to obtain a number of backing strips by cutting deeper into the log – is lost with elm.

Remember that these elm backings were used in the old days. Back then, virtually nobody had a clear idea of how to produce a fine elm bow. Today, we know how (see chapter on Other Bow Woods). So that elm log which could produce backing strips will in fact produce a fine, solid elm bow if the bow is correctly made. For all these reasons, I would submit that backing a bow with elm is essentially a waste of time in the 1990's.

## BAMBOO

Like hickory backing, bamboo backing can turn a board stave into a fine bow. Strips are cut from large-diameter pieces of bamboo. Flatten the inside of these strips and glue the bamboo to the stave with the outside of the bamboo forming the back. With large bamboo, a single strip is wide enough to cover the entire back.

It is important to remember there are hundreds of subspecies of bamboo, with the value for bow-backing varying considerably among the subspecies.

*Top to bottom; a bamboo-backed bow, a piece of bamboo showing the high nodes on the outside, and a piece of bamboo showing the concave section on the inside.*

I believe a reliable test of bamboo is to take a strip and give it a big bend with the outside of the bamboo on the outside of the bend. If it springs right back to its original shape, it is a fine candidate for backing. If it takes a set from such a bend, I do not think it is the best backing material.

If it does take a set, it may be too wet. I once backed a piece of lemonwood with such a piece of bamboo. Years afterward, I tested the bow with a moisture meter. The lemonwood was 9% moisture, the bamboo 13. The string follow in the bow was considerable.

In theory, if the bamboo was only being stretched it would be free of compression strain and not create excessive string follow. For those of us more interested in results than theory, the best course of action is to use the best bamboo we can get.

If the bamboo strip takes a set from a test bend, one option is to take some step to dry out the bamboo. Placing it in a hot box or some other warm place removes moisture. If the bamboo passes the bend test afterward, use it on a bow.

Bamboo can splinter badly on the sides of a backing strip. If a bow narrows at the tips, it would be wise to work tools only in one direction – toward the limb tip.

Splintering is not generally a problem when flattening the inside of the bamboo. Flattening is necessary because bamboo is hollow, and the original strips are sure to have a concave section in the middle.

Several methods work well for flattening the inside of bamboo. A sharp spokeshave or rasp works well. A power sander or planer will also do the trick.

The finished bamboo strip is almost certain to be thinner on the edges than the middle. However, this poses no mechanical problem for a well-designed and built bow.

The tough bamboo can take a very big bend indeed without breaking. The high nodes on the back can be flattened completely and the bow can still work. However, it is proportionately safer to leave the nodes in close to their original condition. They also create what I think is an attractive appearance, plus evidence that the backing is, in fact, bamboo.

I use Weldwood Resorcinol™ and plenty of clamps when applying bamboo to a stave. The clamps should not be tightened too tightly, as this squeezes out too much glue, resulting in a dry, or weak, joint.

## EXTINCT BACKINGS

There are a number of backing types which were common in the old days, but now are as extinct as the Tyrannosaurus.

One of them is the previously mentioned commercial silk backing as developed by Hickman.

Another was called **fiber** in the old days. Specifics on how fiber was made are rare. Most references speak only of compressed wood fiber or Vulcanized fiber. Essentially, it was thick, tough paper. Material of this type seems to have had other commercial applications in the past. Hot-metal typesetting, also quite extinct, required molding lead into mattes made of a material which looked exactly like bow-backing fiber. The fiber was also used for electrical panels and thrust washers on electric motors.

*Fortisan-backed bow from the 1940's.*

Old books say fiber was applied much like rawhide, even to the point of being soaked in water first. I own an old lemonwood bow with a fiber back. Tons of these weapons were produced in pre-fiberglass days. Fiber backings were typically white, brown, black, or gray. (Hot-metal mattes were usually yellow, pink, or pale blue.) In the 1946 book *Target Archery*, Robert Elmer considered fiber backings completely unnecessary in well-made lemonwood bows. But they created a nice appearance, and helped sell bows, and were also used on yew and Osage.

No doubt in an attic somewhere is enough fiber to back a few dozen bows.

Also used in the past was Fortisan™, sometimes called (and spelled) Celanese Fortizan™. (Celanese Corp. developed Fortisan™ during World War II.)

By the early 1950's, Fortisan™ was out of production, replaced by fiberglass. Elmer described Fortisan™ as plastic squeezed through fine holes to produce thread. *Archery, The Technical Side* describes Hickman's experience with Fortisan™. It had a higher elastic modulus than nylon or silk, with a breaking strength over twice that of silk.

Hickman began producing Fortisan™ commercially in thicknesses of 0.025 and 0.037 of an inch, in sheets about 11.5 inches wide and 72 inches long.

*Archery, The Technical Side* recommends that Fortisan™ backing be applied with a pre-stretched tension of under 1.5% .

## BALEEN

A krill-eating whale uses baleen to filter its food from thousands of gallons of sea water. It can also be used to back bows. The baleen I have seen looks just like black horn. It is a mass of tightly compressed hair-like strands. A large whale may have over 300 pieces of baleen in his mouth, from 3 to 12 feet in length.

Unless you have spent the past few years in a cave, you are aware that harvesting whales is as politically incorrect as clubbing baby seals to death. It is also illegal.

The U.S. Fish and Wildlife Service has a law enforcement office in Ann Arbor, Mich. I talked by telephone to a woman at the office who would only identify herself as "Agent Lavin." Lavin said the Marine Mammal Protection Act has banned the harvest of whales since 1972 (except for certain circumstances such as Native American whaling.) It has also been illegal since then to import whale parts, but she said it is legal to possess whale parts that were in the United States before the act was passed. But, Lavin said, a number of whales were named as endangered by the Endangered Species Act of 1973. They include the blue, bowhead, finback, gray, humpback, right, sei, and sperm whales. Interstate commerce of products from any of these whales is banned period, no matter when the whale was harvested, and the government's forensic laboratories can identify the type of whale a piece of baleen came from.

She urges anyone with specific questions on baleen restrictions to contact the U.S. Fish and Wildlife Service.

Baleen has never been common or cheap. In the late 1940's, Elmer said a ton of baleen cost $10,000 – $5 a pound. A pretty stiff price when a good lunch cost 20 cents.

Before whaling was curtailed, thousands of whales were harvested. There may still some of the stuff sitting about here and there. If you found a few pieces in Grandpa's closet, you can back a bow with it. It is almost unbreakable and a strip can be bent significantly without taking a set.

John Strunk has backed bows with baleen. He says baleen often has a faint S-shaped cross section, and the edge may trail off into loose hair. He uses a power disc sander to reduce a baleen strip to uniform thickness. Since the baleen strip is flat, he also flattens the back of the bow, cutting through as few growth rings as possible.

Strunk glued on the baleen with epoxy, wrapped the bow with an Ace™ bandage until the glue dried, then trimmed the edges of the finished backing with a disc sander or file, taking care not to pull hairs out of the baleen during trimming.

It is also worth mentioning a bow can be made with baleen as the belly. To be more specific, a short deeply reflexed composite bow can be made. This type of bow would require a good sinew backing and a wooden core. Since baleen is so rare, a bowyer with a piece or two would be well advised to consider an Asiatic or Arabic composite design. If he produces such a composite bow, he would be a member of a very small fraternity.

## EXPEDIENTS

To use natural materials as much as possible is generally the goal of all makers of wooden bows. This sort of attraction, after all, is essentially what draws people to wooden bows in the first place.

Those who have been active in this pursuit for a number of years usually have enviable stockpiles of wood, sinew, and other materials, plus the right connections to obtain other supplies as needed.

The novice, however, is a different story. Obtaining hard-to-find material is often difficult for him, unless he is prepared to pay what are sometimes significant sums of money. And it is patently unfair to exclude a man from primitive archery simply because he may be low on money.

For these reasons, I would urge this to the novice: If you have to, cheat. The experience will be worthwhile and it will get you by until you can obtain sinew, rawhide, or whatever you lust for.

Walk to the nearest fabric store where for a dollar or two you can buy enough nylon to back several bows.

Rip-stop nylon – used to make parachutes – is so thin as to be almost transparent. Avoid rip-stop and buy the heaviest nylon fabric available. If the weight of the nylon feels about as heavy as the material in nylon backpacks, it will work.

While plenty tough, nylon falls short of sinew or rawhide because it's not as strong and exposure to sun light eventually weakens it. It is probably a bad idea to back a board stave with nylon. But it will work fine on a log stave when the grain has not been cut through severely.

White wood glue works well with nylon, but thin it with hot water until fairly runny. Brush this glue onto the back of the bow. Tie one end of the nylon strip to the handle with string. This enables you to pull on the other end of the nylon, and to keep it under tension as you press the material onto the bow's back. By doing this, you can keep air bubbles out. When the nylon has been pushed against the entire limb, wrap the tip with string. Apply fabric to the other limb in the same fashion.

If the bow's back has bumps and hollows, better wrap the nylon backing until it dries. You can use something as thin as sewing thread.

It is a good plan to brush thin glue over the backing before you wrap it. You can wipe off the excess glue with a cloth, or your hand.

Remove the wrapping after the glue dries. The nylon will now be hanging over the edges of the limbs. But before you trim it, varnish it and let the varnish dry. This is a good idea because nylon can fray considerably when cut. If you varnish it first, and use a razor-sharp instrument (like a razor blade) to trim it, then you can eliminate unsightly fraying.

Leather can also be used, although, like nylon, it is not as rugged as sinew or rawhide. Use the thinnest, toughest leather you can obtain. Glue it on just like a rawhide back.

If you can't afford leather or nylon, chances are you have some brown grocery bags around the house. Glue strips of this to the back of a bow to hold down splinters. (Remember that fiber backing, after all, was little more than very thick, tough paper.) Ron Hardcastle has used epoxy glue to hold down a grocery sack backing. Odds are good wood glue would also be very successful.

So could hide glue. Don't know where to get hide glue? No problem. Just walk down to the grocery store and buy some powdered Knox™ Gelatin. Tim Baker has learned this works just like hide glue if mixed to the same consistency.

In the Fastest-Backing-There-Is category is fiberglass-reinforced packing tape. Cut off a long-piece of tape, put it on the bow's back, trim the edges, done. Ron Hardcastle wins the coveted Bowyer's Speed Demon Award for developing this backing.

As this chapter has shown, there are many answers one can find to solve problems when making wooden bows. The variety of possibilities in wooden bows is so great that no single method or set of instructions can be relied upon to produce acceptable results in every case. The bowyer must be able to think for himself to determine the correct course of action.

That is, in fact, much of the fun and satisfaction of making wooden bows.

# TILLERING

*Jim Hamm*

Up until this point, all of the work which has been done is simply a foundation. Tillering is where the bow-making really begins. And, unfortunately for the beginner, all too often where it ends. As Stewart White, a companion of Art Young and Saxton Pope in Africa in the early part of this century, wrote, "The best way to go at making your first bow is without hope, but with persistence."

Although experienced bowyers delight in telling horror stories, tillering is not really as difficult as it seems at first glance. While it rarely fails to intimidate the first-time bowyer – determining the shape, weight, and in large measure the durability – it is also one of the simplest steps (With tongue firmly in cheek, I once told a gathering that bow-making was easy, just get a log and a hatchet and chop away everything that doesn't look like a bow).

The unnerving art of tillering boils down to one sentence: Take off wood where the limb doesn't bend enough, and leave alone the areas where it bends too much.

That's it. No magic formula. No smoke and mirrors. If at any time during tillering you become uncertain, remember: Take off wood where the limb doesn't bend enough, and leave alone the areas where it bends too much.

Tillering may seem overwhelming, at first, because several things have to be accomplished at once. Each of the two limbs must bend in a proper arc. Both limbs must bend equally. And the bow must be brought to the correct draw weight. The process will be simplified if you keep in mind that the first task is making the limbs bend evenly, with no stiff places or weak hinges. Once the limbs both possess the same, correct bend, then the weight can be adjusted.

To begin with, we'll assume the wood at hand is straight, with no kinks, twists, knots, or other irregularities; these will be dealt with later, after basic tillering has been covered. The silhouette of the bow should be cut out, and the thickness of the limbs reduced with bandsaw, handax, spokeshave, or rasp to about 3/4" thick for a weapon with an average pull of 60 pounds or so.

**Floor tillering** is the first step in the process. Place one tip of the bow on the floor and grip it at the center. Lean into the bow, while watching for a bend in the lower limb and feeling how much pressure must be applied. At this stage, it probably won't bend at all, which means more wood needs to be removed.

Tighten the bow in a vise, belly side up, and take off wood with long, sweeping strokes of a coarse rasp. A sharp 8 or 10 inch rasp, flat on one side and

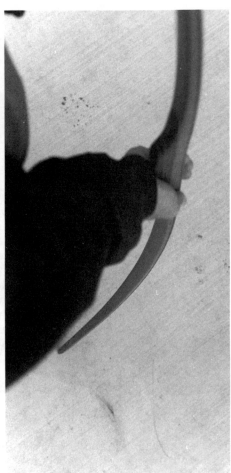

*Ron Hardcastle floor tillers a bow.*  *The bend in the lower limb from his viewpoint.*

rounded on the other, which has a handle, makes the job much easier. Work from both edges with the flat side of the rasp, taking care not to remove wood in only one place. Look down the bow from the tip; humps and low spots should be evident. It is helpful to mark the humps with a pencil so they can be removed to match the rest of the limb.

Take off twenty strokes with the rasp, then floor tiller the bow again. It probably still won't bend. Repeat the process of rasping, then floor tillering, until the limb begins to bend. This may take ten separate times. If you are a beginning bowyer and find yourself saying, "This is taking way too long. I'll get rid of a BUNCH of wood this time, and make this beast bend," then you should carefully put away your tools, fill a large bucket with water, and stick your head in it, because you are well on the way to making a 30 pound bow instead of a 60 pounder.

The difference in thickness between a 60 pound bow and a 30 pound bow is surprisingly small, and the reason is very simple. If you double the width of a bow, it will be twice as strong. But if you make it twice as thick, it will be EIGHT TIMES as strong. It is easy to see that a small amount of wood taken from the belly will make a marked difference in the way a bow bends, especially if the limbs are wide and thin. The point is: *Proceed slowly when tillering.* The most common mistake of a beginning bowyer is making a bow too light, and this is almost always a result of impatience. A beginner is, in effect, groping blindfolded toward the edge of a cliff. Once you've made a few bows you will recognize when far too much wood remains. But this bow-making is not a timed event, so, for now, take it slowly, and check your progress by floor tillering often.

Continue floor tillering and rasping until the limb begins to bend. Repeat the process for the other limb. It is very helpful to have a finished bow, of either wood or fiberglass, about the length and weight of the bow being made, which can be floor tillered for comparison. It will be relatively easy to tell if the bow you are working on is still far too strong, if so, continue the floor tillering and rasping until it is within twenty pounds of the weight desired.

I'm almost hesitant to mention this, but experienced bowyers often use their bandsaws as a "power rasp" during this initial floor tillering, taking off small amounts of wood through judicious, skilled use of the saw. Though this speeds up the process, considerable experience and judgment are needed, attributes the beginning bowyer does not yet possess. So if you have made less than twenty or thirty bows, please stay with the rasp, and avoid the wood-eating, time-saving, bow-destroying bandsaw until later in your career. Trust me on this.

Perhaps a safer option if the rasp is too laborious is a spokeshave, set fine enough to remove only thin shavings. A spokeshave works well on clear straight woods, though with Osage it usually jumps and chatters and leaves washboards in the bow. But during the floor tillering phase of most woods, it is an option you should consider, especially if the rasp seems too slow and you're tempted to take off wood with the bandsaw.

It is advantageous to make the belly of the bow flat rather than with a raised crown, especially with yew, cedar, or any other fairly soft wood. (This is for a flatbow only, the rules are different for an English-style longbow). A crowned belly concentrates the compression on the highest portion, which is fairly narrow, and a wood such as yew, being susceptible to compression fractures, or frets, is more likely to develop these fatal flaws with a crowned belly than a perfectly flat one. The flat belly spreads the compression forces equally across the entire limb, no matter what kind of wood is used, which increases a bow's durability and decreases string follow.

The growth rings on the belly side of the bow should be mentioned. A great deal of time and effort are spent in keeping a single growth ring intact on the back, but, naturally, the rings will be cut through on the belly side as the limb is tapered. At times, with straight, even wood, the rings feathering out on the belly can be used as a rough gauge of the tiller. Ash, hickory, elm, and other normally flawless woods lend themselves to this technique, while Osage and yew do not. The rings should taper to a point in the center of the limb. If they run off to one side, then that side is too thick. If there is an hourglass shaped ring or an island

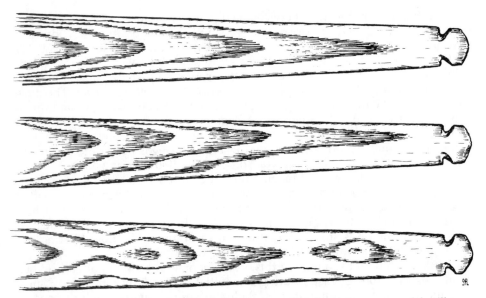

*Growth rings feathering out on the belly of a bow can sometimes be used as a gauge of the tiller. Top to bottom; correct, upper side too thick, and thick places shown by islands of rings or hourglass-shaped rings.*

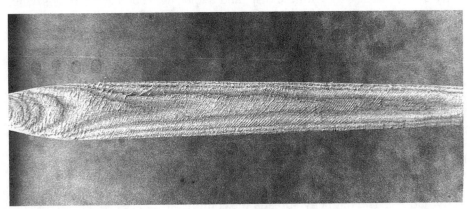

*Belly of an ash bow at correct tiller.*

of ring left, a thick place is indicated, which will be too stiff. Keep in mind that this rough rule of thumb will work ONLY with straight, flawless wood. Twists, knots, or growth rings which are not uniform render this technique useless, if not harmful. But if the wood permits, this is a quick, easy way to tell if the limbs are properly tapered and shaped. (On a historical note, in the 1930's and 40's a bow design which was popular had limbs the same thickness throughout their length. The tillering was done by adjusting the width of the limbs with rasp, scraper, or sander, much like the tillering of a modern fiberglass-laminated bow).

Watch the sides of the limbs carefully throughout the tillering process. They should gradually taper in thickness from the widest part of the bow to the tips. Both sides of a limb should be the same thickness, with no low places or humps.

Once both limbs are bending to some degree, nocks should be cut so the bow can be pulled on a **tillering stick,** or a stick with notches so the bow can be drawn and held at different lengths. Nocks in the bow's tips can be made with a chainsaw file (5/32" works well), a Dremel tool, or even with a pocketknife, though care should be taken to round the edges to prevent damage to the string. Also, be careful not to cut across the back of the bow, thus violating the integral growth ring.

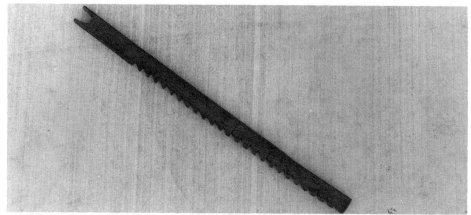

*Tillering stick.*

*Nocks. L - R; narrow self nocks, horn nocks on yew longbow, wide self nock, self nock, and a ring of flax dipped in glue formed into a nock to prevent cutting into the narrow tip of a yew bow.*

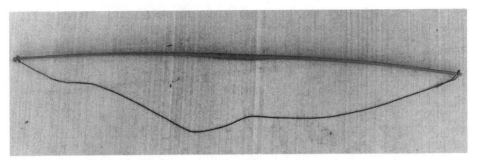

*Long tillering string in place on bow.*

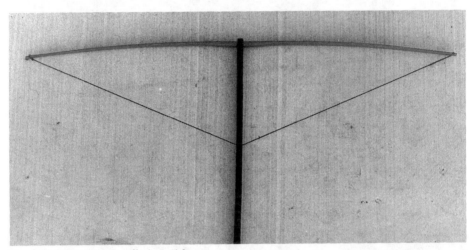

*Bow with long string on tillering stick.*

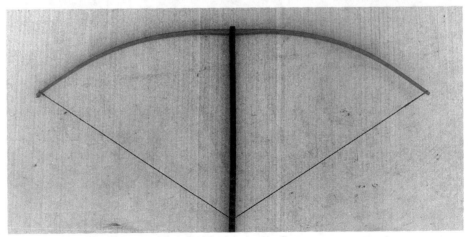

*Tillering string allows bow to be drawn without stringing first.*

At this stage, a long string is used, allowing the bow to be pulled on the stick without being strung first. A genuine, adequate bowstring should be used here, as it is under considerable strain since the bow is still far too strong. You may want to make an extra long string just for tillering purposes: fourteen or sixteen strands of Dacron™ are adequate. Position the center of the bow's handle on the tillering stick and pull the exact center of the string 10 to 12 inches before securing it in one of the grooves. Lean the contraption against the wall and step away from it. The relative bend of the limbs should be more evident. Sometimes it is useful to place the bow and tillering stick on a grid, such as a tile floor or squares drawn on a wall, so the bend will be easier to recognize.

One limb will probably be considerably stronger, or stiffer, than the other. Wood should be removed from the entire length of the stronger limb until both limbs appear roughly equal when the bow is drawn on the tillering stick.

When the two limbs look correct at the shorter draw lengths of ten or twelve inches, the string can be pulled a bit farther. For a bow with a narrow, thicker handle section, the center should remain stiff until the widest part of the bow is reached, then the limb should begin bending gracefully. For a "D" bow, or one without a narrow handle section, the bow should bend throughout its length, with the center perhaps being slightly stiffer, or flattened. With either type of bow the tips should not bend for the last 6" or so, though they need to be thinned and narrowed to some extent to cut down on speed-robbing weight, as explained in the chapter on Performance.

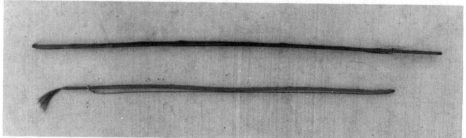

*"D" bows. Note absence of a thicker handle section.*

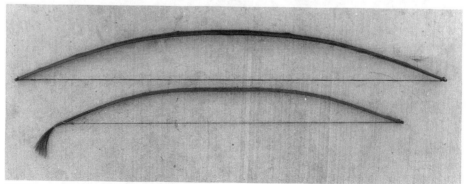

*"D" bows strung, showing how they bend throughout their length.*

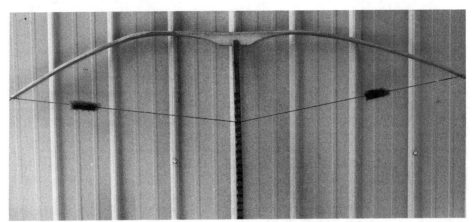

*Bow with a hinge in the left limb. When a hinge appears, a bow should never be drawn any farther until it is corrected.*

During the entire tillering process you should be on the lookout for **hinges,** or an area which bends a great deal more than the wood on both sides of it. A hinge appears as an angular bend, rather than an even, graceful curve. When dealing with hinges, keep in mind the adage we started with; take off wood where the limb doesn't bend enough, and leave alone the areas where it bends too much. Because a hinged area bends far too much, it should be left alone and the wood on either side of it reduced to make the bend correct. When a noticeable hinge appears, never draw a bow any farther, otherwise the hinged area will be permanently compressed and bent. It is a good idea to mark a hinged area on the belly with a pencil, so additional wood won't accidentally be removed there.

A hinge is similar to the weak link in a chain. The weakest part of the bow determines the maximum final weight. There may be a 65 pound hinge in a 75 pound bow. This means when the bow is properly tillered and the limbs are even that it will pull 65 pounds at the most. Or it could be there is a 45 pound

*Plaited loop, above, for the top limb, and an adjustable timber hitch for the bottom.*

hinge in a 65 pound bow, meaning that the maximum weight possible for this bow is 45 pounds. An extreme case such as this will only occur if the bowyer gets in a hurry.

Of course, this has never happened to me – not over a few dozen times. From this long and sometimes sad personal experience, I would like to coin Hamm's Law – *Two minutes of impatience or inattention – 10 seconds if using a power tool – will wreck eight hours of careful work.*

When the limbs pull evenly, the bow is ready to be strung for the first time. A word about strings. I prefer using a timber hitch on the bottom limb and a plaited loop on the top. The timber hitch can be quickly adjusted for length and will not constantly fall off when the bow is unstrung. The fistmele of the bow, or the distance from the string to the back of the handle when it's strung, can be low, about 3 or 4", during these early stages. Later, as the finished weight is approached and the bow is pulled farther, the string should be shortened so the fistmele is 5 to 6", or enough so that when an arrow is nocked the feathers do not touch the bow.

If you find yourself turning purple in the face and blacking out when trying to string a bow, then it is still too strong. I once managed to string a 90# bow while sitting in a chair. I saw Ishi clearly, and was sore for three days afterward. If your bow is too stiff, wood should be removed from both limbs, taking care to keep the bend even and avoid hinges, until the bow can be strung.

Again, the first priority of tillering is to make both limbs bend evenly. When the strung bow has a correct arc, its strength is weighed. A set-up with pulleys, rope, and a spring scale can be used which not only weighs the bow but allows you to view it from a distance. This is the most desirable method. But a bathroom scale is just as accurate and nearly everybody has one readily available. Cut a groove on one end of a two inch by two inch stick to accept the center of the bowstring, and mark the draw lengths on the stick. It is mandatory to screw a four inch by four inch piece of plywood to the lower end of the stick, then glue a piece of sandpaper to the bottom of the plywood to prevent slippage. The stick and bow are placed on the scales and the reading zeroed.

*Bow with uneven tiller. Both limbs bend gracefully, without hinges, but the limb on the right is stiffer, or stronger, than the other.*

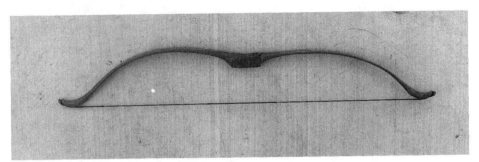

*Recurve with uneven tiller.*

Whichever method is used, bathroom scales or pulley and rope, watch the weight on the scales carefully while drawing the bow. The bow is drawn no farther than half of the finished weight at first, let's say 30 pounds for a 60 pound bow. This weight will be reached at a very short draw length, probably 10 to 15 inches. If the tiller remains even after this first bending, then draw it a bit farther, to 40 pounds, and check the bend. If one limb shows to be stronger at any time during this bending, which is normal, then remove wood from the stronger limb and pull the bow to the same distance again to check the bend. As the limbs approach correct tiller, the differences between them, as well as flat or hinged areas, will be very subtle. Inspect the bow with a critical, meticulous eye.

Once the tiller is even at a given draw length, then the pull is increased in

*Placing the bowstring in the groove on top of the weighing stick.*

*Drawing the bow downward.*

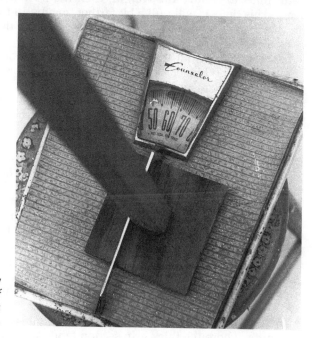

*The weight is measured by the scale. Note square of plywood screwed to bottom of stick to prevent slippage.*

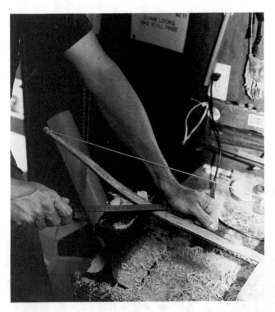

*Rasping wood from the belly of a strung bow held in a vice.*

increments of ten pounds, until the final desired weight is reached. The bow will probably reach 60 pounds at a short draw length to begin with, perhaps 15 to 18 inches. The bow is drawn no farther and more wood is removed equally from both limbs to reduce the weight, then the bow is drawn to 60 pounds once again. This time, it will pull a bit farther, maybe 18 to 20 inches, before reaching the final weight. If the bow is never pulled beyond the finished weight, it cannot be over-strained.

Two thoughts about this method, the first cautionary. The bow limbs MUST be even, with no hinges, before being stressed to this degree. A hinge or even an entire limb which is weaker than the other can take an unnecessary, permanent set. Second, the great advantage to this method is that it is nearly impossible to overshoot the final desired weight and make a bow too light. And the bow is effectively 'broken in' when the final draw length is reached, and will lose very little additional weight.

To restate this procedure: pulling a bow on the scale to its final draw weight, first at a short length and then at increasing lengths as wood is removed until full draw is reached, is an almost fool-proof way to tiller IF the limbs are kept even throughout the process.

From now on, until the bow is finished, draw the bow by hand every time wood is removed. Not beyond its finished weight, but partially draw it eight or ten times since the true effects of wood removal are often not seen until the wood is stressed as it is bent. The wood MUST be stressed by drawing the bow every time wood is taken off so the true bend of the limbs becomes evident. This stressing allows the limbs to show their "real" shape as they respond to the removal of wood.

The most crucial area of tillering a wide-limbed, narrow-handled bow is the **fade-outs,** where the thick grip section fades and blends into the widest part of the bow on each limb. The rounded side of the rasp is especially useful in this area. The photos dealing with the relationship between width and thickness should be studied carefully. The thickness must not be reduced too far back into the handle, thus making the area both thin AND narrow, resulting in a lethal weak place. On the other hand, the limb should not be stiff and unbending far past the widest point, but a gradual bend should begin once the widest point is reached. Smooth, graceful transitions are the rule here, with no abrupt changes in thickness or width.

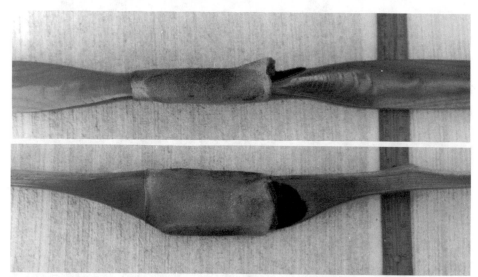

*Fade-outs of handle sections showing correct relationship between width and thickness. Note that ruler is at the widest point of the bows.*

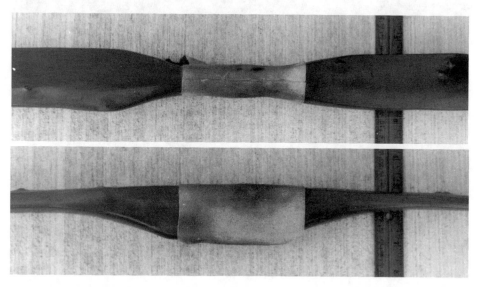

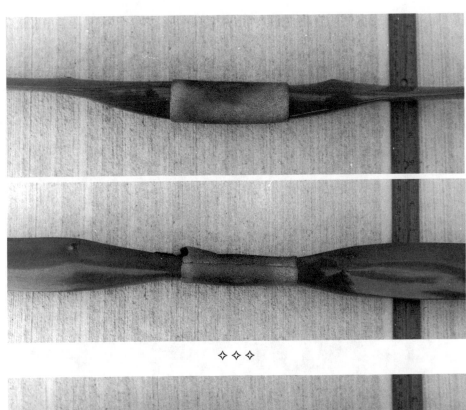

✧ ✧ ✧

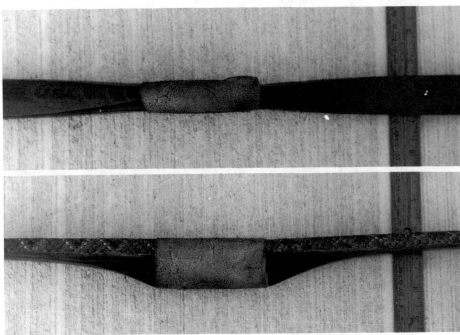

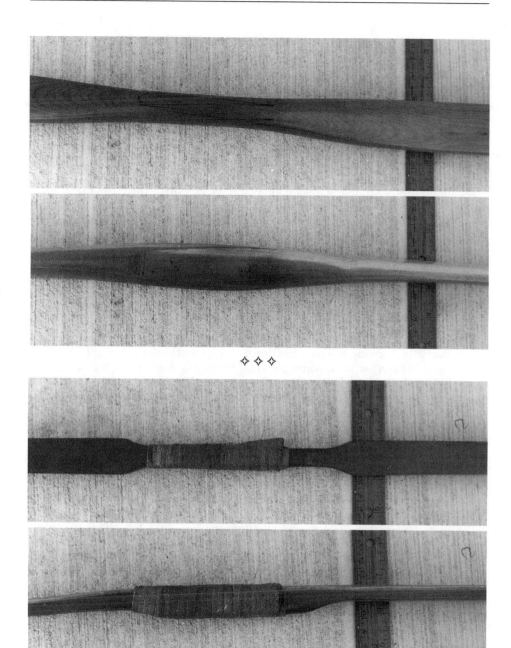

*Incorrect fade-out. Note how bow is still thin as it begins to narrow next to the ruler, resulting in an area which bends too much because it is too weak. With a narrow-handled bow, it should not begin bending until the widest part of the limb is reached.*

To further reduce the weight of the bow, exchange the rasp for a scraper once the draw reaches 20" or so. A cabinet maker's scraper or a sharp pocketknife works well. Because the scraper is more precise and takes off less wood, it makes it difficult to remove too much. This is especially critical with a thin, wide-limbed bow, since a given amount of wood removed from the belly will make a much greater difference than with a narrower, thicker bow. Make long, smooth strokes while holding the scraper at right angles to the wood. If it begins to chatter, or make ridges, change the angle or scrape the wood from the other direction. Knots or twists may require more effort as the wood is usually harder in these areas.

As an alternative to using a scraper, you may exchange the coarse rasp for a fine one, sometimes called a cabinetmaker's rasp. This tool takes off small amounts of wood while keeping the belly perfectly flat, which the scraper sometimes does not. Experienced bowyers often take a bow to finished weight and tiller with a coarse rasp or a spokeshave, but this skill only comes with many years – and numerous aborted bows. So if you are the least bit uncertain, stick with a scraper or at the very least a fine rasp. An effective trade-off is to make one pass with the scraper, check the weight of the bow, then make the next pass with the fine rasp. This keeps the belly perfectly flat while minimizing the chance of removing too much wood.

Whichever tool is used, take off only twenty or thirty strokes from each limb before partially drawing the bow ten times and re-checking the weight. The bow will draw a bit farther now when the final weight is reached on the scale. The bend should also be checked on the tillering stick. It is quite useful to mark the draw lengths on the tillering stick, so the bow can be pulled to the same degree as it is pulled on the scales. From now on, when it is on the tillering stick, the bow should be viewed from both sides, as a limb that appears too stiff from one side may sometimes look perfect from the other.

A few strokes can make a critical difference at this stage so progress should slow to a crawl when approaching full draw length. Continue scraping, gradually drawing the bow farther and farther, until the strength is reduced to about 4 pounds over the final weight at full draw. It is desirable to be at this weight when the bow is first pulled to a full draw; this stresses the limbs less than drawing it at a greater weight and will allow the bow to deliver its best performance. That is why we have slowly and carefully stalked the correct weight. The bow is now pulled to full draw thirty or forty times. Occasionally this will change the tiller slightly. If this occurs, carefully adjust the stronger limb by making only a very few passes with the scraper.

How should the bow look when it is pulled? For a bow with straight limbs, the simplest and most effective shape is a gentle, elliptical bend, with the tips being slightly straighter. A "D" bow, or one without a narrowed handle, will bend evenly throughout its length, with the middle section perhaps a bit stiffer, or flattened. For a narrow, deep handled bow, each limb bends in a symmetrical arc when drawn, connected by the stiff handle section. A recurved bow will appear different at full draw, since the working section of the limb is shortened. Refer to the photos for the proper shape of different bows at different draw lengths.

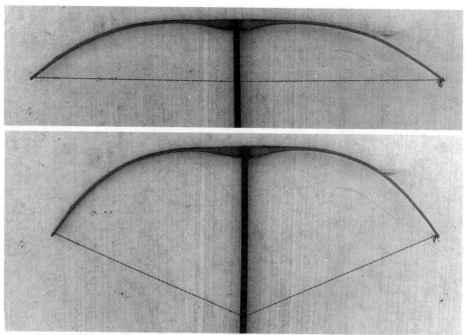

*Correct tiller for a bow with a narrowed handle section. This Osage self bow was made by nine-year-old Reed Hamm.*

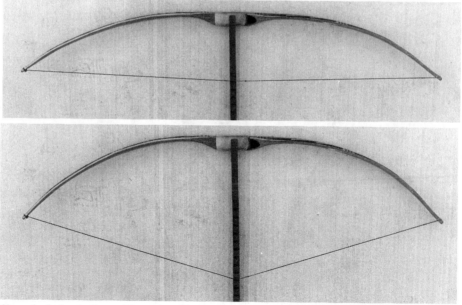

*Sinew-backed cedar bow with correct tiller.*

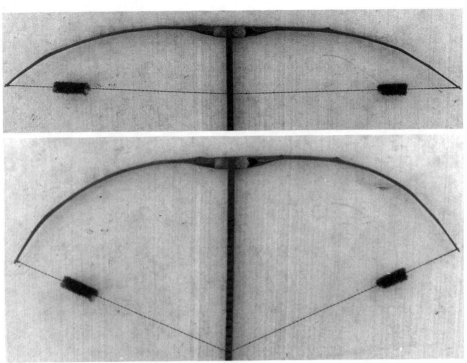

*This bow's tiller is fine, though it is very slightly whip-ended.*

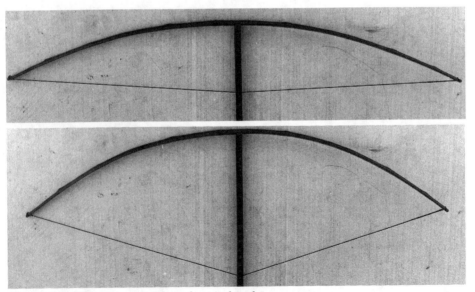

*"D" bow, showing correct bend throughout its length.*

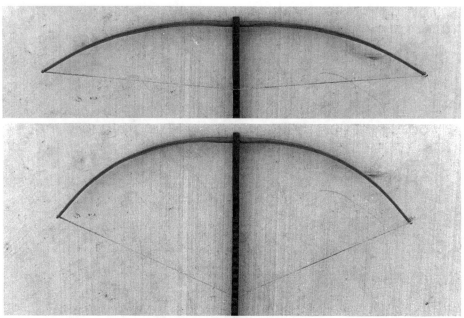

*"D" bow with a slightly thickened, and stiffer, handle section.*

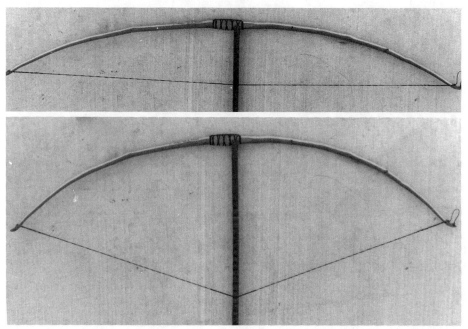

*Yew longbow. Note how lower limb on the left is slightly shorter, and stiffer, than the upper limb.*

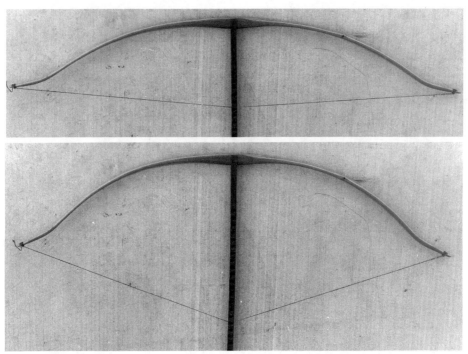

*Yew working recurve.*

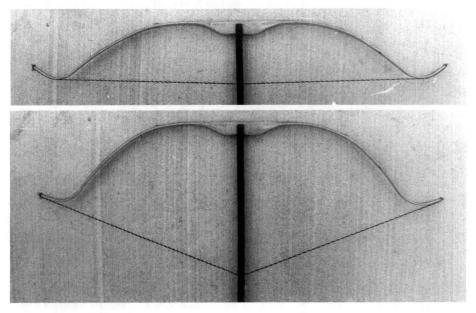

*Osage static recurve.*

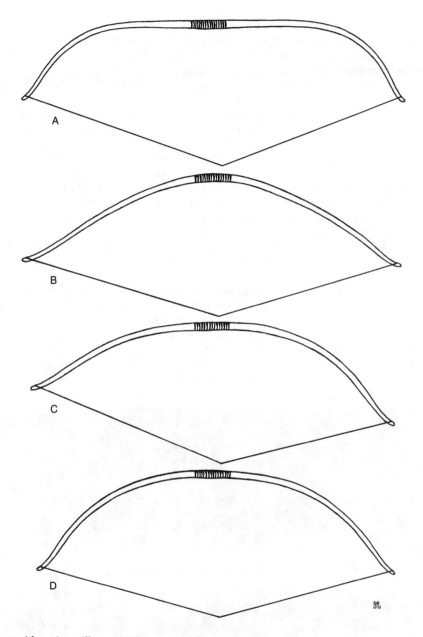

*Bows with various tillers. A) Whip-ended. This bow would have very little hand shock, though it sacrifices some speed and durability. B) Bends in the handle. This bow would likely be named "Destroyer of Cartilage", for the unmerciful hand shock it would have. C) Uneven tiller. This bow would have higher than normal hand shock (though not as much as "B"), and would have a shorter life. D) Correct tiller. This gives the best combination of speed, durability, and hand shock.*

Once the tiller and weight are correct shoot the bow and stop to check the shape every dozen arrows or so. An unbacked bow will normally lose only a couple of pounds if tillered with the method outlined above, with another pound or two lost during sanding and finishing. I prefer shooting a bow a day or two to insure that the tiller and weight remain stable. If so, the tillering is complete and the bow is now ready to finish.

If you have done the final tillering with a fine rasp, or even a coarse one (heaven forbid), the weight of the bow will change very slightly, if at all, when the rasp marks are scraped out prior to sanding. The rough belly, when viewed close up, appears as mountains of wood separated by valleys. Since the belly side is under compression, any wood in a ridge has nothing to push against and so adds nothing to the power of the bow. Though it appears that considerable amounts of wood are being removed with the scraper, this wood performs no work and its removal has little effect on the final weight.

So, this is the tillering process for perfect wood. Slow and steady, with no surprises or pitfalls. Nice, gradual tapers. The ideal remains: take off wood where the limb doesn't bend enough, and leave alone the areas where it bends too much.

But, as you have undoubtedly noticed by now, bow wood is seldom perfect. In reality, it is sometimes contrary in the extreme, shot through with knots, with wrinkled grain, twists, and off-center string alignment.

As disconcerting as these problems may sometimes be, they can be dealt with or allowed for with no detrimental effects. In fact, the realities of working with sun-drenched, wind-blown, rain-nurtured wood is what gives traditional bows their character, and, indeed, is what captivated many of us and drew us to

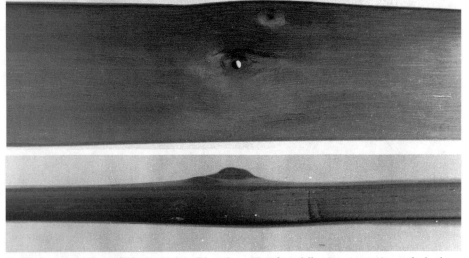

*Knothole entirely through the limb of an Osage bow. Note how following one grain on the back leaves a hump, and also how bow was left slightly thicker on the belly side and slightly wider around the knot.*

natural bows in the first place. A wooden bow has a personality, a *soul*, that is nonexistent in mundane, predictable, boring materials such as aluminum, graphite, or fiberglass.

The most common obstacle encountered is knots. They are caused by small branches, or in the case of Osage orange, by thorns as well, and should be considered as possible weak places in the bow. Nature has, in most instances, compensated for this weakness by growing a bump in the growth ring in such areas. A prime example is Osage. If a stave is from a small tree and a single growth ring well-worked by the bowyer, the back will have a bump, or wart, wherever there is a knot. Usually, the bigger the knot, the bigger the compensating growth and resulting bump. Now, remembering that a bow twice as wide will be twice as strong, but one twice as thick will be eight times as strong, it is evident that a small increase in thickness will result in a tremendous increase in bend resistance, or relative flexibility. In the case of the knots, the additional raised areas on the back of the bow translate to more strength, and less bending, than the rest of the back. This causes less stress in the problem areas, allowing us to make beautiful bows which are shot-full of knots. With this natural compensation, the normal knot requires no adjustment in the tillering being done on the belly side of the bow.

A point to be aware of: If a bow has a great many knots, and therefore corresponding stiff areas, it should be made a bit wider or longer than normal so the diminished working areas of the bow, between the knots, will not be overstrained.

Occasionally, however, a bad knot is flat on the back, with no strengthening bump built in by the tree. Or sometimes a small rotten branch will leave a hole entirely through a limb. In these situations, it is up to the bowyer to protect

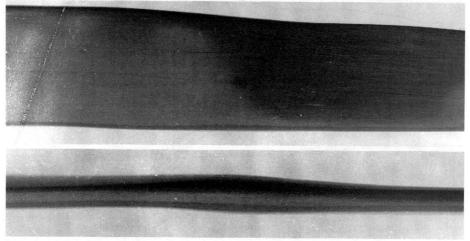

*Knot in an Osage bow in which the tree did not build in extra reinforcing wood on the back. Note the mild "swell" in the knot area from the side view, where the bow was left a bit thicker on the back and belly to compensate.*

these areas by leaving more wood on the belly. Remember, though, it doesn't take much additional thickness, just a very slight swelling in the problem area when viewed from the side.

Another option is to increase the strength by making the bow slightly wider around a problem spot. The radial grain often flows around a knot anyway, much as water flows around a rock in a stream, allowing the bowyer to follow it and compensate for the flaw. Nowhere is it written in granite that the sides of a bow have to be perfectly straight. There is nothing wrong with allowing for problems with the width of a limb, in addition to, or in lieu of, the thickness. Many bows, made from smaller, more challenging trees, will have undulating sides throughout their length. The shooting qualities, by the way, are not affected in the slightest. I have heard old-timers speak in hushed tones of a flight bow from back in the thirties. Made from a snarly piece of Osage, it had wavy sides and a hole entirely through the lower limb, and while the weapon may have looked inferior to some modern eyes, the owner regularly thumped the competition in distance shoots with it.

Even severe problems can sometimes be dealt with by compensating for weakness with more width or thickness. One of Ron Hardcastle's master creations was an Osage self bow with a massive thumb-sized hole right in the working part of one limb. The wood was otherwise perfect, except for that one terrible defect, a defect which would have probably sent the stave to the kindling pile had I been working it. But Ron persevered, using his skill and experience to produce an exquisite, striking bow. The point is: don't necessarily look upon knots, twists, holes, or other flaws as insurmountable, look upon them as beauty marks and simply make allowances.

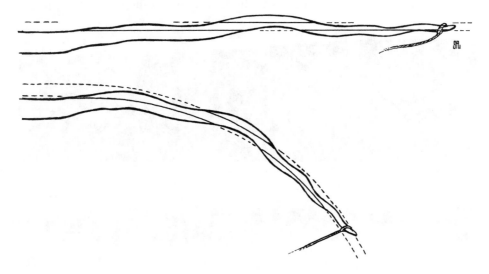

*Method for tillering a "snaky" limb. Draw parallel lines down the side and use them for correct tillering bend rather than using the undulations of the wood.*

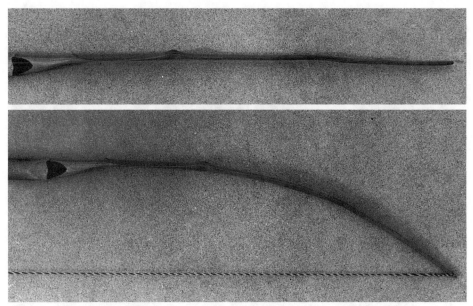

*Limb with mild "snaky" grain.*

A problem occasionally encountered in the real world of wood is a stave with wrinkled grain. Such bows with severe wrinkles were referred to in the old days as **snake bows.** Yew and Osage were the most common woods for these bows and they were, and still are, prized for their character. Such staves are difficult to work to a single grain on the back because of the twists and turns. But they are just as difficult to tiller, the wrinkles appearing as an array of flat spots and hinges. One way to tiller such a bow is to squint the eyes, until the bend of the bow is a blur. The idea is to adjust the average bend of the limbs, instead of worrying about each ripple in the grain, though care must be taken to keep the belly of the bow parallel with the back as it follows the curves. Another option, even better, that Tim Baker has devised, is to draw parallel lines down the side of the bow, and tiller by using the lines for correct bend instead of the undulations of the wood. This allows precise tillering, with every part of the bow doing an equal amount of work. Such pieces of wood are challenging and require consummate skill from the bowyer, but make some of the most desirable, interesting weapons. More often a stave will exhibit only a wrinkle or two. Deal with them in the same manner; tiller for the average bend of the limb and the wrinkle will cause no problems.

Tillering, or taking off wood, is normally intended to reduce the weight of a bow, though there are times when the weight, or stiffness, will need to be increased. One example is when the bow is at the weight desired, but the limbs are out of balance with one weaker, or bending more, than the other. In this case, the weaker limb should be shortened, making it relatively stiffer, and new string nocks cut. How much to shorten the limb? It depends on how much weaker it is, but cutting off 1/2" to 3/4" is a good starting point. Often, this

▲ W. I. King (left), and Chester Stevenson examine "snaky" bows and arrow, circa. 1940 (courtesy Bear Archery and the Fred Bear Museum).

◄ Bow made by Chester Stevenson in the 1940's (courtesy Bear Archery and the Fred Bear Museum).

method brings the tiller into alignment without reducing the weight of the bow any farther. In fact, the weight will sometimes increase slightly.

A more common problem is a bow which turns out too light. There are several options for increasing the weight. One is to sinew-back it. The weight can be increased from 5 to 10 pounds, depending on how much sinew is applied. But be aware that a bow intended to be sinew-backed from the start is not tillered until after the sinew is in place and dried, since such a bow is usually too short to stand the strain of bending without the backing.

Another way to raise the weight is to recurve the tips, which effectively shortens the working part of the bow, making it bend farther, thus greatly increasing the stress. The weight can be raised from 15 to 30 pounds this way, depending upon the length and angle of recurve, though the chances for wood failure are dramatically heightened.

But another, much simpler option exists. An equal amount can be cut from both tips and new string nocks fashioned. The bow remains in tiller and the weight goes up. How much to cut off? Here is a simple formula. For each 1% of the length cut off, the weight will go up approximately 5%. Divide the weight you want by the weight you have. The figure to the right of the decimal is the percentage increase you want. Divide this decimal figure by 5 to yield the percentage the bow should shortened. Multiply this figure by the bow's length to give the amount to be cut off. Take half of this amount from each end.

For example, let's say a bow is 66" and pulls 52 pounds, but was intended to be 58 pounds. Dividing the weight we want by the weight we have yields a figure of 1.1153. The figure to the right of the decimal, .1153, is the percentage increase in weight we want. Dividing this figure by 5 gives the percentage the bow should be cut off, or .023. Multiplying .023 times the bow's length, 66", shows that 1.5" should be cut from the bow, or 3/4" from both tips. The bow will now pull 58 pounds, and if the tiller was even before the tips were cut off, it will remain so.

Naturally, shortening the limbs places more stress on the wood. If the bow design was pushing the edges of the allowable envelope to begin with, then sinew-backing may be the preferred choice, or a combination of shortening the bow and sinew-backing. But most designs have plenty of length and tolerance built in, so this method is a helpful one to know. If for no other reason than this, a wise bowyer designs his weapons an inch or two longer than necessary.

Suppose a bow is both out of tiller and too light. It is possible to cut off unequal amounts from either end, with more being cut from the weaker limb. This can get tricky, though, so unless you're in love with the particular piece of wood it may be best to finish this bow out at a lighter weight. A gift of this bow to a child about ten years old will make you their favorite uncle, neighbor, or father. Bowyers, particularly those just beginning, are very popular among children.

Another factor that may come into play during tillering is string alignment down the bow. With straight, flawless wood and careful layout of the design, the string will usually line up perfectly. Usually, but not always. And, as we have seen, perfect wood is not always available or even desirable, since pieces with flaws have so much character.

First, understand that with a wide, thin, rectangular cross-section, flawless string alignment is commendable but far from crucial. With a longbow, as John Strunk has outlined earlier, string alignment is more critical, but with a flatbow it falls somewhere down the list behind correct weight, proper tiller, and hand-shock just to mention a few more important characteristics. This is not to say that a string grossly out of alignment should not be corrected, and we'll address that presently, but moderate deviations in the string lying down the exact center of the bow will cause not the slightest problem; indeed, they will never be noticed when the bow is shot.

Ideally, when a bow is strung, the string bisects the handle and the limbs. If it lies off to one side, that should be the side the arrow passes across. This is an advantage to the bow limbs being of equal length, the bow can simply be flipped over if necessary, placing the upper limb on the bottom to allow for slight string mis-alignment.

One trick to lining up a narrow-handled bow is to leave the handle at full width until the bow is tillered. The handle doesn't bend anyway, so the extra wood presents no impediment to the process. Once tillering is complete, check the string alignment. If the string is off center, a handle section can now be drawn and cut out to reflect the true position of the string.

At times, the string is out of alignment because of a twist in one limb caused by improper tiller, or to be more precise, improper tapering of the limbs. With a twisted limb, the first thing to check is the thickness on both its sides. If one side is thinner than the other, and therefore weaker, the limb will always twist to the weaker side. To cure this simply reduce the thicker side of the limb until it is equal to the other; the twist will disappear or greatly diminish as tillering progresses.

Once in a great while, however, the string is terribly out of line, lying outside the handle, as a result of crooked wood or a limb twisting when stressed. Ron Hardcastle came up with a technique to correct the problem and together we have fine-tuned it over time. First, look down the string from one end and esti-mate how far that tip has to be moved, in relation to the other, to bring the string into alignment. An inch, maybe, or even two. Plan on moving each tip half of this amount, let's say an inch, for example. Place the shaped, narrowed handle of the bow over a pot of boiling water, then form a tent of aluminum foil over it to help hold in the steam. Turn the bow over after fifteen minutes so both sides will be exposed to the heat. Make sure the steam is localized on the handle so the limbs won't have to be dried.

In the meantime, set up two wooden chucks, with a large "V" or "U" cut out on one end, 18" apart on the edge of a table. Pad the cutout areas, so the bow won't be marred. After thirty minutes of boiling, and no less (this is for Osage – other woods may take up to an hour), place the bow on its edge in the chucks and put a clamp at the center of the handle. A big C clamp will work but a pipe clamp has less of a tendency to slip. It is helpful to have someone hold a ruler against one tip and measure the distance the tip moves as pressure is applied with the clamp. The tip must move 50% more than the desired final measure-ment, an inch and a half to yield an ultimate distance of one inch. Once suffi-cient pressure has been applied with the clamp, leave the bow for at least one

*Steaming and clamping method for correcting limbs which are out of alignment. This bow's string lay more than an inch outside the handle, but after steaming the handle section and applying correct pressure with the clamp, the limbs lined up properly and the string lay down the center of the bow.*

hour, allowing it to cool completely (Paul Comstock recommends with white woods the clamps be left in place twenty-four hours). When the clamp is removed, notice that the bow tips move slightly, this is the reason for going 50% past the desired measurement. The bow can now be strung, and the string alignment should be very close, if not perfect.

A limb with a **propeller twist,** or one that is essentially straight but with a twist in it like a propeller, is sometimes encountered during the tillering stage once a bow is strung. This is not due to improper tillering but is inherent in the particular piece of wood. There are two schools of thought on dealing with this. The first is to shrug your shoulders and ignore it completely. I'm a disciple of this method, and while it may be fairly claimed this is due to natural laziness on my part, I can honestly write such twists do not seem to cause any detectable problems with a bow's performance or shooting characteristics. I don't believe it possible to shoot two identical bows, one with a propeller twist and one without, and differentiate between them. So I've learned to live quite comfortably with this problem.

However, some bowyers look with horror upon such a bow, insisting that it would be more suitably mounted on the front of a Sopwith Camel. If such a twist offends one's sensibilities, it can usually be taken out with heat, though a limb torqued too far is likely to vigorously protest by coming apart. This is the underlying reason why a fairly minor problem such as propeller twist or a string being slightly out of alignment is often easier to live with than to change.

Another final factor to keep in mind is that an unbalanced, out of tiller bow will usually have more hand shock than one which is tillered properly. In fact, if a bow has an abnormal amount of jar when an arrow is released, check the tiller first. Often, too, a bow can be shortened to reduce hand shock, and it doesn't necessarily have to be shortened by much to make a big difference. Sometimes 3/4" cut from each tip will bring about a noticeable improvement.

Every bowyer of any experience, without exception, has made plenty of bows ten or fifteen pounds lighter than intended. Or broken bows during tillering. Or during weighing. Or had a bow turn out far different from what he had in mind. So don't be discouraged by failures or setbacks. Rejoice in the successes and learn from the occasional mistakes, while keeping firmly in mind that the point is creating a useable, long-lasting bow, not necessarily the perfect bow, if such a thing exists.

This wonderful endeavor is more art than science, and the variations in the wood are what make it interesting and fun. After all, if we walked the path of least resistance and resorted to pure science, our bows would have cables for strings. And wheels on the end of limbs made from space alloys. Our fingers would never touch the string, and the shot would be made with the push of a button. The sights would be a laser-generated dot, allowing 60 and 70 yard shots with hollow metal arrows. There would be no trace of natural, honest materials in the entire rig.

The very thought of such a device is chilling, and makes one appreciate the challenges of working with wood.

# FINISHES AND HANDLES

*John Strunk*

When your bow has been tillered and shot 50 or so times, it is ready to finish. Preparing the bow for finishing is an important step. Make sure all scratches, file marks, fingerprints, etc., have been removed. The best way to check this is to take the bow outdoors and use the bright sunlight to help you see. If it is winter time, which is when most of us will be building a bow, then use an artificial light that illuminates the bow surface well. Remember, finish does not cover up flaws but works just the opposite. If there are scratches or file marks on the bow, they will be much more noticeable when you apply the finish.

With yew wood, file and rasp marks are difficult to remove by sanding. One way to deal with this problem is to use a sharp knife and scrape the bow surface prior to sanding. Begin the sanding operation by using 50-grit garnet paper; this has sufficient abrasive quality to remove any tool marks. Proceed through the sanding operation using 80, 120, and 180-grit garnet paper.

One trick to sanding is to dampen the wood using a moist paper towel each time you change sizes of abrasive paper. This raises the grain and results in a smoother surface after sanding. The wood should be allowed to dry approximately a half hour after dampening before further sanding is attempted.

If the yew wood bow is to be unbacked, then the sapwood surface should be burnished. Using a small, polished, smooth stone or small glass bottle as a burnishing tool, rub it firmly back and forth lengthwise along the back of the bow. Apply sufficient pressure to compress the wood grain down into itself. This operation hardens the surface by binding the wood fibers to one another to prevent them lifting as the bow back stretches in the shooting process. Another trick that I've used with the burnishing process is to remove small dents in the bow. Yew wood is a soft wood and is prone to small scratches and dents from daily use. These can be smoothed out as if they never existed by using the burnishing technique. This can be done without damaging the bow's finish.

With Osage orange, which is extremely hard, begin the sanding with 120-grit after all of the rasp marks have been scraped from the wood. The sanding continues to 220, 320, 400, and finally 600-grit. The wood is then burnished, which brings out the fire and color to a remarkable degree.

On light-colored woods, I usually stain the bow before finishing. This is most appropriate for a hunting bow, and also adds to the natural beauty of the wood. On woods such as ash, the stain will penetrate down into its pores and really

*Sign your work before applying the finish.*

enhance the appearance. You may also burnish the wood using fine 5/0 steel wool after the stain has penetrated into the wood. This will highlight the grain of the wood. The best stains I have found for bow work have been a black or brown oil dye by Fiebings™. Although this dye is made for leather, it will work well on wood. Whatever stain you choose, test it first on small wood samples. This gives you the necessary practice in using it; also, you will see if all your finishes are compatible.

There are several methods you can use for finishing your new bow. Let the use and your locality help determine how you proceed. As an example, I live where it rains approximately 80-100 inches annually. I also use my bows year round for hunting as well as for other archery fun. Therefore, my bow finish must be very durable and also as waterproof as possible. When I started making bows, I tried several different types of finishes and found that each has its own advantages and disadvantages.

Whether you use a penetrating type finish or a surface build-up type finish is up to you and your needs. A penetrating finish soaks into the wood and requires multiple applications over a long period of time before sufficient moisture protection is attained. This can take as long as a year of repeated applications to achieve a waterproof finish. They are part of the romance of archery past and are easy to do.

The first penetrating agent for waterproofing a bow was undoubtedly the fat obtained from animals. And while this treatment may be ancient, it is as func-

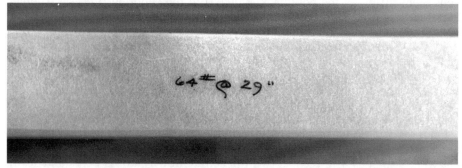

*It is also a good idea to record the weight and draw length on the bow before finishing.*

tional now as it ever was. A modern proponent of this method is Al Herrin, who has used animal fat almost exclusively on bows he has made over many years. He prefers bear grease, but has used fat from deer and even hog (in the form of bacon grease). The fat is heated in a pot until the melted oil rises to the surface, when it is skimmed off and stored in a sealed container. The oil is rubbed on the bow by hand, until the rubbing friction helps it to penetrate, or else the bow is placed in a warm area, such as beside a stove. Al puts several coats on the bow at first, then additional coats twice a year. During hunting season he applies oil weekly, or even daily if the weather is bad. He maintains that animal fat is much more than a last resort; it provides excellent protection from the elements by causing water to bead on the surface of a bow, rather than letting it soak into the wood. While he cautions against using fat on a sinew or rawhide backed bow, he recommends it as a traditional, effective finish for wood.

We read about early archers and hunters anointing their bows with a mixture of tung oil, linseed oil, cedar oils, and French polish. French polish is a combination of shellac and linseed oil. My experience with it has been with wood turnings only, but it takes years of application to impart enough moisture protection.

Tung oil is easy to apply and additional applications quick to do. It leaves a nice luster on the wood and makes it easy to repair small scratches the bow may get. However, I found that any writing I put on the bow quickly vanished because there wasn't any surface build-up of the finish. It also didn't protect the bow from a good day in the rain.

I've also used a mixture of spar varnish, mineral spirits, and linseed oil. A mixture of one-third of each created a satisfactory penetrating finish. I had used this on gunstocks in the past and found that like the tung oil and other penetrating finishes, it required many, many coats to seal out moisture.

While all of the penetrating finishes must enter the wood and fill the pores, requiring a great many applications to be effective, a surface finish is designed to encase the wood in a protective covering. To me these are the best types of finishes for providing protection from continual exposure to moisture. Finishes such as spar varnish, varathane, or polyurethanes fit this category, and are the best type of finishes I have found. The spar varnish takes a long time to dry and is difficult to apply smoothly, though for the do-it-yourself craftsman it works well.

Jim Hamm has had success with making his own varnishes, and explains the method this way; "There are two types of varnish, oil varnish and spirit varnish. The oil varnish is a complicated process of heating tree resins, linseed oil, and thinner to exact, high temperatures over an extended period of time. For the home craftsman, this method is not only laborious, but dangerous, due to the possibility of explosion or fire. The spirit varnish, however, is easy to make and does a nice job of finishing and waterproofing a bow. Gather the pitch from pine or cedar trees from where the sap oozes out of a damaged area on the trunk. Other trees, varieties of fruits, for instance, also have a resinous sap and may well be worth experimentation. The pitch is dried until hard, then crushed as fine as possible with a mortar and pestle. Place the powder in a glass container and add enough 'spirit' to cover it. I used rubbing alcohol and it worked fine, but in the old days turpentine was used, and since turpentine is distilled from pine sap, it may be the better choice (Or, if you're a really hard-core traditionalist, moonshine from your own still could probably be used). The mixture is stirred occasionally over a twenty-four hour period to dissolve the pitch, then strained through an old T-shirt into another glass container. The resulting varnish is a translucent amber color.

To apply it to the bow, I dip a corner of a cotton cloth into the liquid, then rub it smoothly onto the wood. Make sure to cover every portion equally: the only thing worse than no moisture protection is uneven moisture protection. This first coat will dry fairly quickly. When it is totally dry, another coat is applied. After three or four of these coatings, the varnish will begin to build up and appear slick. At this stage, each application will take longer and longer to dry completely, sometimes a day or two. Also, once the finish begins to build up, the wood surface should be gone over lightly with fine steel wool before every application. If the varnish is a bit thick, more spirit can be added and stirred. Usually, six or eight coats of this finish gives a nice gloss and waterproofs the bow. For the hunter, an additional coat can be added before each hunting season, and the sheen on the back of the bow dulled with fine steel wool. In the old days, aniline dyes were added to spirit varnish to stain the wood, and for those hunting with bows made from white woods, such as ash and hickory, the addition of these dyes may be useful.

The only problems I encountered with this home-made varnish was obtaining an even, smooth finish. A number of coats of thin varnish worked better than fewer coats when the varnish was thick. Dust will also stick to the bow, because the finish is tacky during the long drying periods. A clean work area and steel wool between coats overcame most dust problems.

I was a bit dubious when I began experimenting with this finish, but have found it to be very attractive while giving excellent protection to the wood. Best of all, it allows a bowyer to fashion a weapon made entirely by hand, with minimal outside influences or assistance."

While varnishes work well, the one finish I've found that gives the most complete protection to the wood is varathane, such as that made by Flecto™. This is available in an aerosol spray. It goes on quickly, smoothly, and dries dust free in about 30 minutes. I found that the Gloss 90™ product was the best, providing the best penetration and surface build-up. I use five to seven coats without any need for sanding in between. When the last coat has dried for several hours, I sand the surface smooth with 400 wet or dry sanding paper. Further smoothing with (5/0) steel wool removes all the shine and leaves a satin finish.

You can either leave it that way or polish further with a rubbing compound. I use a small amount of pumice powder mixed with cooking oil to polish the finish. Use a small piece of cloth dipped in the oil and then into the pumice. Thoroughly rub down the entire bow with this mixture. This brings out the beauty of your finish.

A coat of paste wax will complete the finishing process, and many hunters take this wax with them into the field. Paul Comstock uses furniture paste wax, and swears by it for protection – even in downpours. If the weather turns sour he simply rubs on a generous coating and keeps hunting. He also applies a coating of wax when the season is over and his bows are put away. The use of wax dates back hundreds of years, as beeswax was used to protect longbows in early England.

One final suggestion about finishes would be to practice your choice on a small scrap of wood like that used in your bow. This will give a good indication of how your finish will look.

Practicality and one's personal needs must be used as a guide when choosing a bow finish. No finish can completely stop the penetration of water over extended periods, only slow it down. The more effective the finish, the longer it keeps water from penetrating the wood. Where you live and hunt should determine what you use. You must judge what will work best for you and go with it.

Finishing highlights and preserves your craftsmanship. Therefore, take as much time as needed to do it right.

## HANDLES

Customs and personal desires determine the style of handle used on a wood bow. If you are making a bow that is to be an authentic replica of a historical weapon, then that should determine all details about it.

Bow handles can also be styled to regulate how the bow bends. By the size and shape of the handle, you can cause the bow to "work" or bend throughout its length. You may want to leave the handle area stiff so that all the bend takes place in the limbs. I like to have the handle work to some degree to give the bow a nice circular shape when drawn.

Handle size and shape should also be relative to the archer's hand size; what allows a comfortable, steady grip of the bow. Another factor to consider is how and where the arrow will be placed. This affects how the arrow will pass by the bow handle; and, therefore, it affects the flight of the arrow.

Shown are several handle styles that represent past designs and some more modern modifications that work well.

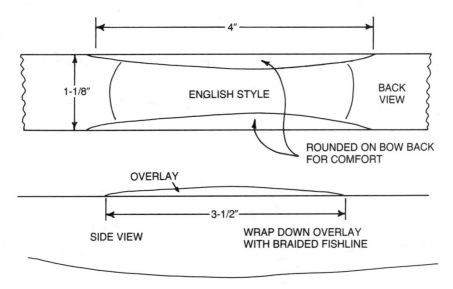

*Grip for an English-style longbow, showing addition of an overlay of leather for a better "feel".*

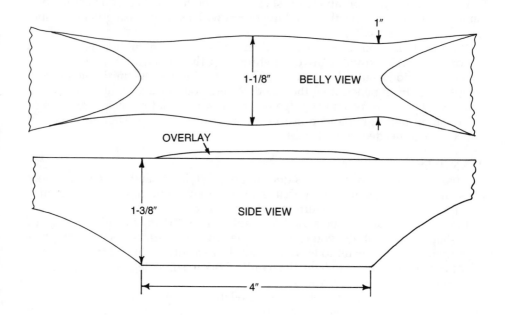

*Handle design for a flatbow.*

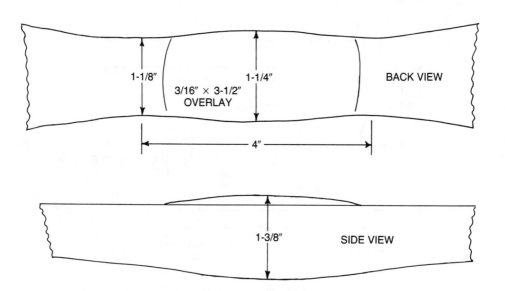

*Modified design for a flatbow.*

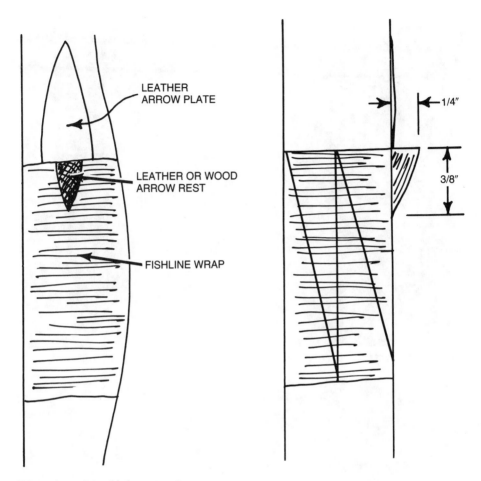

LEATHER
ARROW PLATE

LEATHER OR WOOD
ARROW REST

FISHLINE WRAP

1/4"

3/8"

*Dimensions of an added arrow rest.*

Most early bows had no arrow rest or shelf; the arrow was simply shot across the bow hand. With practice, this method becomes surprisingly accurate, and dates back to the dawning of archery.

An alternative way of designing the bow handle provides a small arrow rest. By cutting into the side of the bow a small, 1/4" wide platform for the arrow may be created. However, caution must be exercised, since this can weaken the grain structure which may result in the bow splitting at that point. I have seen this happen many times even on fiberglass laminated bows; in my estimation, it is not worth the risk.

A safer way to provide an arrow rest involves gluing a small wedge of leather or wood to the side of the bow. Any type of glue, such as Duco™ Household Cement, Elmer's™ Carpenter Glue, or contact cement will suffice. The wedge can be shaped as shown. Later, when wrapping the handle, the wedge will be covered. An arrow rest permits more consistent shooting and should be used by those primarily interested in accuracy.

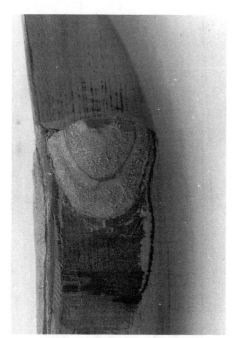
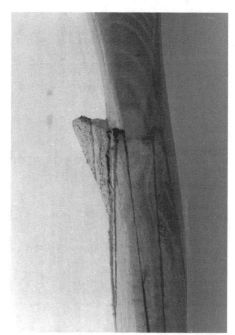

*Side and back views of harness leather glued with contact cement for arrow rest.*

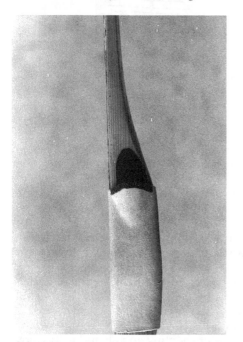
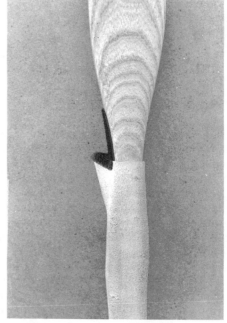

*Side and back views of finished arrow rest after covering with leather.*

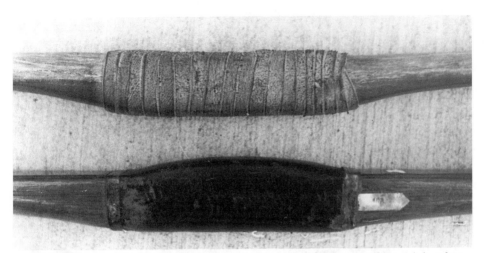

*Handle made by wrapping long leather thong around bow, above. Fifty-year-old bow, below, has colored leather glued over grip. Note mother-of-pearl arrow plate inlet into wood.*

The arrow plate, or where the arrow lays against the bow, can be treated in several ways. The easiest is to glue a piece of leather to the wood with contact cement, or use one of the commercial stick-on clipped calf-hair plates. These soft surfaces help dampen the sound of an arrow's passing, an important consideration to a hunter. In the early part of this century, leather, or even mother-of-pearl or ivory, were inlet into the wood to act as an arrow plate.

In the old days, before a handle was covered with leather, a thin sheet of cork was sometimes glued to the handle to give a softer feel to the grip. A modern take-off on this is to cut up a foam-rubber innersole and glue a piece to the bow

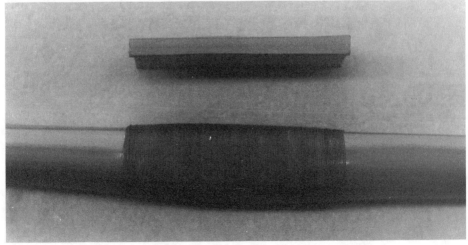

*Overlay of leather glued to back of bow, then wrapped with cord, gives a firm grip.*

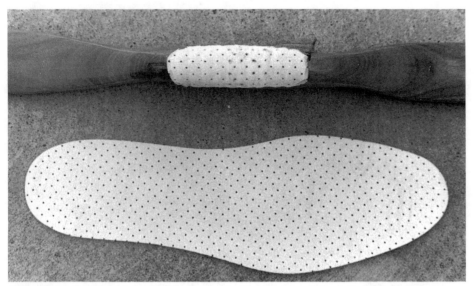

*Thin foam rubber glued to handle, then covered with buckskin, gives a better grip and helps dampen hand shock.*

in the deepest part of the handle, thus imparting a bit of "give". This reduces some of the kick in a bow, and may be a remedy for one with an uncomfortable recoil if everything else about the weapon is satisfactory.

A bow handle can be wrapped with pigskin leather around a small leather wedge and laced with goatskin. First glue and shape the leather wedge, then cut and trim a piece of pigskin to perfectly fit the shape of the bow handle. Be aware that the leather will stretch as you lace it on; therefore, it may be necessary to trim it so that it is slightly less than the circumference of the handle. Then cut

*Sixty-year-old bow with braided fishing line wrapped around the handle, then varnished. This makes a simple, effective, and attractive grip. (courtesy Glenn Parker).*

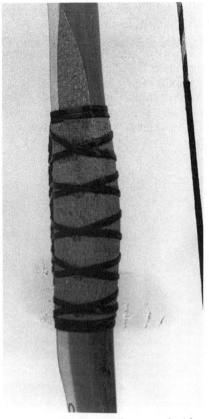
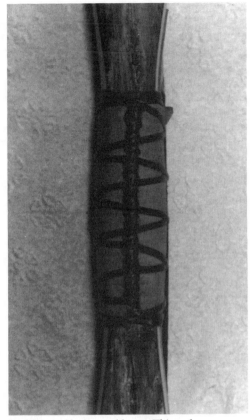

*Side view of leather handle wrapped with lacing thongs. Note leather arrow plate.*

*Back view of lacing and knots. This makes an attractive, secure grip.*

lacing notches into the two vertical edges of the handle wrap using a leather-worker's thonging chisel. These will secure the goatskin lace. Apply contact cement to the area around the wedge and the same area on the leather handle wrap. When the glue has dried, carefully begin attaching the handle leather, forming it around the wedge. Once this is accomplished, wrap the leather around the bow handle and begin lacing from the top to the bottom. It would be up to the bowmaker whether to stop here and secure the ends of the lace to complete the operation, or spiral wrap the lace around the grip as shown in the photograph.

A snakeskin can be applied to a bow handle in small strips approximately 1/2" wide with contact cement. Cover the handle area of the bow and the back side of the snakeskin strips with contact glue. Once the glue has dried, begin at the bottom of the handle and slowly wrap the snakeskin in a spiral fashion up the bow handle. It may be necessary to have two or three (or more) strips of snakeskin to cover the area. The snakeskin wrapping should begin approximately 1" below and travel 1-1/2" above where the handle wrap will be applied later.

Finish the upper and lower edges of the snakeskin with nylon fishing rod wrapping material. Spiral wrap the lace around the handle to fit the size of your hand. This will cover approximately 4" of the snakeskin wrapping.

Perhaps the easiest type of grip is to glue on a piece of buckskin, using contact cement. Or braided fishing cord can be wrapped around the handle then sealed with varnish, as was sometimes done in the early part of this century.

As you can see, there are many popular handle designs. Copy a style if it fits your bow design, but be sure it fits your hand size. Experiment and use your own ideas. After all, the handle, like the bow, is your creation. As long as function and style work in harmony with one another, you can't go wrong.

# SELF ARROWS

*Jay Massey*

"For good shooting," Maurice Thompson wrote in 1878, "everything depends upon the arrow. No matter how true your aim, how staunch your bow, or how steady your hand, you cannot hit regularly without perfect arrows."

How true – and how often we archers seem to forget this simple fact!

So many archer/craftsmen – myself included – spend countless hours working a handmade bow to perfection. We shape it carefully and tiller the limbs in perfect harmony and finally polish and finish the bow until it glows like a jewel. Then, when it comes time to shoot our shiny new bow, we hastily grab a handful of arrow shafts from the bin, fletch them up, and off we go.

Of course, our bow casts the arrow like a bullet – an arrow which, all too many times, will flirt ever so slightly as it sails toward the mark, missing it by inches.

There's an old archery adage which goes something like this: Any old stick will do for a bow, but a heap of work goes into making a good arrow. There's a good bit of truth to that statement.

Making a set of accurate hunting, field or target arrows from scratch is indeed a heap of work. I'm talking about building the entire arrow here, not just assembling the "store bought" components with a tube of glue. The arrow-making I'm referring to involves cutting and seasoning your own wood, reducing the shafts to the proper diameter, cutting the nocks, gluing or tying on the fletching, and so on. After making a matched set of a dozen arrows from scratch the work of bow-making suddenly doesn't seem so formidable.

## ARROW WOODS

In arrow-making, as in bow-making, there are many problems to be solved and decisions to be made. The first problem confronting the arrowsmith is to select a suitable wood from which to make the shafts.

Which wood to use? Each archer seems to have his own personal preference. Ishi's favorite was hazel wood; Saxton Pope and Art Young almost always used birch. The medieval English longbowmen preferred ash, birch and oak – at least for war; the ancient Turks used mostly pine. Many American Indian tribes preferred dogwood over all others.

So, which arrow wood is best? Hardly any experienced archer would be so bold as to volunteer a hard-and-fast rule in answer to that question!

The truth of the matter seems to be that no one arrow wood is ideal for all situations. For example, the ancient Turks and the medieval English longbowmen selected drastically different woods for their arrows. The Turks preferred a type of pine; the English longbowmen apparently liked ash better than any other woods available. Who was right and who was wrong?

Both – and neither.

Turkish archery evolved from the type of archery used by the horse-mounted archers of the steppes of central Asia. Those ancient horse-archers used short, powerfully-reflexed composite bows – made of horn, wood, sinew, bone and glue – which were capable of shooting arrows great distances. These horse-archers were the light artillery of their day. Their style of warfare came into use several thousand years ago by such nomadic, warlike peoples as the Scythians, then was imitated by countless others, including the Huns and Mongols, who came close to conquering all of Europe and Asia. Hordes of horse-mounted archers would charge in, release showers of arrows, and then wheel about and gallop safely out of range of the opposing forces, which were often made up of spear-wielding foot soldiers. Long range warfare was ideal for these horse-archers, for they traveled light and wore little protective armor. With such tactics, it was better to shoot arrows from 300 yards or more rather than to risk in-fighting at close range.

The short, reflexed composite bow was ideal for shooting from horseback, and the Turks developed it to its highest state. Their flight records – 800 yards and more – could not have been reached with heavy arrows made from such woods as ash or birch.

But on the British Isles, the English longbowmen opted for the dense, heavy arrow woods. These medieval archers commonly shot wooden bows that ranged from 80 to 150 pounds and were capable of casting heavy shafts tipped with huge broadheads or armor-piercing bodkins. Heavy shafts penetrate deeply and the longbow, of course, handles them well. Roger Ascham, the 16th century author of *Toxophilus*, wrote that of all woods, ash was best because it was "hevye to geve a great stripe" – meaning a hard blow.

So, both the heavy shafts used by the English longbowman and the much lighter arrows used by the Asiatic horse-archer suited the particular circumstances. Each represented the ideal arrow material for their respective uses.

Another factor which determined which arrow wood would be used was availability of the material. Ishi's favorite arrow wood – hazel – probably was the result of his having felt it was the best arrow wood growing in his immediate area. Hazel is, in fact, a fine arrow wood – one of the best for making arrows from shoots of young trees. It undoubtedly worked well for his purposes. Some American Indians preferred river cane, which is heavy and tough and commonly grew all over the southeastern United States. It too, makes good arrows. Perhaps Saxton Pope and Art Young came to prefer birch simply because it was not only tough, but readily available in dowel form during their time.

Today, we have a vast selection of fine arrow woods growing in North America. Nearly any straight-grained, moderately strong wood can be used to make arrows. The known list of good domestic arrow woods includes Sitka spruce, Douglas fir, Port Orford cedar, birch, dogwood, osoberry, ocean spray, chokecherry, osier (called "red willow," but actually a dogwood), hazel, river cane, serviceberry, snowberry, syringa, wild rose, ash, hickory, black locust, Osage orange, oak, maple, cascara, Phragmites reed, red elderberry and even willow. Good imported arrow materials include bamboo from Southeast Asia, ramin from Malaysia and Norway pine.

Like those of many other archers, my first arrows were made from birch dowels bought from the bins of a local hardware store for 25 cents apiece. I sorted through hundreds of dowels for just a couple dozen, choosing them for straightness and stiffness, or spine. Nowadays, the "birch dowels" you find in most hardware stores are actually ramin wood, which comes from Malaysia. This wood also makes good arrow shafts. Real birch dowels, however, are hard to come by these days, and if you want birch you'll probably have to cut them yourself.

If you truly want to make your arrows the traditional way, you should make the dowels yourself anyway, using either lumber from a supplier or material

*Arrow Materials – (left to right) finished hand-planed shafts of Sitka spruce, bundles of river cane and ocean spray shoots, and two slabs of air-dried Sitka spruce.*

you have cut yourself. Otherwise, you can purchase the bare shafts – of Port Orford Cedar, Douglas fir, Sitka spruce or other arrow wood – from an archery supplier. But by doing this, you'll miss out on much of the fun (and much of the work!) of traditional archery.

There are two ways to make self arrow shafts from scratch: either cut the shafts in the round (from such shrubs as dogwood, river cane, osoberry, wild rose, etc.), or cut the arrow blank from a solid chunk of wood. By **self arrows,** I'm talking about an all-wood arrow made from one piece of wood. **Footed** arrows – arrows constructed mostly of softer, more fragile woods and having a hardwood foreshaft – will be covered in a subsequent volume.

My own experience in arrow-making (arrow-assembling, actually) began with fletching birch dowels by hand and cutting in the self nocks. But soon I was looking for more accuracy and so graduated to using matched sets of bare Port Orford cedar shafting which I purchased from various archery dealers. After that, I tried compressed Port Orford cedar shafts (Forgewood shafts produced by Bill Sweetland, which were much stronger and heavier than regular cedar), and then went on to fiberglass. After I grew tired of fiberglass I began making my arrows from ramin dowels (sold as "birch" dowels in most building supply outlets) and Douglas fir. During the past few years I've used Sitka spruce almost exclusively.

Once I even bought a dozen aluminum shafts and tried them out. I found these to be the worst possible choice for roving, field and hunting. The cold metal had an awful feel to it in below-freezing weather, but what I really hated about aluminum was that after taking a shot in the woods I could never be certain whether the shaft was straight. To me, aluminum arrows seemed to represent the type of bowhunter who doesn't care a whit about the history, traditions, and romance of archery, but is only interested in racking up an impressive number of game kills – using, of course, the latest high-tech archery equipment to make the task easier.

One day, in a fit of anger, I gathered up the aluminum arrows which had been polluting my home and shot them far out into the murky, glacial waters of a tidal arm north of Anchorage. The ugly mud flats seemed a fitting resting place for the despicable things.

Not long afterward I even stopped using fiberglass shafts and went back to wood arrows for good.

Since I began making my own arrow shafting from scratch, I've come to prefer Sitka spruce above other woods. This is truly a magical American arrow wood that, for reasons I cannot comprehend, never seemed to catch on with archers. Among its many attributes are superior strength, consistency (both weight and spine), straightness of its grain, and its availability (at least for anyone living near the West Coast).

Articles from the old American Bowman Review, reprinted in Dr. C. N. Hickman's book, *Archery – The Technical Side,* rated the best arrow woods to be Sitka spruce, Douglas fir, Norway pine and Port Orford Cedar – in that order. Of the four, Port Orford cedar seems to have emerged as the favored arrow wood among traditional archers. After having put three of these arrow woods to considerable use – I've never tried Norway pine – I've come to suspect that Port

Orford cedar gained its popularity because of one attribute: its pleasant aroma. Cut into a cedar shaft with a tapering tool and you'll see what I mean. Its smell grabs you instantly and produces a feeling of nostalgia for the old traditional archery. The smell of Port Orford cedar is to the archer what gun oil is to the rifleman.

But for that wonderful aroma, I'd never use Port Orford cedar. The wood isn't nearly as strong as Sitka spruce or Douglas fir. It's also somewhat light in weight, if you prefer shafts of 600 grains and more. For that matter, Sitka spruce is also on the light side, yet it has other qualities which more than offset this. Douglas fir is heavy and is the strongest of the three, but from what I gather, seems to lack one important thing: consistency.

Consistency is, or perhaps should be, one of the primary considerations of the make-it-from-scratch arrowsmith. It's exasperating to fell a tree, cart home the log and saw it up – only to discover that the dowels you cut from it will spine anywhere from 40 to 100 pounds! Simplified, "spine" refers to the stiffness of the arrow material. An arrow spined for an 80-lb bow is far too stiff for a 40-lb bow, and will fly wide of the mark.

The thing that amazes me about Sitka spruce is that I've made shafts at random from a variety of wood from different geographical locations and invariably the spine seems to fall within the usable range. If I split out or saw a batch of two dozen shafts from a Sitka spruce log, and then reduce them to 11/32 or 3/8 dimensions, I can expect that at least three-quarters of them will spine between 60 and 80 pounds. And the weight never seems to vary more than about 50 grains at the most – even though I'm planing down the shafts by hand. This means I don't have to waste hours whittling out a batch of shafts and then toss half of them into the fireplace.

Other things I like about Sitka spruce are its resiliency and its strength. The wood is used not only in guitar tops, but in airplane spars! I'm convinced it's twice as strong as Port Orford cedar; at least it's only half as apt to break if I'm out stump-shooting. I remember a buck deer I once shot on Kodiak Island with a Sitka spruce shaft and how, as the deer ran wildly through 50 yards of solid tag-alders, I could see the shaft protruding from the deer's chest and hear it whacking loudly against the brush. I followed the blood trail through the alders and found the entire shaft lying a few feet away from the deer. Except for a few scratches near the fletching the shaft was in perfect condition. When I've shot big game with Port Orford cedar arrows the shafts seem to break against the first bit of shrubbery.

The operator of a sawmill near Seward, Alaska once told me that during his 30 years of lumbering in Minnesota, Washington and Alaska, he'd never found any wood of similar weight which would even come close to the strength of Sitka spruce. As he stood in his mill yard and talked about various woods, he pointed toward a large Sitka spruce log about four feet in diameter. "See that log over there? I can cut through it with a chainsaw and leave only an inch of wood and when I go to lift it with the loader, she won't break at the cut. She'll split out an inch of wood that'll run the entire log!"

The proof of the pudding is in the eating, they say, and I only know that since I began using Sitka spruce, I've broken far fewer arrows when out roving. Plus, my accuracy has improved a good deal.

Other things I like about this spruce is its straight grain and its tendency to stay straight without warping. This is especially true of shafts which have been split from the log rather than sawn. The long fibers of the wood have something to do with this. In various museums around the Pacific Northwest and Alaska you'll see lots of aboriginal arrow shafts made of Sitka spruce. Most of them are as straight as the day they were made. One of the oldest arrows ever found, a 10,000 year old shaft found in Germany before World War II, was split from a log. So shafts made in this way are as traditional as they come.

Another good thing about spruce is it's easily worked with edged tools. A sharp hand plane shaves through it smoothly, with little gouging.

So, there you have my prejudice toward Sitka spruce. There may be other woods out there in other parts of the country which are equally good. Oklahoma bowyer Al Herrin has some Cherokee arrows of black locust which were made in the old style – split out from the log and finished with a knife. They're some of the finest-looking arrows I've ever seen. I doubt any North American hardwood would surpass them for strength.

## THE "NATURAL" SHAFT

Most American Indian groups didn't bother making split-timber shafts, but instead used what might be termed natural arrow shafts – that is, shafts made from small shoots and saplings. Such arrows have gained an ill-deserved reputation for being inaccurate and inefficient, perhaps because of the crooked aboriginal arrows we see gathering dust in museums. Arrows made from shoots tend to warp over time and must be straightened periodically. But if they are straightened and kept straight, a well-made natural arrow can shoot as well as a fine target arrow.

In *The Witchery of Archery*, Maurice Thompson tells of a hunting trip he once took with a Seminole Indian – a trip in which the Indian outshot him even though Thompson was using his finest bows and custom-made arrows. In describing the Indian's archery gear, Thompson wrote, "His arrows were a wonder of exact work."

And in the book *Lions in the Path*, Stewart Edward White tells of a flight-shooting contest between Saxton Pope and an African man. Pope was shooting his heavy yew longbow and finest flight arrows while the African used an aboriginal bow and his regular hunting arrows. The African's arrows, apparently made from shoots, shot a distance of 243 paces – several yards further than Pope's flight arrows. Very much surprised, Pope switched to his heaviest yew longbow and they shot again. This time he managed to beat the African – who still was using his standard hunting shafts – but only by about 10 yards.

So there's no question that arrows made from shoots can be efficient and accurate if they are well-made and kept straight. Such arrows are also very strong and durable, especially when made from shoots like dogwood, hazel, osoberry, river cane, ocean spray and chokecherry.

One big advantage to using shoots for arrows is that they can be made quickly and easily. There's no splitting or sawing or planing to be done. Just cut the shafts, bundle them together and let them season for a couple of months. Then straighten them with heat, scrape off the bark and finish them. When thoroughly seasoned, these naturally round shafts will become tough and very hard to break.

In selecting the shoots, look for those which are at least 3/8-inch diameter at the base, for the shaft will be somewhat smaller once it is dried and the bark removed. Cut them six or eight inches longer than your normal arrow length. Most arrow woods will check somewhat at the ends during drying and you can cut the ends off later. Arrow shoots cut during the winter, when the sap is down, will check less than those cut in spring and summer.

After cutting the shoots, put them in bundles of a dozen or so, wrap them loosely with tape or rubber bands and then place them in a cool, dry place to season. The shafts will continue to toughen with age, but they should be ready to use within two or three months. Leave the bark on during the initial seasoning.

After the shafts are partially seasoned, the bark should be scraped off with a sharp knife. Shoots of some types of wood will check badly if the bark is removed immediately after cutting. When thoroughly dry, the shafts should be straightened and finished by sanding or planing with a fine hand plane to remove irregularities. They are then ready to be made into arrows.

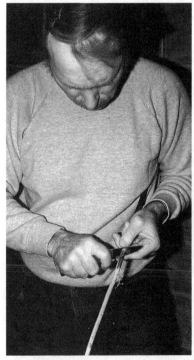

*After initial drying, the shoots can be scraped clean of bark, using a sharp knife.*

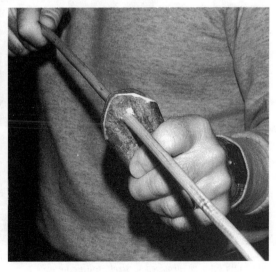

*The shoots are then heated and straightened. This arrow straightener was made by drilling a hole through a piece of caribou antler.*

## RIVER CANE

River cane grows over much of the southeastern and midwestern U.S. and was widely used by many American Indian groups for making good arrows. An old archery supply brochure put out in the 1920's by master bowyer E.F. Pope of Woodville, Texas, – he provided Osage staves and bows for Art Young – lists prices for his finest bows and arrows. The most expensive arrows listed in the brochure were Pope's Special Flight Arrows – made of southern cane – which sold for $2 each. Pope's Osage hunting arrows, made of clear Osage and fletched with eagle feathers, sold for $20 per dozen. His hickory hunting arrows cost $15 per dozen. E.F. Pope (apparently no relation to Saxton Pope) and other early archers knew the value of good cane arrows, yet this fine arrow material is hardly used at all today.

One of the reasons could be that cane, being hollow, requires that you make a separate foreshaft which is inserted at the pile end – at least when using modern or Indian-style tie-on heads. Heads with round tangs, such as the ancient cast bronze points from Asia, were simply inserted directly into the cane or bamboo and bound with sinew or thread. Actually, a hardwood foreshaft isn't that difficult to make and fit, so don't let this little detail deter you from using river cane shafts. The nock can either be cut in directly above a joint or it can be made from a separate block of hardwood inserted and glued into the nock end.

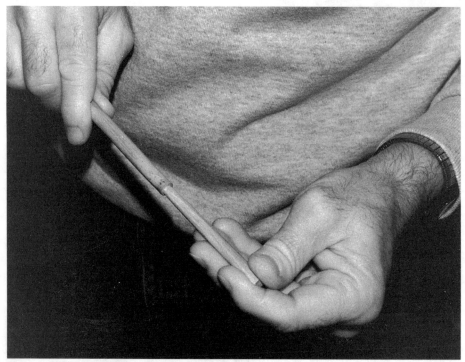

*The foreshaft of a river cane arrow should be made of hardwood and fitted into the pile end. The joint will later be wrapped securely with sinew.*

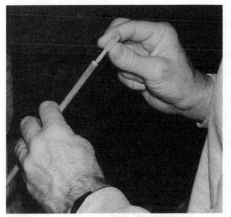

*Nocks can be cut directly into the river cane, but it's better to use a nock insert which is fitted and glued in. This nock insert is of Osage orange.*

River cane shoots should be cut and bundled to season for at least six months before using. The outer skin of this material is tough and dense and it dries more slowly than other types of natural shoots. Select the straightest cane and cut them extra long, then do some initial straightening before putting them aside to season. Cane shafts can be straightened either while green or after they are seasoned, but the task, as I have recently discovered, is easier just after they are cut. An entire batch of green cane can be quickly straightened by placing them

*River cane shafts can be smoothed and straightened by "ironing" on a grooved, heated stone.*

atop a heated wood stove for fifteen or twenty minutes. Be sure to place some sort of spacers to keep the cane from direct contact with the hot stove. If your woodstove is wide enough you can heat the entire length of cane evenly throughout. After they are warmed, they can be straightened in a flash, but don't try to get them 100% straight the first time; do it in two stages. Otherwise you might fracture the cane at the nodes or weaken it. Once straightened, cane shafts seem to hold their shape remarkably well. After they are seasoned you can work down the joints or nodes to smooth the shaft.

Some Indian groups were known to use grooved and heated stones to smooth the nodes. The stones were first heated, then the cane shaft was dipped in water, placed in the groove and "ironed" out with a downward pressure and a rotating motion. The grooved stone should be heated so that the moistened shaft will "smoke" when it is pushed along through the groove, but not so much that it will scorch the shaft. This method will give the cane shaft a more even diameter and also straighten it at the same time.

## THE SPLIT-TIMBER SHAFT

The first step in making the split-timber shaft is to obtain your raw material – Sitka spruce, Douglas fir, cedar, hickory, black locust or whatever. You can either buy the wood from a lumber dealer or go out in the woods and cut it yourself. Unlike wood which is to be used for bows, arrow material can be completely air-dried and ready to use within a matter of weeks. You needn't bother with splitting the log and waxing the ends as in treating bow wood. With arrow wood, the raw log need only be sawn up into boards or split out into "shakes" an inch or two wide. The decision to split or saw is your own. I've made arrow

*Splitting out an arrow blank is easy with straight-grained wood such as Sitka spruce.*

*The first step in making the split-timber shaft is to plane one side of the blank perfectly flat.*

*Check to see that all sides of the square dowel are straight and true.*

shafts both ways. Splitting is more wasteful of lumber but it allows you to follow the grain precisely; sawing is quicker and easier and saves on material.

Some woods will check and warp as they are being air-dried, so you'll have to experiment to see which ones will and which ones won't. Happily for me, Sitka spruce has almost no tendency to warp during drying; I've taken green-sawn boards two-inches thick and **stickered** them in a pile in a dry attic and not had 10 percent of them show any warping.

After splitting or sawing, the boards should be stickered, which means to alternate layers of the boards with small strips of scrap wood which allow the air to circulate freely between the layers. Place the first layer of boards on two rows of scrap wood, leaving an inch or so of space between each board. Then place more scrap wood "stickers" on top of the boards as a spacer between the next layer, and so on. As the wood dries, the boards should be turned over and alternated every week or so. This helps control warping. Stacked this way in a dry area, the boards will be ready to use within a few weeks. No matter whether you split or saw, the boards should be thoroughly dry. If you immediately cut up the green boards into small square arrow blanks, without giving the wood a chance to dry, your arrow blanks will almost certainly warp.

Splitting the arrow blanks from the board can be done easily with a large knife and the butt of a hand axe or a maul. Using the blade as a splitting froe, split off one-inch chunks of the board. If the wood is straight-grained, this will be no problem. If the grain isn't straight your only choice is to saw out the blank on a table saw or a band saw which is set up with a cutting fence. Next, the blank will be reduced with a hand plane to a square dowel of exact dimensions. For hunting-weight shafts, this will be about 3/8-inch or so, depending on the type of wood you're using. Shafts made from hard woods such as birch, black locust or Osage orange will be smaller than those of say, Sitka spruce or fir, for any given spine.

For now, your goal will be to reduce the arrow blank to a dowel which is 3/8-inch square. This square dowel can be cut out quickly with a table saw; if you have a small power planer, the work can be done in a flash.

If you've chosen to split out the blank, you'll end up with a long splinter of wood which is anything but square. To make a square dowel from it simply place the blank down on a flat surface and use a hand plane to flatten one side perfectly flat and true. Check to see that it is by sighting down along the edge, or by placing it on a flat surface. Once you have one surface perfectly true, place this side down on the work bench and then reduce its opposite side to the desired 3/8-inch thickness. Now plane the other two sides of the blank in the same manner and suddenly you have a square dowel. A template made from plywood or a scrap of lumber will allow you to check the dimensions of your dowel as you work it.

With an easily-worked wood such as spruce, this hand-planing can be done within 10 or 15 minutes. With a tough, hard wood such as Osage orange or hickory it will take longer. With the harder woods, be sure to set your plane to a fine adjustment in order to avoid gouging.

After you have your square dowel, the next step is to make it round. This is

*A template made from a piece of 2 X 4 allows you to quickly check the dimensions of the 3/8-inch square dowel.*

*Planing off the four edges of the square dowel gives you an...*

*...eight sided shaft. Planing off the remaining edges produces a sixteen-sided shaft, which is essentially round.*

*During final sanding, the diameter of the shaft is checked by fitting it through a hole drilled in the template.*

surprisingly easy. Simply place the square dowel on edge – or in a 90-degree trough made by nailing together two small boards – and shave off the uppermost edge with a small hand plane. Experience will tell you how much wood should be removed.

Now turn the dowel over and shave off the other three edges as you did the first one. You now have an eight-sided dowel. From there, it's a simple matter to shave off the remaining edges, thus making the dowel sixteen-sided. For all practical purposes, the shaft is now round and can be finished by sanding, first with medium-grit and then with fine-grit sandpaper. Bumps and irregularities in the shaft can be removed by placing it down on a perfectly flat surface and sanding it with a small hand-sander as the shaft is rapidly rotated. During the

*John Strunk's arrow maker, a worthwhile investment if you plan to make many self arrows. With a rounded blade in the plane it only takes off excess wood, when it stops removing shavings the shaft is the proper size.*

final sanding, the diameter of the shaft should be checked by inserting it through a hole drilled in a chunk of wood. If the shaft is too large, it can easily be sanded down to the desired dimensions.

If you've done the job right, the shaft will not only be perfectly straight but also uniformly round throughout its length. Tapered or barreled shafts are easy to make when you're using this method; simply plane off a little more material at the ends when you're initially shaving the sharp edges from the square dowel.

As you can readily see, the process of making a hand-planed shaft can be speeded up considerably by sawing the rough boards to the 3/8-inch square dimension rather than splitting them. I've found it takes less than half the time to make an arrow shaft by sawing – a maximum of 15 minutes, compared to half an hour or so when splitting. If you're sawing, a dozen arrows can take up to three hours; the splitting method can require twice as long.

Six hours might seem a long time to spend making a dozen shafts, but, as I mentioned before, the wood I use does not break easily. I doubt that I break more than half a dozen shafts the entire summer during my roving and stump-shooting. I rarely go through more than a dozen shafts during the entire year, from spring on through the hunting season.

Granted, six hours is a lot of time to spend on making a dozen shafts – which still have to be finished and painted and fletched. But what else would you do with those six hours – watch television? Sit in a bar? No thanks. Let the high-tech boys brag about taking their "P & Y" bucks with their laser-blade-tipped XXY-21000 metal shafts and their compound shooting devices. I'll take the good old-fashioned satisfaction and contentment which comes from taking a deer with tools I've created with my own hands.

*If no spine-tester is available, the shafts can be flexed by hand to test for spine or stiffness.*

## ARROW SPINE & WEIGHT

Up to now, nothing has been said about weighing the shafts and testing them for spine or stiffness. The most precise way to weed out unwanted arrow shafts – before you've gone to the trouble of fletching them up – is to use a spine tester. This device is a good investment if you plan to make many arrows. If you don't have a spine tester, you can test your raw shafts by "feel" – flexing them for comparison against an arrow which is spined for a known draw weight. After some practice, you should be able to guess the spine of an arrow within 10 lbs or so. After you finish fletching a batch of shafts and adding the points, you should shoot them repeatedly under controlled conditions in order to watch their flight. An arrow which is crooked or of the wrong spine will show those defects within a few shots. Mark them and either put them aside or throw them away. Be careful not to let the culls get mixed in with your good hunting arrows!

Shafts which vary greatly in weight should also be avoided because an arrow which deviates more than about 50 grains from its kin can throw off your accuracy. When I make a new batch of arrows, I like to weigh them as soon as they are fletched – before adding the points. That way I can match one of my lighter broadheads to a shaft which is a bit heavy. My split-timber shafts of Sitka spruce weigh between 375 and 425 grains after they are fletched and cut to length. My homemade broadheads run anywhere from 160 to 190 grains. So with Sitka spruce, my finished hunting arrows run between 550 and 600 grains. When shooting at 35 yards and under, I can't tell the difference in 50 grains of arrow weight. However, if I've been shooting Sitka spruce arrows and then pick up one of my old ramin shafts that weighs 650 grains, I'll shoot low even at 20 yards.

## TYPES OF NOCKS

Now that you've taken the cold plunge into the frigid and demanding waters of traditional arrow-making, and now that you've invested several hours in making up a batch of raw shafts, you're ready to add a most important feature to your arrows: the nock. I make my nocks by first sawing a 1/2-inch deep slot in the shaft – this can be done with two or three hacksaw blades taped together – and then enlarging it with a small rattail file. When the nock slot will almost, but not quite, fit onto my bowstring, I put aside the rattail file and then finish enlarging it with fine-grit sandpaper until the nock "snaps" onto the string with just the slightest of pressure. If the nock is too small and fits too tightly, it may break when the string is released. If the nock is too large for your bowstring, your arrow may fall off at a crucial moment.

The nock can be made plain – cut directly into the wood itself – or it can be elaborate, cut from a separate piece of hardwood or horn and then glued onto the shaft. No matter which type you use, the nock of the finished arrow should lie perpendicular to the edge grain of the shaft. In other words, the grain layers of the shaft should lie at a 90-degree angle to the bowstring. This takes

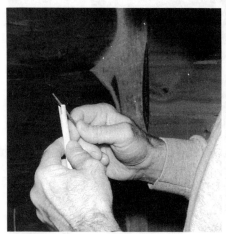

*Arrow nocks are made by sawing a slot in the shaft and then enlarging it with a small rattail file. Final work on the nocks will be done with fine sandpaper.*

*Finished arrow shafts, ready to be fletched.*

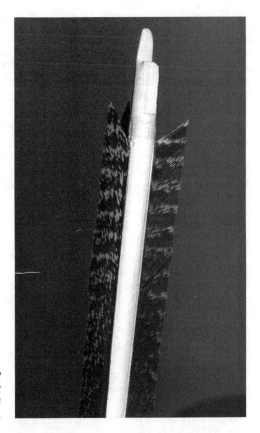

*One of only two self nocks broken by the author during his years of using such nocks. Note that the nock split out only as far as the sinew wrapping.*

advantage of the maximum strength of the wood because the shaft will be under severe stress when the string is released at full draw.

Nocks cut from a separate piece of hardwood or horn and glued onto the shaft add a beautiful touch to a handmade arrow, but they aren't at all necessary if your shaft has a diameter of 11/32-inch or greater at the nock end. This is true even when you're using a softer wood such as cedar, spruce or fir. But if you're concerned about the strength of your self nocks, you can wrap the last inch of so of the shaft with sinew or fine thread set in glue. Silk thread, though not easy to find these days, works great for this and also for wrapping on feathers. Arrows used by many Asian archers were wrapped with silk thread.

Turkish-style arrow nocks, which were rather bulb-shaped and larger than the rear part of the shaft, were glued onto the shaft separately. Afterward, the last bit of shaft was carefully wrapped in fine sinew to a point nearly half-way up the throat of the nock itself. The bottom of the nock was cut out after the sinew had dried, actually cutting through the sinew on two sides of the shaft. Such nocks were apparently able to withstand the extreme shock of very powerful composite bows.

I've found self nocks to be sufficiently strong, even without such reinforcing, for bows ranging up to 75 lbs. During the years I've used self nocks, I've broken only two, even though I have never reinforced the wood in any way. One arrow – from the first batch of self-nocked arrows I ever made – had a crooked grain to the wood which ran completely off the shaft just below the nock. Of course, this nock split out on the second or third shot. The only other nock I have broken did so for unknown reasons, though I've always suspected I may have hit it earlier with another arrow and partially fractured it. But overall, two broken nocks from tens of thousands of arrows shot isn't bad. Over the years I've broken dozens of plastic nocks, including a few of a make which were supposedly unbreakable.

However, if you're still afraid of self nocks, you can cut a slot in the arrow, parallel to the wood grain (perpendicular to the nock itself), and then glue in a thin strip of horn or hardwood. This will greatly strengthen the wood at the nock. Or you could just wrap the last inch or so of the arrow with sinew, right up to the base of the nock.

### FINISHING & SEALING THE SHAFT

Before fletching your batch of new arrow shafts, you'll want to first cut them to your draw length. Measure from the bottom of the nock throat down to the base of your broadhead. Don't forget to allow for the inch or so you'll lose when tapering or slotting your shaft for the point or broadhead. The draw length of your arrows is a strictly personal thing, depending on what type of bow you're using, your shooting style and so on. With most of us, this draw length will be between 26 and 29 inches.

Back when I was shooting fiberglass-laminated recurved bows, I used an open, deliberate style of shooting, with a draw length of 29-1/2 inches. After switching back to a longbow and a bent arm style, my draw length dropped to 28-inches. Now that I've gone entirely to shorter, Indian-style bows (my favorites are all 56 inches long, overall), my draw length has shortened even further, to 27 inches.

So, your draw length is purely personal and may take some experimentation. If it feels natural and comfortable for you, don't let anyone tell you to adhere to a hard-and-fast rule on arrow length.

After the arrows have been cut to length, you're ready to finish by painting them, dipping them in lacquer or otherwise coating the wood to keep out moisture. I've tried a dozen different methods of sealing arrow shafts and most of them have worked very well. I now use the easiest: rubbing the shaft with several coats of Watco™ Oil or French polish. Watco Oil, found in most hardware and paint stores, has a Tung oil base; French polish can be made by mixing one-part linseed oil to one-part shellac. Both the Watco Oil and the French polish will protect the shafts without adding a shiny finish – which is anathema to the hunting archer. Nearly all of the commercial arrow lacquers will result in a shiny finish, which is a good reason to avoid them. Painting the shafts is fine, provided the paint has a matt or semi-gloss finish.

If you plan to dip your shafts, you can make an inexpensive dipping tube from 3/4-inch pipe, capped at one end and with a bell at the top. However, I think hand-finishing and hand-painting is more traditional and more fun. Ideally, arrow-making should be a wintertime project, so why rush it?

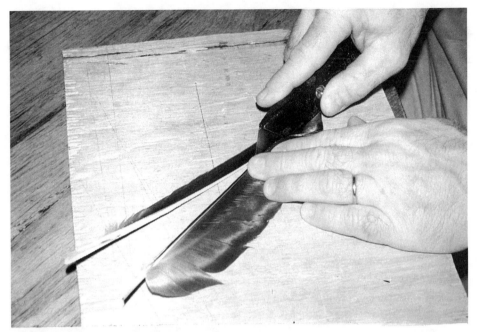

*Full-length feathers are first split with a sharp knife and then the bases are ground flat by sanding.*

## FLETCHING

Time for another decision – which type of feathers to use for the fletching. I've come to prefer two types: gray-barred wild turkey feathers for general hunting and roving and the time-tested "gray goose wing" – from wild Canada geese – when hunting in rainy and inclement weather. The wild turkey feathers are sturdier and hold up better for knock-around use in dry weather, while the wild goose feathers are much better in wet conditions. The oil content is far greater in the goose feathers and this makes them superior to all others for wet climates.

Glues are another matter. Natural glues, such as animal hide glue or spruce pitch, are preferred when you want to duplicate primitive archery methods. However, if you want to glue on the fletching and never have to worry about it coming off, you can use the modern adhesives. My personal preference is contact cement, which, in my opinion, is the strongest of all for hunting use.

In any case, I always tie on my fletching, both fore and aft, with fine sinew thread soaked in warm hide glue. I then coat the sinew wrapping with spruce pitch or a synthetic finish of the type used to coat fishing rod wrappings. Nothing is more bothersome than having your feathers come off when you're out on a remote hunting expedition. With the methods I've developed over years of trial and error, I never have to worry about it.

The feathers can be affixed to the shaft either by hand, setting them 120-degrees apart, or with a more accurate fletching jig. The first method requires either some excellent hand dexterity or the assistance of a trained octopus! This

*Tying on Canada goose feathers with sinew soaked in warm hide glue.*

is one area of work when you need four hands. Nevertheless, the job can be done rather quickly with a bit of practice.

Three things to watch for as you go about your fletching: first, be sure the base of your feather has been trimmed or ground flat and true; second, make sure your "cock" feather is set on at right angles to the arrow nock and bowstring; third, be sure you do not mix right-wing and left-wing feathers on the same arrow. An arrow fletched this way will flirt and gad about, sometimes dangerously. If you set your feathers onto the shaft at an angle, or with some helical twist to make the arrow spin, be sure the rough, or underside, of the feather angles into the wind.

I always use full-length, natural feathers. I first split the base of the feather with a sharp knife and then grind down both the base and the inside edge of the base with a small hand sander. If I'm in a hurry, I'll often sand down the feathers with a small drum sander – mounted in an electric drill press – and then fletch the arrows with a fletching jig. After setting a feather into the clamp, I coat the bottom of the feather liberally with contact cement and immediately push it down against the shaft to transfer some of the cement onto the shaft. I quickly lift the clamp back up again and allow the cement to dry for 10 minutes or so until it is no longer tacky. After the glue is dry to the touch, I clamp the feather down onto the shaft for a moment, remove it from the fletching jig and smooth it down with my forefinger. Then I'm ready to apply the second feather. A batch of arrows can be fletched this way within minutes.

Arrows fletched with
wild turkey and
Canada goose.

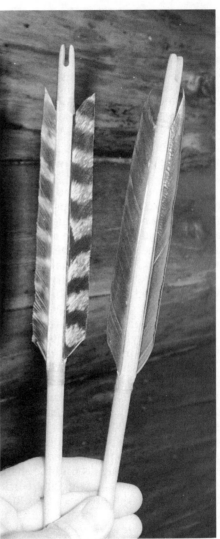

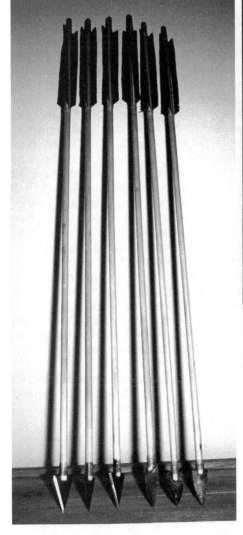

Finished arrows,
ready for the hunt.

If I want to make a batch of truly primitive-style arrows, I forgo all of the mechanized aids – the electric saw to cut out the shaft, the electric sander to grind the base of the feather, the fletching jig to glue on the feathers, etc. – and do it all by hand. This is no problem; it just takes a bit longer. One of the most time-consuming steps is tying on the feathers.

This task seems easier when you wrap the tail-ends of the feathers first, then wrap the front-ends. I start with the cock feather, placing it on the shaft and then taking a couple of wraps around its tail-end with sinew made moist and limp with warm hide glue. Then I add the second feather, wrap twice around it and add the third. When I have all three aligned properly, I wrap around and around the shaft with sinew. The sinew will dry quickly and hold the tails down.

Next, I coat the base of the cock feather with warm hide glue, align it on the shaft and take a couple wraps around its front-end. The second and third feathers should be coated with glue and wrapped down as you did the tail-ends. You can make adjustments to the three feathers as you wrap the sinew. Incidentally, the ends of the sinew wrapping need not be tied off; the threads will just naturally lie tightly against the shaft as the sinew dries and shrinks.

Let the sinew wrappings dry for a day or so, then weatherproof them by coating as described earlier. The feathers can now be trimmed, using a commercial feather-burner, a pair of scissors (my preference) or even a sharp knife. Your arrow is now finished except for adding the point.

Traditional-style blunt points can be made from horn or bone, drilled out to fit over the shaft. Tie-on broadheads, cut from spring steel or old saw blades, will work as well as the finest modern steel broadhead. Two things to watch out for if you opt for the tie-on style broadheads: first, be sure your steel isn't so thin that it will curl back on itself upon hitting a rib of a game animal; and second, be sure to set the tang into the shaft solidly, perpendicular to the grain, and wrap securely with sinew so that the head doesn't split the shaft upon impact. I've never had a problem with either, because I always use steel thicker than .080 thick with the tie-on heads and I always set the tang into the slot with pitch or cement and then wrap around the shaft securely with sinew.

So now you've made your first batch of handmade arrows – completely from scratch! And in the process of building them, you've built something within yourself – a bit of knowledge, a little more patience, a new-found skill – and a strengthening of the will.

Someone once said that the true test of the hunting archer is whether he can go out into the woods, make his own tackle from materials found in nature and then put meat on the pole. You now know that you could do it, if you had to.

How many modern-day archers can truthfully say that?

# A COMEDY OF ARROWS

*Jim Hamm*

I'm invisible. Once again.

Becoming invisible is addictive, I suppose, like wooden bows, and for all I know it may be bad for the liver. But it's certainly good for sneaking up on deer. At least that's the plan. The deer have been feeding through an area of live and white oaks, not a half mile from my house, and I intend to be invisible within twenty yards of the buck. I think he's a buck, anyway, judging from the sign.

I don't pretend to be much of a tracker, but the last few days it's been easy to see where the deer have been moving among the trees, picking up early fallen acorns and even plucking them from the lowest branches. And one of the deer is considerably larger than the others. I haven't actually seen any of them, but this largest one's tracks show him to be wider at the shoulders than at the hips. Which leads me to believe that he's a buck. The register of the tracks will tell the story, if you can find where they've walked in a straight line, though the system is far from infallible.

So I've circled around the area to the south and ease into the north wind, hoping that the deer are there and that one of them is, indeed, a buck.

The leaves rustle only slightly as I pick my way among the trees with moccasined feet. The rain which proceeded the present cool front has made stalking conditions nearly ideal by wetting the ground and tempering the corn-flake dryness of the fallen leaves. The wind helps, too, rattling the trees and bushes to give plenty of background noise.

There are times when I can't sneak up on a train wreck, but today everything feels right; the cleanness of the air, with just a hint of the edge of coming winter to it; the distant squawking of Sandhill cranes as they circle to gain altitude, a big flock by the sound of them, pushed south by the front; the bright colors of the changing leaves, blood red on the sumacs and red oaks, shimmering yellow on the elms.

It's a nice time to be moving silently, invisibly, through the woods, even if the deer aren't. I haven't a clue what time of day they are coming for acorns, though I suppose a better tracker would be able to tell. For all I know, they come in the middle of the night and are a mile away right now. But I think not; it will be easier for them to find acorns on the ground with some light.

I flex the bow slightly, feeling the pent-up tension in the string, as if it were alive. The name on the bow, "Old Ugly," is fitting. Made from a small Osage tree full of knots, the bow is designed very loosely after one found in a peat bog in Denmark, the Holmegaard bow, which is thousands of years old and fairly massive and broad. Someone once commented that if I ever got my pickup stuck, "Old Ugly" would make an excellent pry bar. Perhaps. But it has certainly made an excellent bow, complete with a knothole entirely through the upper limb. It's a peep sight, I tell the agnostic compound shooters, though if they thought about it they would realize such a sight would place an arrow into the ground about five feet in front of the shooter. The compound crowd finds it hard to understand why anyone would go to so much trouble making such a bow. It's too difficult, they say, and for them it unquestionably would be. Traditional bows aren't accurate, they claim, though I manage to hold my own with them on a 3-D course. My bows are archaic, they say, a thing from the past. And I thank them very much.

When pressed, I tell them it is a challenge, that anyone can kill game with a space bow. But there is more to it even than that, I sense, something more difficult to explain to a non-believer. Wooden bows seem to pluck at a primal chord within some men, much as rabbits trigger an inborn instinct within beagles, an ancient, innate sense which cannot be taught but may be simply honed if it exists. Many modern hunters, with both rifle and compound bow, seem to have been born without it, and would hunt with a Cobra gunship if only it was legal.

It seems the men who are drawn to hand-made bows feel compelled to fit into the natural rhythm, instead of trying to overpower or circumvent it with gadgets and technology. To these men, making their own tackle lets them step further into the reality that is wilderness and wildness, and for a time, at least, freedom. Such men have become predators in the truest and best sense, instead of simply killers...

A squirrel chatters at me from a nearby tree. I stop. Long minutes pass. The deer should be just ahead, if they're here at all. I take an infinitely slow step. Then another. The squirrel apparently has lost interest, for he remains silent.

The sun slips below the horizon as I gently feel the way with the thin rawhide of the moccasin soles. Slow. Take it carefully now. Move deliberately and smoothly. Motion is an even bigger giveaway than noise. Pause every few steps to search the trees ahead.

The woods seem empty where I expected to find the deer, save for the fussing of a distant blue jay and the sighing of the wind in the trees. Finally relaxing from the tense stalking crouch, I stand erect, stretch, and take two steps.

I freeze, one foot in mid-air, when there is sudden motion just ahead and to the right. Forty yards away a deer feeds head-down under a tree. With an almost electric jolt of recognition, I realize that it's a buck, though I can't see any antlers. His shape and body language are dead giveaways. Where he came from, I haven't a hint, since I've peered beneath that very tree at least a dozen times.

Gently, I lower the raised foot. The deer snaps his head up, looking off to the left, ears as alert as radar antennas. His antlers are wider than his ears, I see now, dark brown but with polished ivory tips. Now I know who's been demolishing the small willow trees along the creek. He looks to be a three and a half year old, with about eight points. He's heavy and sleek, not a huge buck, but a nice trophy – especially with an archaic bow. I consciously resist staring at him too hard, having come to believe that deer somehow sense a predator intently watching them. At least, it seems to make them nervous.

Easy now, be patient, I tell myself. Be disciplined. My heart doesn't appear to be listening, and is beating at a rate well into the triple digits.

He cocks one ear back, flicks his tail, then continues searching the ground for acorns. I let out a long breath I hadn't realized was being held. How to get close to him? He may come this way, eventually, but the light is fading and in twenty minutes it will be too dark to shoot. The only way to get a shot is to move in on him. There is a cedar bush to the left and ahead, and while his head is down I step carefully to place it between us.

Moving forward from behind the screen of the bush, more confident now since he can't possibly see me, I start the inner dialogue, "Pick a spot. Concentrate on a spot," in preparation for the shot. After ten eternal minutes I make it to the cedar tree, with no eruption of a fleeing deer, and peer through the lacy foliage.

He's twenty-five yards away, licking his flank, broadside.

Pick a spot. My heart rate is off the scale; my one hope is that I can get off a shot before it explodes.

He glances around, flicks his tail, and puts his head down.

Pick a spot.

Slowly, the draw begins. My stomach thinks I just leaped from the top of a building. My knees have inexplicably turned to tapioca pudding.

The index finger of my right hand touches the anchor spot at the corner of my mouth. I slowly lean out just past the edge of the cedar, then the arrow is gone.

Time stands still. Maybe not perfectly still, because I can see the arrow spinning in the air as it wobbles briefly, then recovers. But I've certainly entered a time warp where everything moves at a crawl. In slow motion, the buck lifts a front foot to take a step. There is no sound except the soft hiss of the arrow. I'm still concentrating on the spot just behind his shoulder where the hair is a shade darker.

But the arrow seems a bit high. Perhaps a lot high.

Time returns to normal as the feathers flick harmlessly across his withers. He blasts into motion, bucking like a horse in the rodeo, trying to shake the unseen assailant which has crept inside his defenses.

Fifty yards away he stops, staring back in my direction, disbelief written all over his face. His shoulders quiver like coiled springs.

"You better watch out, brother," I croak at him, "there are some real predators in these woods."

He obviously believes me, bounding madly away now, tail flared wide. He dodges from sight, his feet drumming the earth for a moment longer.

Silence returns.

The few clouds overhead glow an incandescent orange from the light of the dying sun. My heart-rate is slowing to the level of red-line. Perhaps I won't have the Big One today, after all. A cricket chirps softly, then louder, more confidently. My hands begin to tremble.

I find my arrow buried in the earth beyond where he stood. Not a trace of blood or hair; a clean miss, just as I thought. Wiping the dirt from the shaft, I replace it in the back quiver, then unstring "Old Ugly."

The clouds subside to a lovely, iridescent blue as I start the walk back home. A few stars wink on, right on schedule, against the fading polished-copper glow to the west.

Sights, a string release, and a dozen other miracles of modern invention would undoubtedly have made the hunting easier today, a kill more certain. But once having fashioned a wooden bow and taken it into the woods with deadly intent, a kill, strangely enough, no longer seems so necessary. Sure, I was trying hard to plant feathered death inside the buck, and will perhaps try again on another day. But while this afternoon would be considered a failure by most standards, I suppose, it somehow doesn't strike me that way at all. I can't help smiling while strolling in the deepening twilight, for there is, indeed, a predator in these woods.

# BIBLIOGRAPHY

Ascham, Roger, *Toxophilus; The School of Shooting*, 1544.

Baugh, Dick, *A Cordage-backed Bow*, Bulletin of Primitive Technology, Spring, 1992.

Callahan, Errett, *Archery in the Arctic*, Bulletin of Primitive Technology, Spring, 1991.

Clark, William, and Lewis, Meriwether, *The Journals of Lewis and Clark*, 1804-1806.

Comstock, Paul, *The Bent Stick; Making and Using Wooden Hunting Bows*, Delaware, OH, 1988.

Duff, James, *Bows and Arrows*, MacMillan Co., New York, NY, 1927.

Elmer, Robert P., *Archery*, Penn Publishing Co., Philadelphia, PA., 1926.

   – *Target Archery*, Alfred A. Knopf, New York, NY, 1946.

Hamm, Jim, *Bows and Arrows of the Native Americans*, Bois d'Arc Press, Azle, TX, 1989.

Henery, Alexander, *The Journal of Alexander Henery*, Astoria Journal, 1814.

Heizer, Robert F., and Kroeber, Theodora, *Ishi the Last Yahi - A Documentary History*, University of California Press, Berkeley, CA, 1979.

Herrin, Al, *Cherokee Bows and Arrows - How to Make and Shoot Primitive Bows and Arrows*, White Bear Publishing, Tahlequah, OK, 1989.

Hickman, C.N., Nagler, Forrest, and Klopsteg, Paul E., *Archery: The Technical Side*, National Field Archery Association, 1947.

Hoadley, R. Bruce, *Understanding Wood*, The Taunton Press, Newtown, CT., 1980.

Hodgkin, Adrian Eliot, *The Archer's Craft*, A. S. Barnes and Co., New York, NY, 1940.

Hunt, W. Ben, and Metz, John J., *The Flatbow*, Bruce Publishing Co., New York,NY, 1936.

Klopsteg, Paul E., *Turkish Archery and the Composite Bow*, Private Printing, 1934.

Lambert, Arthur Jr., *Modern Archery*, 1929.

Massey, Jay, *The Book of Primitive Archery*, Bearpaw Publications, Girdwood, AK, 1990.

   – *The Bowyer's Craft*, Bearpaw Publications, Girdwood, AK, 1987.

National Association of Glue Manufacturers, *Animal Glue in Industry*, 1951.

Pope, Saxton, *Hunting With the Bow and Arrow*, G. P. Putnam's Sons, New York, NY., 1925.

Riggs, Jim, *Make Your Own Hide Glue*, Bulletin of Primitive Technology, Fall 1991.

Schmidt, Jeffrey R., *Animal and Fish Glues*, Bulletin of Primitive Technology, Fall, 1991.

Silsby, Scott K., *Mummy Varnish, Spruce Gum, and Other Sticky Stuff*, Bulletin of Primitive Technology, Fall, 1991.

Thompson, Maurice, *The Witchery of Archery*, 1879.

White, Stewart Edward, *Lions in the Path*, Doubleday, Page, and Co., 1926.

Wilke, Philip J., *Bow Staves Harvested from Juniper Trees By Indians of Nevada*, Journal of California and Great Basin Anthropology, 1988.